# *My Daily* WORD OF TRUTH

Dr. Todd Stinnett

My Daily Word of Truth

Copyright © 2021 Todd Stinnett

All Rights Reserved.

Unless otherwise noted, Scripture taken from the New King James Version®. Copyright © 1982 by Thomas Nelson. Used by permission. All rights reserved.

ISBN 978-1-940645-91-9

Greenville, South Carolina

PUBLISHED IN THE UNITED STATES OF AMERICA

## Dedication

This book is dedicated to:
— My parents, who first taught me the word of truth,
— My wife and children, who have stood by me as I've ministered the word of truth,
— My parishioners, who have intently listened to me preach the word of truth, and most of all,
— My God, who alone is the Author of the word of truth.

## Preface

I was blessed to grow up in a Christian home with parents that pointed me to Jesus. I was also blessed to spend my childhood in a church that proclaimed the Gospel and preached the Word. When I was almost seven years old, my parents invited my pastor to come and have a conversation with me and my brother. My pastor lived just down the street and I can distinctly remember him walking to my house on that beautiful spring day in 1984.

After we exchanged pleasantries, my pastor took my brother into the den of our house. After several minutes had passed, I didn't know exactly what they were talking about, but I was certainly curious. It wasn't long before my brother came back into the living room and my pastor invited me into the den. Once I was seated, he pulled out a child's tract and explained the Gospel to me. I was heartbroken as he confronted me with my sin, but I was equally elated to learn that Jesus had paid my debt. That day, by God's grace, I became a child of God through faith in Jesus.

I'd love to say that I became a great student of the Bible immediately after I was born again, but that would be a lie. It wasn't until I got to our church's youth group that I began to take more seriously the study of God's Word. The greatest thing our youth minister ever did for us was to teach us spiritual discipline — specifically using prayer and Bible study as a means of loving God and growing in the Lord. Because of his godly influence, I remember buying myself my very first study Bible and a daily devotional book when I was just a youth.

It wasn't long before I began to sense the call of God into full-time ministry, and in the summer of 1995 I announced my call to the church. After several years of education, I accepted the call to pastor my first church in late 2001. For about twenty years I've been pastoring local churches and doing all I can to point people to Jesus. In those twenty years I've noticed something — many professing Christians do not have an adequate understanding of God's Word. Because they don't know how to wield "the sword of the Spirit" (Ephesians 6:17), they often wind up depressed, defeated, and discouraged.

The book is nothing short of an attempt to turn back the biblical illiteracy that prevails in our churches. We desperately need revival in our churches and awakening throughout our culture, but neither will come until God's people return to the Scriptures. Only the Word of God has the power to make dry bones live (Ezekiel 37) because it is "living and powerful, and sharper than any two-edged sword, piercing even to the division of soul and spirit, and of joints and marrow, and is a discerner of the thoughts and intents of the heart" (Hebrews 4:12).

This book is no substitute for the Word of God, but by using it I believe you will become better acquainted with Scripture. Use it on a daily basis, spend time in prayer, and don't be surprised when God begins to do some amazing things in your life and through your life. Our world desperately needs you to dedicate yourself to God and "the word of truth" (2 Timothy 2:15).

Dr. Todd Stinnett<br>
*Soli Deo Gloria*

*My Daily*
# WORD OF TRUTH

## January 1 — The Person God Blesses

> *"Blessed is the man who walks not in the counsel of the ungodly, nor stands in the path of sinners, nor sits in the seat of the scornful; but his delight is in the law of the Lord, and in His law he meditates day and night." (Psalm 1:1-2)*

Everybody wants to be blessed, don't they? In our materialistic culture, we tend to say that a person is "blessed" when he has a nice house, nice cars, a good job, a big salary, etc. Some look beyond the material and say that a person is really blessed when he has a caring spouse, lovely children, and a loving home. Blessing really goes further than any of these because a man can have all those things and still not be completely blessed of the Lord.

True blessing is the peace that comes with knowing your sins have been forgiven. It's the assurance that comes with knowing if you don't wake up in the morning, you've got nothing to fear because you'll awaken in the presence of Jesus. It's the wonderful blessing of knowing that God works all things together for good to those who love Him (Romans 8:28). The man who is truly blessed does not desire to walk in the paths of sin. Rather, he desires to be in the world but not of the world.

In today's verses, the psalmist tells us how a truly blessed man overcomes the wiles of the devil: "His delight is in the law of the Lord." In other words, a righteous man cherishes the Word of God. He reads it and studies it to determine the will of God. He uses the Word as ammunition against the devil. Not only that, but he meditates on what he has studied so that truth can continue to rise within him. As a result, "he shall be like a tree planted by the rivers of water" (Psalm 1:3) — blessed of the Lord!

## January 2 — Satan's Oldest Tactic

*"Now the serpent was more cunning than any beast of the field which the Lord God had made. And he said to the woman, 'Has God indeed said, "You shall not eat of every tree of the garden"?'" (Genesis 3:1)*

The devil is a powerful adversary and not to be taken lightly. Peter said, "Be sober, be vigilant; because your adversary the devil walks about like a roaring lion, seeking whom he may devour" (1 Peter 5:8). Several Old Testament (Isaiah 14 and Ezekiel 28) and New Testament passages (Revelation 12:4) lead us to believe that Satan was a powerful servant of God in heaven (Lucifer). Jude 6 implies that Lucifer and a third of heaven's angels were banished from heaven for rising up against the Lord.

Having been cast to the earth, the devil knows his time is short. Even the demons know who Jesus is (Mark 5:1-20), and they know they are defeated at the end of time. With that being the case, the only real pleasure Satan has in his miserable existence is to try and take others to hell with him. One of his best tactics in tempting humans and leading them to hell is to get them to question the Word of God: "Has God indeed said? Did God really say that? Did He really mean it?"

Because Satan convinced Adam and Eve to doubt the Word of God, they fell into sin. And just because Satan won the victory with our ancestors does not mean he's finished with us. He wants you in hell just as bad as he wanted Adam and Eve. Here's what we must do — when the devil comes to cast doubt on the Word, we must *know* the Word and *respond* with the Word like Jesus did (Matthew 4:1-10). Only in using the Sword of the Spirit can we overcome our enemy the devil.

## January 3 – The Confirmation of the Son

*"When He had been baptized, Jesus came up immediately from the water; and behold, the heavens were opened to Him, and He saw the Spirit of God descending like a dove and alighting upon Him. And suddenly a voice came from heaven, saying, 'This is My beloved Son, in whom I am well pleased.'" (Matthew 3:16-17)*

No Christian denies that Jesus was born to the virgin Mary and her betrothed husband Joseph. Neither would he/she deny that Christ grew in wisdom and stature, and that He even shocked the religious leaders of His day. These were all signs of Christ's Messiahship, but the ultimate confirmation came at the Jordan River. A man named John the Baptist was providing a baptism of repentance to prepare the way for Jesus, and many came to him to renounce their sins.

On one particular occasion, a man named Jesus came to John at the Jordan. When John saw Him, he said, "Behold! The Lamb of God who takes away the sin of the world!" (John 1:29). Jesus then asked John to baptize Him, just as he had already done for so many others. John immediately protested — "I need to be baptized by You, and are You coming to me?" (Matthew 3:14). Jesus replied that it was necessary to "fulfill all righteousness" (Matthew 3:15), so John consented.

As soon as Jesus was baptized, the Bible says the heavens were opened and the Spirit of God descended like a dove and rested upon Him. John had already confirmed Jesus' identity, but the confirmation of the Holy Spirit was much greater! And if that weren't enough, a voice rang out from heaven — "This is My beloved Son, in whom I am well pleased." In that one moment, the entire Trinity — Father, Son, and Holy Spirit — confirmed that Jesus alone is the anointed Son of God.

# January 4 – Christ's First Message

*"From that time Jesus began to preach and to say, 'Repent, for the kingdom of heaven is at hand.'" (Matthew 4:17)*

Think of all the great messages Jesus ever preached. Who can forget the Sermon on the Mount (Matthew 5-7)? In that great sermon, Jesus explained how He fulfills the righteous requirements of the Law and provides us the true interpretation of the Old Covenant. We know there are times when Jesus preached to thousands along the hillsides of Galilee. There were times He preached in the temple. You could even make the argument that Jesus preached from the Cross!

Have you ever wondered about the content of Christ's very first message? Most people would probably guess something like, "Love one another," or, "Judge not, lest you be judged." As important as those messages might be, as soon as Jesus completed His baptism and His forty-day temptation at the hands of the devil, there was one message on His mind — "Repent, for the kingdom of heaven is at hand." The first recorded message Jesus began to preach was a very serious call to action.

What does it mean to repent? It means "to change" or "to turn." In this case, Christ is talking about turning from one's sins and turning to Him in faith. That turn from sin to the Savior will result in an obvious change in one's life. No longer bound to sin, he/she will be able to live for the glory of God. Why did Jesus think repentance is so necessary? Because "the kingdom of heaven is at hand." Our Lord Jesus could return at any moment. When He returns, what will He find you doing?

## January 5 — What the Rainbow Really Means

*"And God said: 'This is the sign of the covenant which I make between Me and you, and every living creature that is with you, for perpetual generations: I set My rainbow in the cloud, and it shall be for the sign of the covenant between Me and the earth.'" (Genesis 9:12-13)*

The rainbow is quite prominent in our present culture, but the meaning has changed drastically in the last few decades. The rainbow flag was popularized as a symbol of the gay community by San Francisco artist Gilbert Baker in 1978. Since the 1990s, its symbolism has been transferred to represent the extended "LGBT" (lesbian, gay, bisexual and transgender) community. Baker's original rainbow contained 8 colors, but the LGBT community has used only 6 colors since 1979.

What is the true meaning of the rainbow? God created Adam and Eve, placing them in the beautiful Garden of Eden. Sadly, they chose to sin and thus affected the whole of creation and passed a sin nature along to the rest of us. Several generations later, the world had become so wicked during Noah's day that God decided to cleanse the earth of sin. Noah built an ark, his family of 8 entered, God shut the door, and for forty days and nights it rained.

After the flood waters subsided, God commanded Noah and his sons to be fruitful and multiply (Genesis 9:1). God also gave them a promise — "Never again shall all flesh be cut off by the waters of the flood; never again shall there be a flood to destroy the earth" (Genesis 9:11). So then, the rainbow is not a symbol of homosexual pride, though the devil has certainly hijacked it for that purpose. The rainbow is an everlasting reminder that we have a merciful God who keeps His Word.

## January 6 — God's Covenant with Abraham

*"Now the Lord had said to Abram: 'Get out of your country, from your family and from your father's house, to a land that I will show you. I will make you a great nation; I will bless you and make your name great; and you shall be a blessing. I will bless those who bless you, and I will curse him who curses you; and in you all the families of the earth shall be blessed.'" (Genesis 12:1-3)*

About 3,800 years ago, God approached a man named Abram who lived in a city called Ur in the region of Mesopotamia. Basically, Abram lived with his family in the modern-day land of Iraq. In his sermon from Acts 7, Stephen tells us Abram was called by God to leave his family and follow the Lord's leadership. Abram relocated his family to Haran (modern-day Turkey), and God prompted him to leave once more — this time at the age of seventy-five.

When Abram was called to live in Haran, he really didn't know where he was going. God simply said He was calling him to go to "a land that I will show you." I'm sure this was not easy for Abram. His home city of Ur was a thriving metropolis of the ancient world, and I'm sure his home in Haran was comfortable as well. God called Abram out of his comfort zone and commanded him to take a leap of faith. God still does the same thing with each of us today.

When God commanded Abram to begin his journey toward the land of Canaan, He made him a timeless promise — "I will make you a great nation." The nation birthed through Abram's lineage is Israel: Abraham, Isaac, and Jacob, whose name was changed to Israel. What's the significance of this promise? It proves once more that our God is a covenant-keeper and that He still has a special plan for His people. Every Christian should continue to bless God's chosen people, Israel.

## January 7 — Prophet, Priest, and King

*"Then Melchizedek king of Salem brought out bread and wine; he was the priest of God Most High. And he blessed him and said: 'Blessed be Abram of God Most High, possessor of heaven and earth; and blessed be God Most High, who has delivered your enemies into your hand.' And he gave him a tithe of all." (Genesis 14:18-20)*

After God made His covenant with Abram, it wasn't too long until he began to reside in the Promised Land. Abram's nephew, Lot, lived to the east, and Abram pitched his tents in the west. In the process of time, Lot was taken captive by a conglomeration of armies that came against the inhabitants of his new home. Being the great man he was, Abram gathered his servants and retrieved his nephew, along with much spoil from the hands of his enemies.

As Abram returned home from battle, the Bible says at least two kings came out to greet him, and among them was Melchizedek. He is unlike any other king in the Scriptures. He shared three distinct roles — prophet, priest, and king. How do we know? The Bible says he was "king of Salem." Further, "he was the priest of God Most High." In other words, he performed priestly duties in the worship of Jehovah. He didn't serve the Canaanite gods that were worshiped all around him.

Our passage says Melchizedek blessed Abram and prophesied over his life. Abram acknowledged Melchizedek's unique position as prophet, priest, and king by giving him "a tithe of all" — one tenth of all he had. What is the significance of Melchizedek? I believe the Lord permitted Abram to encounter Melchizedek in order to point Him to Jesus. Jesus Christ is the TRUE Prophet, Priest, and King who will reign forevermore. Each of us should surrender all that we have to Him today!

## January 8 — How to Eliminate Worry

*"But seek first the kingdom of God and His righteousness, and all these things shall be added to you." (Matthew 6:33)*

In His famous Sermon on the Mount, Jesus addressed the subject of worry, encouraging His followers not to worry about material things, even the daily necessities of life — food, clothes, etc. Instead, He challenged them to consider the birds of the air and the flowers of the field. They neither "toil or spin," yet the Father takes care of them and arrays them with His beauty. Christ wanted His followers to understand that they are worth much more than birds and flowers.

The words of Jesus remind us that God knows exactly what we need and exactly when we need it. We spend far too much time worrying about material needs, financial burdens, vocational problems, etc. Worry doesn't do one thing to change our situation. As Jesus asked, "Which of you by worrying can add one cubit to his stature?" Worrying does nothing to help us, and in fact it hurts us. Medical experts agree that worry produces stress, and stress can lead to high blood pressure, among other problems.

Instead of worrying about things beyond our control, Jesus commands us to "seek first the kingdom of God and His righteousness." In other words, make God and His work your highest priorities — loving Him with all your heart, soul, mind, and strength. If we seek Him above all else, He has promised to take care of all our needs. So then, what are you worried about? Instead of worrying, start praying! Trust in His power and He will supply all your needs (Philippians 4:19).

# January 9 — Judge Not

*"Judge not, that you be not judged." (Matthew 7:1)*

A few decades ago, if you were to ask most Americans to quote one verse of Scripture, they probably would've quoted John 3:16 — "For God so loved the world ... ." As a child I distinctly remember seeing "John 3:16" on poster boards and signs at sporting events all across America. I don't see John 3:16 plastered across our culture quite like I used to. Instead, the verse most Americans would probably quote would be today's verse — "Judge not, that you be not judged."

Why do so many people, even lost people, have this verse memorized and quote it from time to time? Because it's generally become a way of saying, "Keep your nose out of my business, and I'll keep my nose out of yours." Is that really what Jesus intended with this verse? With this exhortation, Jesus was really rebuking hypocrisy. Jesus warned against being overly concerned about the "speck" in someone else's eye while being unconcerned about the "plank" in our own.

It is certainly true that we should not pass judgment on things we have not investigated, especially if there is sin on our own doorstep. Christ commands us to deal with our own sins, "then you will see clearly to remove the speck from your brother's eye." With that said, we must judge the words and works of others as we seek to live for Christ. Later in this chapter, Jesus said, "You will know them by their fruits" (Matthew 7:16). Premature judgment is a sin, but careful consideration is a must. Ask God to help you recognize the difference between self-righteous judgment and Spirit-filled discernment.

## January 10 – The Sins of Sodom and Gomorrah

*"And they called to Lot and said to him, 'Where are the men who came to you tonight? Bring them out to us that we may know them carnally.'" (Genesis 19:5)*

Sodom and Gomorrah were ancient cities that came to God's attention because of their rampant wickedness. In today's verses, their wickedness was on full display, culminating with the men of the city desiring to have homosexual relations with the angelic visitors that came to stay with Lot. He begged the men of the city not to act so wickedly, but they would not be deterred. They nearly beat down Lot's door in their attempts to violate his visitors.

Through four millennia of Jewish history and two millennia of Christian history, virtually no one within those faith communities attempted to justify homosexual behavior. Disciples within both groups pointed to passages such as the one we're considering today as evidence that homosexuality is a lifestyle displeasing to the Lord. Fast forward to the 21st century. Not only is the culture advocating for the homosexual lifestyle, but some who claim to know Christ even argue that it is not unbiblical.

They claim that Sodom's sin was not homosexuality but rather inhospitality. While Sodom was certainly guilty of many sins (Ezekiel 16:49), the culmination was that they "committed abomination before Me" (Ezekiel 16:50). What was that abomination? Jude says they were given over to "sexual immorality and gone after strange flesh" (Jude 7). Sodom and Gomorrah's primary sin was sexual immorality, and for it they were destroyed. America needs to pay close attention! May God help us to repent of our sins before we suffer the same judgment!

## January 11 — Trust in the Lord

*"Trust in the Lord with all your heart, and lean not on your own understanding; in all your ways acknowledge Him, and He shall direct your paths." (Proverbs 3:5-6)*

Trust is defined as "firm belief in the reliability, truth, ability, or strength of someone or something." A popular team-building exercise of the '80s and '90s was the "trust fall." Typically, a group of people stood in two lines, facing one another, with their hands extended outward. It was their job to catch a colleague who stood on a table or platform as he/she fell into the arms of friends standing below. The exercise was designed to create more trust between co-workers.

In today's verse, God commands us to trust Him with all our hearts. Is the Lord talking about some sort of blind trust, similar to falling into the arms of those we can't see? Not quite — instead, the Word tells us that trusting the Lord means "lean not on your own understanding." Just because God has commanded you to do something that doesn't make sense doesn't mean you should cease to trust Him. Trusting God means leaning on His Word and not on our own ideas.

Solomon also tells us that trusting the Lord means acknowledging Him in all our ways. So then, trusting God means I surrender my life to Him at all times — not just when it's convenient, easy, inexpensive, comfortable, etc. Trusting God means vowing to seek and serve Him habitually. And how does God reward our trust? "He shall direct your paths." In other words, God will bless your childlike trust by navigating you through life's turbulent waters and providing all your needs.

# January 12 – Only the Sick Can Be Saved

*"When Jesus heard that, He said to them, 'Those who are well have no need of a physician, but those who are sick.'" (Matthew 9:12)*

No one really enjoys a visit to the doctor's office. Why? Because he might tell you that you need to lose weight. He might give you a shot. He might deliver bad news that will change the course of your life. For those reasons, we try to stay out of the doctor's office. Can you imagine a person who is not sick wanting to go to the doctor for no reason? "Go ahead, doctor, just see if you can find something." Of course not! Typically, only those who need medical attention visit the doctor.

Today's verse comes just after a conversation that Jesus had with the Pharisees. They were upset because "many tax collectors and sinners came and sat down with Him and His disciples" (Matthew 9:10). The Pharisees felt that no true rabbi would keep company with such sinners. Jesus confronted the Pharisees with their self-righteousness — "those who are well have no need of a physician, but those who are sick." Christ came to save those who are sin-sick!

That begs the question, "How many people are sin-sick?" Of course, *everyone* is sin-sick and in need of a relationship with Jesus Christ. In today's verse, Jesus was not trying to say that the Pharisees were "well" — far from it. He was simply saying that while God's grace is extended to every sinner, it is reserved for those who acknowledge their need for it. If you don't think you're sick, you'll never receive God's grace. But if you know you need the Great Physician, He will make you completely well.

## January 13 – Where Are the Workers

*"Then He said to His disciples, 'The harvest truly is plentiful, but the laborers are few.'" (Matthew 9:37)*

Some people love work. They love to set their alarm clock, jump out of bed, scarf down some breakfast, and get to the job. Some people love to work because they love their job — they're passionate about what they do. Others love to work because they love to reap the rewards — handsome pay for hard work. Sadly, some enjoy work because it takes them away from people they'd rather not be around. It's a shame when someone would rather be with colleagues than family or friends.

Generally speaking, there are a good number of people who don't care for work. Why? Because it's work — it requires effort, time, forethought, and perseverance. Some able-bodied people prefer not to work, content to live off whatever bones are thrown their direction from the government or charities. The fact is that God designed our bodies for work, as we see from Adam and Eve in the Garden of Eden (Genesis 2).

Jesus used the analogy of a harvest — "the harvest is plentiful, but the laborers are few." In this case, He was speaking of souls — men and women who need Christ. There are many people that need to be reached, but sadly there are very few willing to reach them. Why is that? We're game for a party or a dinner date but not so eager to reach the lost. God forgive us! Let's roll up our sleeves and get busy reaching others for Christ, praying that God would send out even more workers with us (Matthew 9:38).

## January 14 — Serpents and Doves

*"Behold, I send you out as sheep in the midst of wolves. Therefore be wise as serpents and harmless as doves." (Matthew 10:16)*

Studies indicate that about half of Americans are scared of snakes, and that's probably not too surprising. Just look at them — they're scaly and slimy. They lurk in hidden places. They strike sometimes when you don't even see them. And when they do, they can sink their fangs deep into your skin. That's especially bad if the snake is venomous! But give the serpent his due — he is very crafty and stealthy. He's a wise hunter who knows just when and how to strike.

On the other hand, consider beautiful doves. They are a universal picture of peace and purity. As a pastor, I've officiated many funerals. Sometimes at the graveside, after I've said a few words, a caretaker will be there with a basket of doves, which are released into the air. The doves are a beautiful picture of someone's soul ascending into the heavens. I think we can all agree that doves are beautiful and harmless.

In today's verse, Jesus commands us to emulate both serpents and doves. When He sent His disciples out to minister in His name, Jesus commanded them to be "wise as serpents." In other words, understand where you are, who you belong to, and consider the appropriate time to speak and act. On the other hand, we should be "harmless as doves." As we utilize shrewdness and ingenuity in serving Christ, we should always be peacemakers who yearn to bring others to Jesus.

# January 15 – Confessing Jesus or Denying Him

*"Therefore whoever confesses Me before men, him I will also confess before My Father who is in heaven. But whoever denies Me before men, him I will also deny before My Father who is in heaven." (Matthew 10:32-33)*

Has anyone ever been ashamed to be associated with you? That's a very hurtful experience. It usually goes something like this — you make friends with someone and everything appears to be going great. But your new friend has some old friends who may not care for you that much. When it's just the two of you, your friend treats you great; but when your friend sees the others coming, he/she acts like they don't know you. He/she refuses to acknowledge you in front of others.

There are some people who treat Jesus that way. They're fine talking about Jesus and singing about Jesus when they go to worship, but then they have trouble mentioning Him to classmates and coworkers throughout the week. Or how about the politician who panders to the church on Sunday but votes like a pagan on Monday. The Apostle Paul said, "I am not ashamed of the Gospel of Christ," but sadly many people who profess to know Jesus often act like they don't.

Understand this — if you're not willing to identify with Jesus before men, He will not identify with you before the Father in heaven. Instead of hearing Him say, "Well done, good and faithful servant," you will hear Him say, "Depart from me, you worker of lawlessness — I never knew you." Some portions of Scripture are tough to understand, but this one is not. Either make your stand with Christ before the world, or prepare to join the vast majority of the world in hell at the end of time.

## January 16 — Friend of Sinners

*"The Son of Man came eating and drinking, and they say, 'Look, a glutton and a winebibber, a friend of tax collectors and sinners!'" (Matthew 11:19)*

It's no secret that the religious establishment of Jesus' day did not like Him. I'm sure there were a variety of reasons, but they all seem to swirl around selfishness. If the Pharisees and Sadducees had accepted Jesus as God's Messiah, they would've lost their power and prosperity in Israel. Why? Because they had ceased teaching the true Word of God and had started emphasizing the traditions of men. Sadly, some "churches" are still doing that today — usually the ones closest to dying.

In today's verse, Jesus quoted the religious leaders, and of course, we know they meant their words as an attack. But in this case, their words have some manner of accuracy. We know Jesus was not a glutton or a winebibber — He was the one and only Son of God and a man of great self-control. But the last clause in their criticism is true — Jesus is a friend of tax collectors and sinners. Just think of all those He impacted — Levi, Mary Magdalene, lepers, harlots, etc. Even me and you!

No one was too wicked that Jesus was not willing to befriend them and reach them with the Gospel. Jesus never participated in sin (Hebrews 4:15), but He did meet sinners right at their point of need. Sadly, too many churches have been preaching to the lost without meeting them where they are. I'm convinced if we will join Christ in befriending "tax collectors and sinners," more of them will be transformed by the Gospel. Let's meet people where they are and do all we can to point them to Jesus.

## January 17 — The Great Physician

*"Great multitudes followed Him, and He
healed them all." (Matthew 12:15)*

After the baptism of Jesus and the initiation of His public ministry, it didn't take long for people to see that there was something special about Him. No one taught like He taught. No one touched who He was willing to touch. No one challenged the religious establishment like He did. There was one thing that really captivated the crowds — His healing power. Folks from all across Israel, and even beyond Israel, came to see Jesus, and He had the power to heal them all.

Let's briefly remember just a few of Christ's healing miracles. Of course, we know He opened blind eyes, deaf ears, and mute mouths. Those who came to Him with withered hands walked away with hands wide open. Those who couldn't walk for decades were able to take up their beds and walk away. Those ostracized because of leprosy were healed and granted re-entrance back into their homes. Even the dead were raised back to life!

Jesus had a holistic ministry — teaching people the Word, preaching the kingdom of God, and healing every disease among the people. I'm quite sure that not every healing miracle of Jesus is recorded in Scripture, but the ones that are cause us to stand in awe of God. What is the greatest disease Jesus ever healed? That's easy — sin-sickness. With His own blood, Jesus paid the price for our sins and purged our wicked souls. The Great Physician is the only One who heals both our bodies and our souls!

## January 18 — Generosity

*"Do not withhold good from those to whom it is due, when it is in the power of your hand to do so." (Proverbs 3:27)*

Have you ever done a job, only to be ripped off when payment time came? A classic example is a waitress who serves a large party with high demands. At the end of the meal, the server expects a nice tip for her service. Instead, she gets a couple of bucks — perhaps a 2 percent tip on a $100 meal. That is exasperating. When we do a good job, we expect to be rewarded accordingly. Even the Bible says that "the laborer is worthy of his wages" (Luke 10:7).

It upsets us when people are stingy, but I wonder if it angers us just as much when we are greedy toward others? Today's verse gives a clear command — "Do not withhold good from those to whom it is due." If someone has served you well, you should be quick to reward. In all things, the "Golden Rule" should apply — "And just as you want men to do to you, you also do to them likewise" (Luke 6:31). Give to others as you would want to be given to you.

The command comes with a caveat: "When it is in the power of your hand to do so." Sometimes the spirit is willing, but the wallet is empty. Generosity is not just monetary — there are many ways you can show you gratitude to someone else. But if you receive a service, knowing someone is expecting remuneration, you should be prepared to give generously. For instance, if you can't afford to tip, you can't afford to eat out. Giving is the only time it's good for a Christ-follower to be a liberal!

## January 19 — Beware of Jealousy

*"His brothers envied him, but his father*
*kept the matter in mind." (Genesis 37:11)*

I bet you're familiar with the story of Joseph. What an amazing story it is! It all started with a young man who was dearly beloved by his father, Jacob (Israel). The Bible says, "Now Israel loved Joseph more than all his children, because he was the son of his old age. Also, he made him a tunic of many colors" (Genesis 37:3). Clearly it was not wise for Jacob to play favorites with his children and to give Joseph special treatment, so he bears some of the blame for what happened to his son.

Yet, the way Joseph's brothers dealt with their father's favoritism leaves much to be desired. The Word says, "They hated him (Joseph) and could not speak peaceably to him" (Genesis 37:4). In the process of time, Joseph's brothers crafted a plan to get rid of him and make it look like a wild beast killed him. The brothers took Joseph, lowered him into a pit, removed his coat of many colors, and finally sold him into slavery for twenty shekels of silver.

Why would a group of brothers even consider such a horrible plan? Because they were consumed with jealousy. They yearned for the favor that their father showed to Joseph, and when they couldn't garner their father's special love, they decided to take matters into their own hands. The lesson is simple — jealously will poison us from the inside-out. May God help us to be content with all He's done for us — "godliness with contentment is great gain" (1 Timothy 6:6).

## January 20 – Losing All to Gain Everything

*"The kingdom of heaven is like treasure hidden in a field, which a man found and hid; and for joy over it he goes and sells all that he has and buys that field." (Matthew 13:44)*

Jim Elliot was born in Portland, Oregon, on October 8, 1927. Later in life, he attended Wheaton College and prepared for a life of missionary service. In the early '50s, Elliot began the process of relocating to Ecuador where he would dedicate his life to reaching the Quechua people, including the "Auca" (savages). On January 8, 1956, a group of Huaoroni warriors killed Elliot and four of his companions as they were attempting to build relationships and reach the natives for Christ.

Seven years before his death, Elliot wrote these words in his personal journal — "He is no fool who gives what he cannot keep to gain that which he cannot lose." Elliot's words remind us of Jesus' words from about 2,000 years earlier. Jesus said the kingdom of heaven is like treasure hidden in a field — and clearly not just any treasure. The extravagance of the treasure is so high that a man would rebury the treasure in a field and then sell everything he has to go and buy the field.

Jim Elliot exemplified these words of Christ. He was willing to give up everything he had — even life itself — for the opportunity to gain heaven and lead others to Christ. I wonder, what would you be willing to lose in order to gain heaven? Your job? Your friends? Your money? Your life? "What will it profit a man if he gains the whole world, and loses his own soul?" (Mark 8:36). Jesus is worth much more than anything you will ever lose for His sake.

## January 21 – In the Hands of the Master

*"Now those who had eaten were about five thousand men, besides women and children." (Matthew 14:21)*

The value of something often depends on the person handling it. For instance, a basketball in my hands is worth about $20. A basketball in the hands of Kevin Durant is worth about $40 million a year. In my hands, an Epiphone guitar is worth about $700. In the hands of the great B.B. King, the same guitar ("Lucille") is worth about $10,000. In my hand, a scalpel is worth about $10, but in the hands of a skilled surgeon a scalpel is worth thousands more.

After the death of John the Baptist, Jesus was grieved and desired to get away from the crowds. Yet, the crowds were so taken with Him that they followed the Teacher all the way to a hillside on the Sea of Galilee. When Christ saw the crowds, He was moved with compassion for them and began to heal their diseases. As the sun began to set, no one had eaten. Christ instructed His disciples to feed the multitudes, but all they could find was one small boy with five loaves and two fish.

In my hands, five loaves and two fish would hardly feed my family of eight. That would've been a problem 2,000 years ago, because as today's verse says, there were 5,000 men on the hillside with Jesus, not counting the women and children. In the hands of Jesus, five loaves and two fish were enough to feed well over 5,000 with twelve baskets left over. Everything changes in the hands of the Master. As the old hymn says, "Little is much when God is in it." Place the "loaves and fish" you have in the hands of the Lord, and prepare to be amazed with all that God will do!

## January 22 – When the Foundations Are Destroyed

*"If the foundations are destroyed,
what can the righteous do?" (Psalm 11:3)*

I am certainly not a trained builder or contractor, but I have a pretty good idea about some things. Among them is the vital importance of how a foundation is laid when a building is erected. If the footers are wrong and the block is laid incorrectly, everything laid on top of the foundation is going to suffer. On the other hand, if great care is taken to make sure that the foundation is right, it can support a building for many years.

In today's verse, David is in an all-too-familiar place. Once again, he's on the run from his enemies. The enemy had his arrows pointed at David and was ready to shoot. David felt like the "foundations" of his life were falling apart. Do you ever feel that way? Maybe you've lost your job. Maybe you're concerned about a wayward child. Maybe you've gone through a painful divorce. It's easy to feel like everything is about to come crashing down.

David did the best thing anyone can do when it feels like life is falling apart — he lifted his eyes to the Lord. He reminded himself, "The Lord is in His holy temple … the Lord tests the righteous … . His countenance beholds the upright" (Psalm 11:4-5, 7). No matter what you're going through, remember God is still in charge. No matter how wicked our culture becomes, remember God is still in control. Pray and ask God to deliver you from your trials and to sustain you until the deliverance comes! As a loving Heavenly Father, He cares for all those who belong to Him!

# January 23 – The Providence of God

*"Do not therefore be grieved or angry with yourselves because you sold me here; for God sent me before you to preserve life. ... it was not you who sent me here, but God; and He has made me a father to Pharaoh, and lord of all his house, and a ruler throughout all the land of Egypt." (Genesis 45:5, 8)*

Joseph was a bright young man who enjoyed the favor of his father when he was sold into slavery by his brothers. Joseph's journey after his enslavement was not easy. First, he ended up in Potiphar's house where he found favor in the eyes of his master. Joseph also caught the eye of his master's wife who attempted to proposition him for sex on a number of occasions. After Joseph refused her advances, she falsely accused him, and Joseph was thrown into prison.

But even from prison, Joseph didn't lose hope. Because he was a man of God, the Lord caused Joseph to find favor with the keeper of the prison. He actually placed Joseph in charge of the other prisoners. In the process of time, it was revealed that Joseph was an interpreter of dreams. When it was discovered that Joseph had a God-given gift, he was commanded to come and interpret dreams for Pharaoh himself!

Pharaoh was so impressed with Joseph and his interpretations that he made him second in command over the kingdom of Egypt. Is it possible that someone orchestrated all these events? Joseph said it was God who sent him to Egypt — through slavery, false accusations, imprisonment, etc. Joseph realized that sometimes God allows "bad things to happen to good people" so that He can use them for His glory! Keep persevering through trials — God has a purpose for your pain!

# January 24 — Faith That Won't Be Denied

*"But He answered and said, 'It is not good to take the children's bread and throw it to the little dogs.' And she said, 'Yes, Lord, yet even the little dogs eat the crumbs which fall from their masters' table.'" (Matthew 15:26-27)*

One of our biggest problems is that we often give up too soon. When the food isn't very satisfying, we give up on diets. When the early mornings and hard work get a little intense, we give up on exercise. When the long nights of study get wearisome, we give up on school. The old saying is that the greatest darkness is just before the dawn. That might be the case, but too often we miss the sunrise because we're not willing to persevere in the midst of the night.

Up until the 15th chapter of Matthew, the ministry of Jesus had been directed primarily at His own people Israel. He even said, "I was not sent except to the lost sheep of the house of Israel" (Matthew 15:24). But there was a Gentile woman who was willing to believe that Jesus was the all-powerful Messiah He claimed to be. She had a daughter who was severely demon-possessed, and she sought the help of Jesus because she believed He could exorcise her daughter's demons.

Jesus tested the Gentile woman's faith — "It is not good to take the children's bread and throw it to the little dogs." Of course, Jesus was not calling the woman a dog, but indicating that up until now His message had been dedicated to the Jews, not the Gentiles. The woman did not give up — "even the little dogs eat the crumbs which fall from their masters' table." Because of her unwavering faith, Jesus marveled and healed the Gentile woman's daughter. Today, believe God CAN do all things, and don't give up until He intervenes!

# January 25 – What A Fool Believes

*"The fool has said in his heart, 'There is no God.'" (Psalm 14:1, 53:1)*

Michael McDonald and Kenny Loggins wrote a song called "What A Fool Believes" that was later recorded by The Doobie Brothers in August 1978 and released in January of 1979. The song reached #1 on April 14, 1979, and won a Grammy in 1980 for "Song of the Year." The song tells the story of a man who is reunited with a former love interest. He attempts to rekindle a romantic relationship that never actually existed in the first place. Poor pathetic fool.

The song reminds us that fools have believed a lot of things. But believers know there's nothing more foolish than denying God's existence — "The fool has said in his heart, 'There is no God.'" At first glance, the verse doesn't seem to be accurate. There are many highly educated, intelligent people who claim to be atheists. Yet, we need to understand that "foolish" doesn't mean the same thing as "unintelligent." There are many foolish-intelligent people in the world today — they simply refuse to believe the truth.

The most foolish thing a person can do is believe that there is no God. Why? Because the evidence of God's existence is everywhere you look. The Bible says, "The heavens declare the glory of God" (Psalm 19:1). Not only that, but the intricate design of the universe points us to an all-powerful Designer, just like a watch points to the existence of a watchmaker. Yes — there is a God, His name is Jehovah, and His Son is Jesus. Any fool can be made wise through faith in Him.

# January 26 — When Disobedience Is Obedience

*"But the midwives feared God, and did not do as the king of Egypt commanded them, but saved the male children alive." (Exodus 1:17)*

When you think of the Book of Exodus, you can't help but think of Moses. He was the primary figure who emerged to deliver Israel from their bondage in Egypt. But before Moses, there were two little-known midwives named Shiphrah and Puah. In their day, Pharaoh grew very concerned about the sheer number of Jews, so he concocted a plan to start eliminating them. He commanded the midwives to kill all the male children born to the Hebrew women but to spare the females.

The midwives chose the path of civil disobedience — "the midwives feared God and did not do as the king of Egypt commanded them, but saved the male children." Maybe you've always heard it said that Christians should obey the law of the land, and that's true. Romans 13 says, "Let every soul be subject to the governing authorities … whoever resists the authority resists the ordinance of God, and those who resist will bring judgment on themselves" (vv. 1-2).

When is it acceptable to "break the law" or to disregard appointed rulers? When the governing authorities command you to do anything that requires you to disobey the Lord, then you must object. Why? As the apostle said, "We ought to obey God rather than men" (Acts 5:29). Disobedience to civil authorities might cost you a great deal. Many believers have lost their lives because they refused to deny the Lord and His Word. But at the end of time, obedience to God is all that will really matter.

# January 27 – Biblical Conflict Resolution

*"If your brother sins against you, go and tell him his fault between you and him alone. If he hears you, you have gained your brother. But if he will not hear, take with you one or two more, that 'by the mouth of two or three witnesses every word may be established.' And if he refuses to hear them, tell it to the church. But if he refuses even to hear the church, let him be to you like a heathen and a tax collector." (Matthew 18:15-17)*

Today's verses lay out the process of what is typically called church discipline. Really, they are guidelines for biblical conflict resolution. What am I supposed to do if someone has wronged me — talked behind my back, betrayed my confidence, etc.? First, you are to "go and tell him his fault between you and him alone." Don't go gossip to someone else — that's usually the worst thing you can do! Ninety-nine percent of conflicts get out of hand because people don't talk directly to one another.

If you attempt to resolve your differences with your brother and he will not listen, only then do you need to enlist the help of others. "One or two more" can serve as witnesses and aid in the resolution of the conflict. If your friend refuses to hear the witnesses, as a last resort the matter is to be brought before the church. This should only be a last resort as fallen humans tend to take sides, rather than considering the Scripture. The church should adjudicate every matter based on the Bible.

If your brother will not receive the correction of the church, then he is to be disciplined by the church, which usually means he is disfellowshipped. The breaking of fellowship with an unrepentant sinner is not for a vindictive purpose but so that the brother can come to the end of himself and be encouraged to repent (1 Corinthians 5:5). Why is this so important? Most major conflicts would be avoided if believers learned to settle their differences with one another rather than gossiping to someone else.

## January 28 – The Danger of Unforgiveness

*"So My heavenly Father also will do to you if each of you, from his heart, does not forgive his brother his trespasses."* (Matthew 18:35)

Have you ever wondered how many times you should be willing to forgive someone who has wronged you? If so, you're in good company, because Peter wondered the same thing — "Lord, how often shall my brother sin against me, and I forgive him? Up to seven times?" (Matthew 18:21). Peter probably thought he was being gracious because the rabbis taught that you only had to forgive an offender up to three times.

Jesus answered, not seven times, but "up to seventy times seven" (Matthew 18:22). Of course, Jesus didn't intend for us to keep an account of forgiveness up to 490 times. He used hyperbole to teach that we should always be willing to forgive someone who is genuinely repentant. He then used a parable to make the point. He said there once was a king who was settling accounts with his servants. He found one servant who owed 10,000 talents — about 2 billion in today's dollars!

The king could've put his servant in debtor's prison, but instead he chose to forgive the debt. Afterwards, that same servant found a fellow servant who owed him 100 denarii — about $3,200 — almost nothing in comparison to what he had been forgiven. Ironically, the servant refused to forgive the debt of his friend. When the king found out, he was enraged and delivered the wicked servant to the torturers. The point — it's very selfish and dangerous to be unforgiving when we've been forgiven so much! If someone has asked your forgiveness, grant them forgiveness today!

## January 29 – God's Plan for Marriage

*"So then, they are no longer two but one flesh. Therefore what God has joined together, let not man separate."* (Matthew 19:6)

Lots of folks have questions about marriage and divorce, and so did the Pharisees in Christ's day. On one occasion they asked, "Is it lawful for a man to divorce his wife for just any reason?" (Matthew 19:3). Jesus responded by taking the Pharisees back to the Garden of Eden. God's plan for marriage is seen there in Genesis 2:24 — "A man shall leave his father and mother and be joined to his wife, and they shall become one flesh." Marriage happens when a man leaves his family and cleaves to his wife.

Because God is the One who makes one from the two, Jesus said that men are not to dissolve what God has joined together. Among the Pharisees there were two schools of thought. Some felt that a man could divorce his wife only for reasons of sexual unfaithfulness, while others felt that divorce was justified for any reason. The words of Jesus help us understand that divorce is really never God's plan for marriage. It's His desire that a man and woman are joined together for life.

The Pharisees were quick to respond, "Why then did Moses command to give a certificate of divorce, and to put her away?" (Matthew 19:7). Jesus responded that God permitted a certificate of divorce, not because it's His perfect will, but because of the hardness of men's hearts. Jesus explained that divorce for any reason but adultery was sexual immorality. Later, the Apostle Paul added abandonment to the list (1 Corinthians 7:15). Ultimately, God's plan for marriage is lifelong faithfulness, "'til death do us part."

# January 30 – The Last Will Be First

*"So the last will be first, and the first last. For many are called, but few chosen." (Matthew 20:16)*

Jesus spent much of His ministry addressing the Jews — those who had the Law and covenants but had not always acted on them. Jesus once told a parable about a vineyard owner who hired laborers to work in his vineyard. The owner hired some at daybreak, but others he hired at 9 a.m., noon, 3 p.m., and even as late as 5 p.m. The owner promised each worker that he would pay them a fair wage for honest work.

When the work was done and it was time for pay, the owner commanded his steward to pay the laborers beginning with those who came the latest. Shockingly, the owner paid the same amount to those who came at 5 p.m. to those who came at daybreak. One might expect the first workers to get paid first and to get paid the most. It's not surprising that the first workers complained about the remuneration — "These last men have worked only one hour, and you made them equal to us" (Matthew 20:12).

The owner rebuked the complainers by reminding them that they agreed to one day's wage. The first workers despised the owner's generosity, but he responded, "Is your eye evil because I am good?" (Matthew 20:15). The parable is symbolic, as it seems the Jews represent those who've been in the vineyard all day, and Gentiles represent those who've only been there a short time. The message is clear: The same grace is available to every person regardless of their lineage or background. The Gospel is the power of God to salvation for all who will believe (Romans 1:16).

## January 31 – Our Passover Lamb

*"And they shall take some of the blood and put it on the two doorposts and on the lintel of the houses where they eat it." (Exodus 12:7)*

When God delivered His people Israel from their Egyptian bondage, He showed many signs and wonders to Pharaoh and the people of Egypt. Among them, the Nile turned to blood, pestilence was rampant, and frogs even overtook the land. The greatest of the ten plagues was saved for last — God vowed to kill the firstborn among the Egyptians. The plague was overwhelming, and as a result, Pharaoh finally agreed to release the Israelites from slavery.

As God prepared to send judgment on the people, He gave some clear commands. He instructed all the Israelites to take an unblemished lamb, kill it, and place the blood of the lamb on the doorposts and the lintels of their homes. Why? Because God Himself was going to pass throughout the camps of Egypt and Israel. Only those houses covered by the blood of a spotless lamb would escape judgment. In those cases, the Lord would "pass over" the house.

When the Lord passed through the camp, the death rate was 100 percent among the firstborn of Egypt, but the Israelites avoided God's wrath because of the blood. As Christians, we also have a Passover Lamb. No, we don't have to slaughter a lamb and smear blood across our doors. But, when John the Baptist saw Jesus, he said, "Behold! The Lamb of God who takes away the sins of the world!" (John 1:29). Through His own blood, Jesus spares all believers from the wrath of God.

## February 1 — God Can Make a Way

> *"And Moses said to the people, 'Do not be afraid. Stand still, and see the salvation of the Lord, which He will accomplish for you today. For the Egyptians whom you see today, you shall see again no more forever. The LORD will fight for you, and you shall hold your peace.'" (Exodus 14:13-14)*

Growing up in church, we used to sing this little chorus: "God will make a way where there seems to be no way. He works in ways we cannot see. He will make a way for me. He will be my Guide, hold me closely to His side. With love and strength for each new day, He will make a way." Is that true? Is God really able to make a way where there seems to be no way? For the answer to that question, let's ask the children of Israel.

Released from their Egyptian captivity by the mighty hand of God, the Israelites made their way toward the Promised Land. A major obstacle stood in front of them — a body of water called the Red Sea. To make matters worse, Pharaoh changed his mind about releasing the Israelites. Instead, he banded his armies together and pursued them into the wilderness. Israel was trapped between the Red Sea and the strongest army in the ancient world.

God's people needed a way through to the Promised Land, but there was no way of deliverance. That's exactly when God likes to step in. Moses encouraged the people not to fear because they would "see the salvation of the Lord." You know the rest of the story — God miraculously parted the Red Sea, the Israelites crossed on dry ground, and the Egyptians were destroyed when the water came crashing down. Are you facing an impossible obstacle today? Take it to God — He's still a Waymaker!

## February 2 – God Is My Provider

*"And the children of Israel ate manna forty years, until they came to an inhabited land; they ate manna until they came to the border of the land of Canaan." (Exodus 16:35)*

Having been delivered from slavery and spared from death at the hands of the Egyptians, you would think that the Israelites would've been eternally grateful. Sadly, that was not the case. Just days into their journey toward the Promised Land, their cheers turned to jeers — "Oh, that we had died by the hand of the Lord in the land of Egypt, when we sat by the pots of meat and when we ate bread to the full!" (Exodus 16:3). Just a little bit of hunger made the Israelites forget how bad they had it in Egypt.

Being the merciful God He is, our Lord heard their complaints and promised to provide food for them. Six days a week, God provided what they called "manna." In Hebrew, manna means "what is it," because the people hadn't seen anything quite like it before. Scripture says it was "like white coriander seed, and the taste of it was like wafers made with honey" (Exodus 16:31). The people were to collect manna every morning and then enough for two days on the sixth day.

It's an amazing demonstration of God's provision that He gave them manna to eat for forty years — all the way until the time they took possession of the Promised Land. God provided every need they had, and the same is true for us as well. We don't have a single need that God does not provide — food, clothes, shelter, work, etc. Every good and perfect gift comes from Him (James 1:17). Let's always be thankful to God for the tender mercies He showers on us daily.

## February 3 — Supporting My Brother

*"Moses' hands became heavy; so they took a stone and put it under him, and he sat on it. And Aaron and Hur supported his hands, one on one side, and the other on the other side; and his hands were steady until the going down of the sun. So Joshua defeated Amalek and his people with the edge of the sword." (Exodus 17:12-13)*

Moses was an amazing man of God, but he was still human. He needed help just like we need help. On one occasion, the Israelites went to war against the Amalekites. Moses instructed Joshua to take the armies of God into battle while he went up on the mountain to intercede on their behalf. Moses took Aaron and Hur with him, and while they looked on, Moses held "the rod of God" in his hand. As long as he held it high, the Israelites were victorious over their enemies.

As we all know, your arms get heavy when you try to hold them up for an extended period of time. Moses grew weary trying to hold up his staff, and when he lowered his arms to try and get some rest, the Israelites started losing. Aaron and Hur saw what was happening and they took action. First, they put a stone under Moses so he could sit and rest. Next, both of them got on either side of Moses and held up his hands.

The results were amazing. With Aaron and Hur assisting Moses, the Israelites won a decisive battle over the Amalekites. What if Aaron and Hur had decided to let Moses go it alone? It's pretty certain that Israel would've been routed on their way to the Promised Land. The point is clear — we need the help of others and they need our help too. When we got saved, God put us in the Body of Christ. As brothers and sisters in Christ, let's do all we can to hold up one another's hands.

## February 4 — Fire on the Mountain

> "Now Mount Sinai was completely in smoke, because the LORD descended upon it in fire. Its smoke ascended like the smoke of a furnace, and the whole mountain quaked greatly." (Exodus 19:18)

Most everyone is familiar with the Ten Commandments. While many Christians probably couldn't name each of the commandments, even lost people have a general idea of what they represent — no stealing, no lying, no adultery, etc. What most people probably don't recall are the circumstances surrounding the giving of these commands. They didn't just fall down from heaven into Moses' hands. There was a much more awesome demonstration of God's glory.

When the children of Israel reached Mount Sinai, God instructed Moses to come up on the mountain to receive the Law. Prior to his ascension, Moses saw to it that a boundary was set around the base of Mount Sinai so that no one could approach the mountain or attempt to climb up. God strictly warned Moses and the Israelites that anyone seeking to ascend the mountain would be struck down by God Himself. For that reason, no one dared approach the mountain as God dealt with Moses.

The scene was extraordinary as "Mount Sinai was completely in smoke, because the LORD descended upon it in fire." The thick smoke was actually a protective barrier between the people and the Lord, so that they could not gaze on His glory. The presence of God shook the mountain. What are we to take from this awesome scene? We should understand that our God is holy and awesome and that there is none other like Him. He is worthy of our best worship and our unconditional obedience!

## February 5 – The Sin of the Scribes and Pharisees

> *"Then Jesus spoke to the multitudes and to His disciples, saying: 'The scribes and the Pharisees sit in Moses' seat. Therefore whatever they tell you to observe, that observe and do, but do not do according to their works; for they say, and do not do.'" (Matthew 23:1-3)*

Most everyone loved Jesus during His earthly ministry, at least for a while. The sick and the outcast were especially drawn to Jesus, because in Him they felt something they had never before experienced. Unfortunately, many of those who loved Jesus for a while fell away later (John 6:66). In the end, it was really just Jesus, His mother, His disciples, and a few friends. But there were two groups who had disdain for Jesus from the outset of His ministry — the scribes and Pharisees.

Both groups represented the religious leaders of the day. Jesus even acknowledged that both scribes and Pharisees "sit in Moses' seat." That is, they had received a holy inheritance and they had the right to instruct the people in the Law of Moses. For that reason, Jesus instructed His disciples to observe their teachings but not to follow their example. Why? Because "they say, and do not do." In other words, they preach the Word, but they don't live the Word.

Of course, the overarching sin of the scribes and Pharisees was blasphemy — they denied that Jesus was the Christ and attributed His work to the devil (Matthew 12). But the manifestation of their blasphemy was hypocrisy. They felt they were at liberty to place heavy burdens on others without lifting their fingers to carry a single one (Matthew 23:4). We need to learn from their wickedness — just like the scribes and Pharisees, we will suffer God's judgment if our walk doesn't match our talk.

## February 6 — General Revelation

*"The heavens declare the glory of God; and the firmament shows His handiwork." (Psalm 19:1)*

Seminarians are often charged with the task of studying theology. A popular course among those preparing for ministry is "Systematic Theology." Basically, systematic theology takes the great doctrines of the faith and organizes them into categories of study and analysis. Key to any study of theology is the doctrine of "general revelation," which asserts that God revealed His existence to every person in the world through more general or indirect means.

Today's verse provides us with just one way God reveals His existence to every member of the human race: "The heavens declare the glory of God; and the firmament shows His handiwork." How can someone look at the blue sky and the white clouds and conclude that there is no God? How can someone look over the expansive horizon and determine that it all just popped up out of nothing? Twice the Psalms tell us, "The fool has said in his heart, 'There is no God'" (14:1; 53:1).

Through His creation, God has revealed His existence to the human race so that no man can stand before Jesus on the day of judgment and make excuses (Romans 1:20). And being the benevolent God He is, Jehovah also provided a general revelation of Himself in the conscience of every person (Romans 2:14-15). In essence, God has made it impossible to deny His existence. Down deep, everyone knows there really is a God. Sadly, many choose to suppress that truth in unrighteousness (Romans 1:18).

## February 7 — Special Revelation

*"The law of the L*ORD *is perfect, converting the soul;*
*The testimony of the L*ORD *is sure, making wise the simple;*
*The statutes of the L*ORD *are right, rejoicing the heart;*
*The commandment of the L*ORD *is pure, enlightening the eyes;*
*The fear of the L*ORD *is clean, enduring forever;*
*The judgments of the L*ORD *are true and righteous altogether."*
*(Psalm 19:7-9)*

After establishing the general revelation of God to every human being, the psalmist David then moves to demonstrate that God utilizes an even greater form of revelation. This greater form is called "special revelation," and in this case it's a reference to the Word of God. Just look at all the things David said about God's Word! First, he talks about the perfection of God's Law. It is through the Law that a man becomes aware of his sin and gains the opportunity to repent and be converted to Christ.

He also refers to the Word as the testimony of the Lord. The testimony of God's Word is certain, and as such it makes wise men out of fools. David also calls Scripture "the statutes of the LORD." God's Word clearly directs us to and through God's perfect will, and we find that obedience to those statutes causes our hearts to rejoice. And, of course, we know Scripture is filled with "the commandment of the LORD," which is pure, helping us to understand the difference between right and wrong.

David also calls Scripture "the fear of the LORD," in the sense that Scripture teaches us a holy reverence for God, which is "clean." The fear of the Lord endures forever because God will never cease to be holy. The psalmist finishes with "the judgments of the LORD." Clearly, God's judgments are "true and righteous altogether" because our God does not lie (Titus 1:2). These truths show us that God has gone into great detail revealing Himself to His creation.

## February 8 — Staying Power of the Word

*"Heaven and earth will pass away, but My words will by no means pass away." (Matthew 24:35)*

Think about all the things that come and go. So many things have very little staying power. Take fashion, for instance — when was the last time you saw someone walking around in a pair of bell-bottoms? How about hairstyles? You don't see quite as many Afros these days as you did in the '70s. Think about interior decorating. The '70s also gave us burnt orange shag carpet and lime green cars. These days, most homes are built with hardwood floors, and lime green is something you find in the fruit basket.

Even leaders come and go — presidents, prime ministers, kings and queens — they all run their course. But there is one King who was, and is, and forevermore shall be. His name is King Jesus, and not only is He eternal, but His Word is timeless as well. While talking about the end of time during His Olivet Discourse, Jesus wanted everyone to understand that His Word is trustworthy. Though heaven and earth will pass away, Jesus says, "My words will by no means pass away."

What does that mean for us as followers of Christ? First, we can take confidence in everything God has said. Times and trends change, but the Word of God will never be wrong. Also, it gives us hope that God has a plan for the future. Much prophecy has been fulfilled, but there is much yet to be completed. We can trust that every word of Jesus will come to pass. Instead of building our lives on the shifting sands of change, let us always cling to the timeless Word of God.

## February 9 — Where Is Your Trust?

*"Some trust in chariots, and some in horses; but we will remember the name of the* Lord *our God." (Psalm 20:7)*

Trust is defined as "firm belief in the reliability, truth, ability, or strength of someone or something." People place their trust in lots of things. Of course, just about everyone has another person or multiple people that they trust — parents, children, siblings, coworkers, etc. We also place our trust in law enforcement and emergency personnel. And, of course, people place their trust in material things such as houses, cars, appliances, etc.

Today's verse reminds us that many people place their trust in military prowess and strength. Chariots and horses might not seem too great in the 21st century, but 3,000 years ago they were the instruments of modern warfare. In our contemporary culture, we relate more with planes, guns, rockets, etc. Americans place a great deal of confidence in our military, and rightfully so. Our military is the finest in the world. No other country can rival our battle resources.

It's fine to trust in military power, but if our confidence ends there then we've got a big problem. Even great armies have fallen on the field of battle. During the American Revolution, minutemen often turned back the most powerful army in the world! Rather than placing our trust in warriors and weapons, we must place our faith in Almighty God. When armies have done all they can do, God can surpass them to accomplish the impossible. Trust Him with every detail of your life!

## February 10 – Not All Calves Are Gold

*"And he received the gold from their hand, and he fashioned it with an engraving tool, and made a molded calf. Then they said, 'This is your god, O Israel, that brought you out of the land of Egypt!'" (Exodus 32:4)*

Israel followed the leadership of the Lord as they made their way to the Promised Land, and what an amazing journey it was! On the way, they had seen God part the Red Sea. They had tasted manna from heaven and water in the desert. God had even promised to establish His covenant with the people, and in doing so He called Moses to return to Mount Sinai so He could give him the Law. It was quite a bit of information, so Moses stayed on the mountain with the Lord for forty days.

Israel had agreed to serve the Lord and keep His commands, but when Moses was delayed in coming down, the people instructed Aaron to "build a god." Just a thought — if your god requires construction, he's probably no god at all, but I digress. It was typical for the ancients to worship idols, and the Israelites had spent 400 years in a land that was steeped in pagan worship. When Aaron should've resisted the people, he took the coward's way out and made a golden calf.

It was not a pretty picture when Moses came down from the mountain. He rebuked the people, ground the golden calf to powder, and made them drink it! The story should remind us that while some idols are made of gold, many others are not. We tend to make idols of possessions, relationships, jobs, salaries, etc. You may not be worshiping at the feet of a golden calf, but that doesn't mean you're not worshiping an idol. If there is anything in your life higher than God, that is your idol! Make certain that God is the highest priority of your life!

## February 11 – Bringing My Best to Jesus

*"And when Jesus was in Bethany at the house of Simon the leper, a woman came to Him having an alabaster flask of very costly fragrant oil, and she poured it on His head as He sat at the table. But when His disciples saw it, they were indignant, saying, 'Why this waste? For this fragrant oil might have been sold for much and given to the poor.'" (Matthew 26:6-9)*

Answer this question honestly: Do you think most Christians bring their very best to Jesus? There are many ways we could formulate an answer, but let's consider just the area of giving. How well do most Christians give to the work of the Lord? On average, Christians give about 2.5 percent of their income to the local church. During the Great Depression about 100 years ago, Christians were giving 3.3 percent of their income to churches at a time when it was difficult to give anything at all!

Today's verses tell the story of a woman identified as Mary in parallel gospel accounts. Nothing in the text suggests that this dear woman was wealthy, but when it came time to bring something to Jesus, she brought her very best. John the Apostle tells us she offered the Savior a pound of costly oil of spikenard. The oil was valued at one year's wages because it had to be derived from the nard plant of Northern India. It would be hard to find a more costly gift!

When the disciples saw the gift, they felt it was a waste. They argued it could be used for the poor, but they were only concerned about themselves. Jesus rebuked the disciples and praised the woman's generosity. Mary probably didn't have much to bring to Jesus, but she brought the best she had. Maybe you and I are the same way, feeling we have very little to present to God. Take the first and best of what you have and give it to Jesus. Instead of giving Him what's left, let's bring Him our best!

## February 12 — When God's People Brought Too Much

*"So Moses gave a commandment, and they caused it to be proclaimed throughout the camp, saying, 'Let neither man nor woman do any more work for the offering of the sanctuary.' And the people were restrained from bringing, for the material they had was sufficient for all the work to be done — indeed too much." (Exodus 36:6-7)*

Many people have chronicled the giving woes within local churches. It's very rare that churches have all the resources they need to do the Lord's work effectively. Many times cuts have to be made because there simply is not enough to work with. The problem is probably twofold. First, some Christians don't understand biblical tithing — it's a problem of ignorance. On the other hand, many Christians do understand biblical tithing, but simply choose not to practice it — a problem of obedience.

It's no secret that the Israelites had their problems. On more than one occasion, God had called them a "stiff-necked people." Yet for all their problems, on this occasion they got it right. When the time came for the tabernacle to be constructed, Moses collected an offering for the sanctuary. The people brought so many materials to Moses that he had to take unprecedented action — he had to command God's people to stop giving because they brought too much!

I've grown up in church and pastored several churches. I have never said, nor have I ever heard a pastor say, that God's people needed to stop giving. Wouldn't that be something, though? Just once in my ministry I'd love to address the church and say, "Hey guys, you've been so generous that we don't have any more room for your offerings. Please don't give anymore!" As unlikely as that seems, it's not impossible. When all God's people begin to take their giving seriously, there will be more than enough.

## February 13 — The Fear of the Lord

*"The fear of the Lord is to hate evil; pride and arrogance and the evil way and the perverse mouth I hate." (Proverbs 8:13)*

Humans are afraid of lots of things — too many to count. Some phobias are more common than others. For instance, one of the most common phobias in the world is the fear of public speaking. It causes some people to sweat, break out in hives, and even forget what they were going to say. Another fear high on the list is the fear of heights. For that reason, lots of people avoid roller coasters. And of course, many people fear bugs, insects, spiders, snakes, etc.

Most people you ask would probably not say they are afraid of God, but the Bible talks at length about "the fear of the Lord." What exactly does it mean? Most of us would associate fear with emotion — anxiety, despair, nervousness, etc. While a healthy fear of God is certainly emotional, it's much more than what you feel. The fear of the Lord is actually much more concerned with what we do. Basically, a holy reverence for God's presence will prompt you to take action for His glory.

Solomon gives us a good idea of what holy fear looks like — "the fear of the Lord is to hate evil." What does that mean? He explains — "pride and arrogance and the evil way and the perverse mouth." Evil involves unholy thoughts, actions, and words. Someone who fears the Lord turns from evil and exemplifies holiness. And the good news is that a person who fears the Lord never has to be afraid of anything else. "In all your ways acknowledge Him, and He shall direct your paths" (Proverbs 3:6).

## February 14 — Holiness to the Lord

*"Then they made the plate of the holy crown of pure gold, and wrote on it an inscription like the engraving of a signet: HOLINESS TO THE LORD. And they tied to it a blue cord, to fasten it above on the turban, as the Lord had commanded Moses." (Exodus 39:30-31)*

Theologians often attempt to summarize portions of God's Word for the sake of simplicity and learning. Here's one such summary — the Old Testament magnifies the holiness of God, while the New Testament emphasizes His great love. Follow me on this for a moment. There are two main attributes of God — holiness and love. God's holiness demanded a punishment for sin, and His amazing love provided the sacrifice we needed. God's love is only understood against the backdrop of His holiness.

Of course, the holiness and love of God are readily visible in both testaments because He is the same yesterday, today, and forever (Hebrews 13:8). But holiness is a predominant theme of the Old Testament, especially with the giving of the Law. What is holiness? In Hebrew, the word is *qodesh,* and it means "separateness." The Law was given to mankind to teach us one thing — God is separate from sin, and those who long to enter His presence must separate themselves from sin as well.

That brings me to today's verses. Through the Mosaic Law, God instructed the Israelites to prepare special garments for the priests. Among those garments was a turban adorned on a golden plate with the following inscription — HOLINESS TO THE LORD. At the pinnacle of the priestly service — the most important place in Israel — God wanted everyone to know that He is holy. Reflecting on God's holiness, the Apostle Peter quoted the Old Testament to provide us with a vitally important reminder — "Be holy, for I am holy" (1 Peter 1:16).

# February 15 — The Day the Veil Was Torn

*"And Jesus cried out again with a loud voice, and yielded up His spirit. Then, behold, the veil of the temple was torn in two from top to bottom; and the earth quaked, and the rocks were split, and the graves were opened; and many bodies of the saints who had fallen asleep were raised; and coming out of the graves after His resurrection, they went into the holy city and appeared to many." (Matthew 27:50-53)*

You're probably familiar with many of the details surrounding Christ's crucifixion — how He was arrested by the Pharisees, condemned by the Romans, and brutally beaten and mocked by the soldiers. You probably know that Jesus carried His cross to Calvary and died for the sins of mankind at the place of the skull. You might know that He hung on the cross for about six hours and that He finally died. But do you know exactly what happened when Jesus took His final breath?

According to the Gospels, the last words to come from the mouth of Jesus were "Father, into Your hands I commit my spirit" (Luke 23:46). Having cried out in anguish, the Bible says He took His last breath. At that very moment, something amazing occurred — "the veil of the temple was torn in two from top to bottom." The "veil" was the curtain that separated the holy place from the most holy place. Historically, the Ark of the Covenant had been in the most holy place behind the veil. The most holy place was the place of God's presence.

Why did God choose to tear the veil when His Son died? I believe it was God making a statement to us — through the blood of Jesus we can now have access to God. Prior to this time, only the High Priest could enter the most holy place one time a year. God wanted us to know that we no longer need a priestly mediator because King Jesus is now our Mediator! The spontaneous resurrection of many around Jerusalem at the death of Jesus is further proof that He alone is the Son of God!

## February 16 – The Assurance of a Shepherd

*"The Lord is my shepherd; I shall not want." (Psalm 23:1)*

These are some of the most familiar words in all the Word of God. Psalm 23 comes to us from David — a ruddy shepherd boy whom God appointed to be the King of Israel. Having been a shepherd throughout his early life, it's only appropriate that David used the analogy of a shepherd and sheep to bring us one of the most beautiful passages in the Scripture. He begins by identifying his shepherd — "the Lord is my shepherd." Clearly, that is a reference to Jehovah — and, of course, our Savior Jesus, who identified Himself as "the Good Shepherd" (John 10:11, 14).

So many things about our Good Shepherd are reassuring. Let's think about all He does. First, the psalm says He is our *Leader*. Verse 5 says He holds a staff in His hand. Shepherds had a crook on the end of their staff so they could lead the sheep. "He leads me beside the still waters" and "He leads me in the paths of righteousness." Not only that, but our Shepherd is our *Provider* — "You prepare a table for me ... You anoint my head with oil ... my cup runs over." He provides all our needs!

And of course, our Shepherd is our *Protector*. Just as our Shepherd carries a staff for direction, He also carries a rod for our protection (v. 4). Even as we walk through "the valley of the shadow of death," Jesus promises to go with us and to ward off all enemies. Reflecting on all the comfort and assurance a shepherd brings, David finished with an amazing truth — "Surely goodness and mercy shall follow me all the days of my life; and I will dwell in the house of the Lord forever" (v. 6).

## February 17 — Who May Come to Worship?

*"Who may ascend into the hill of the Lord? Or who may stand in His holy place? He who has clean hands and a pure heart, who has not lifted up his soul to an idol, nor sworn deceitfully."* (Psalm 24:3-4)

In today's psalm, David explores the extent of God's sovereignty and asks some critical questions. He begins with a declaration — "The earth is the Lord's and all its fullness" (v. 1). Simply stated, everything belongs to God — He is sovereign over everything in the world. As such, He is worthy of worship and praise. But that begs the question — who may ascend into the holy hill of the Lord, or who may stand in His holy place?

To understand these questions, we need to understand something about Jewish worship. The Jews worshiped in Jerusalem on top of Mount Moriah — the place where Abraham was willing to sacrifice his son Isaac thousands of years ago. When the ancient Jews went to worship, they had to ascend the southern steps to make their way on top of the temple mount. And even prior to climbing the steps, they had to wash themselves in the *mikveh* located at the base of the southern steps.

Not just anyone could ascend the temple mount and approach the presence of God. Preparation had to be made in order to worship the Lord. I fear this is something we miss in our 21st century worship. Ask yourself, before coming to worship, do you ask God to forgive your sins (clean hands) and to change your heart (a pure heart)? Before coming to worship, do you denounce all idols and pledge your allegiance only to Christ? If so, you're just the sort of person God is looking for in worship.

# February 18 – As One Having Authority

*"Then they went into Capernaum, and immediately on the Sabbath He entered the synagogue and taught. And they were astonished at His teaching, for He taught them as one having authority, and not as the scribes." (Mark 1:21-22)*

There are many types of preachers. Some preach for the right reasons, and some preach for the wrong ones. Some preach to glorify God, and some preach to promote themselves. There are true men of God, and there are false teachers — and in the 21st century, the line seems to have blurred between the two. Some say a preacher should not try to preach with any authority. Rather, he should consider the perspective of his audience and make some inductive comments based on their experience.

I imagine there were just about as many false teachers in Christ's day as there are today. The Pharisees, Sadducees, and religious leaders of the day were often among them. Often, they preached the traditions of men with very little reference to the Word of God. Yet, when Jesus came, everything changed. After His baptism, temptation, and the selection of some early disciples, the Bible says Jesus went to Capernaum and taught the people on the Sabbath.

Immediately, those listening in the synagogue noticed the difference. Christ wasn't like all their other teachers. I'm sure many of the rabbis who taught in the synagogue simply repeated what they heard from the religious leaders in Jerusalem. Jesus was different — "He taught them as one having authority." He didn't meander around talking about traditions and guidelines. He dove into the Word of God and preached in the power of the Holy Spirit — something preachers must still do today! The authority always rests in the Word of God.

## February 19 – The Focus of Our Worship

*"By those who come near Me I must be regarded as holy; and before all the people I must be glorified." (Leviticus 10:3)*

If you were to ask most Christians about the object of worship, I'm sure they would respond with "God" or "Jesus." Of course, they are correct — Jehovah is the object of our worship, and we approach Him through the blood of His Son Jesus. But if you asked those same Christians about the emphasis of our worship, you'd probably get a variety of answers. Thankfully, God has not left us to wonder about all He desires for us and Himself in worship.

Today's verse takes us back to an occasion about 3,400 years ago, when God had established the priesthood and was guiding the children of Israel through the early days of worship. Aaron (Moses' brother) and his descendants were God's appointed priests, but within that priesthood there were clear commands that God expected his priests to follow. On one occasion, Nadab and Abihu were not mindful of those expectations, and they experienced the wrath of God as a result.

Aaron's sons "offered profane fire before the Lord" — that is, they made an offering to the Lord which He had not commanded. God explained the death of both young men to their father — "by those who come near Me I must be regarded as holy." Aaron's sons disregarded God's holiness when they disobeyed His commands. Furthermore, God said, "Before all the people I must be glorified." So then, let us learn that our worship must always emphasize God's holiness and declare God's glory. Anything less simply won't do.

## February 20 – Bringing My Friends to Jesus

> *"Then they came to Him, bringing a paralytic who was carried by four men. And when they could not come near Him because of the crowd, they uncovered the roof where He was. So when they had broken through, they let down the bed on which the paralytic was lying. When Jesus saw their faith, He said to the paralytic, 'Son, your sins are forgiven you.'" (Mark 2:3-5)*

After Jesus initiated His public ministry, He made the seaside city of Capernaum sort of a "ministry headquarters" over the course of the next years. On one occasion, He came to Capernaum, and the Scripture says, "It was heard that He was in the house" (Mark 2:1). I wonder if people get the impression that "Jesus is in the house" when they visit our homes, our churches, our jobs, etc.? When Jesus is in the house, everything changes. Oh, the difference our Savior makes!

When word spread that Jesus was near, everyone flooded the home to capacity — standing room only. That was bad news for a paralytic whose four friends intended to bring him to Jesus. When they arrived at the home where Jesus was staying, there was no way into the home through the door, the windows, etc. The four men were so desperate to get their friend to Christ that they took urgent action — they broke through the roof and lowered him down.

Jesus was impressed by their faith in action. "When Jesus saw *their* faith, He said to the paralytic, 'Son, your sins are forgiven you.'" If we're not careful, we can read right over that. Jesus didn't just honor the paralytic's faith — He honored the faith of his four friends as well! Because of their faith, Jesus healed the man by His miracle-working power. Think about it — some of our friends are sin-sick and in desperate need of Jesus. Will we do all we can to bring our friends to Christ?

## February 21 — The Necessity of Hard Work

*"He who has a slack hand becomes poor, but the hand of the diligent makes rich. He who gathers in summer is a wise son; he who sleeps in harvest is a son who causes shame." (Proverbs 10:4-5)*

Have you ever had one of those mornings where you're nestled in your bed, dreaming a great dream, with the sound of a steady downpour falling on the roof? And then it happens — your alarm goes off! You've got a decision to make — you can lay there and continue to enjoy the warmth of a comfy bed, or you can get up and get to work. Those are the moments we want to listen to our flesh and just stay in bed, but we know that obligations demand that we rise and get to work.

In today's verses, Solomon warns against laziness, while at the same time commending the value of hard work. Those who are lazy "become poor" and "cause shame." I'm sure we've all known able-bodied people who refuse to work. They wait on their parents or the government to provide for their needs. In the process, they often have to beg from others just to supply their necessities. That's not to mention what laziness does to our reputation while bringing shame to our families.

Solomon reminds us that "the hand of the diligent makes rich." Of course, we know it's not the goal of the Christian life to get rich. In fact, service to God might often impoverish us, but it's in those times we learn there is much more to being rich than monetary wealth. Yet, work enables us to provide for our needs and it demonstrates our wisdom. Those who work hard are able to lay aside resources that can be used in the future. As Christ-followers, let's commit ourselves to work hard each day for God's glory.

## February 22 – The Only Unforgivable Sin

> *"Assuredly, I say to you, all sins will be forgiven the sons of men, and whatever blasphemies they may utter; but he who blasphemes against the Holy Spirit never has forgiveness, but is subject to eternal condemnation."* (Mark 3:28-29)

Think of the vilest sins a person could ever commit. I think we'd have to place murder high on the list. Someone once said that murder takes away everything that a person has and everything that he's going to have. I think we'd also have to place the abuse of innocent children high on the list. When someone harms the most vulnerable among us, they deserve to be punished. The sins are too many to name — lying, theft, bribery, pornography, etc.

There's one thing all those sins have in common — every one of them can be forgiven. You might think, "Really? Even a pedophile can be forgiven?" The answer is yes — any person who turns to Jesus Christ in faith is forgiven of ALL their sins — past, present, and future. Every sin is placed under the blood of Jesus when we surrender our lives to Christ. That said, there's only one sin God will not forgive. Jesus called it blasphemy against the Holy Spirit.

What is blasphemy? It's refusing to believe the Holy Spirit's testimony about God and His Son Jesus. The Pharisees were guilty of blasphemy because they attributed the work of Christ to demons. Consequently, Jesus said they would be eternally condemned. So then, if a person dies without believing the Spirit's testimony and placing their faith in Jesus, they will receive the same condemnation. To that end, don't die an unrepentant blasphemer — believe the Holy Spirit's testimony and place your faith in Jesus today!

## February 23 – How We Come Into God's Presence

*"And the LORD said to Moses: 'Tell Aaron your brother not to come at just any time into the Holy Place inside the veil, before the mercy seat which is on the ark, lest he die; for I will appear in the cloud above the mercy seat." (Leviticus 16:2)*

Just after the Exodus, God told Moses that his brother Aaron and his sons would serve as priests before the Lord. Shortly thereafter, Aaron and his sons began their priestly service. Aaron's sons made a critical mistake — they offered an incense offering to God that He did not ask for. As a result, both of them were killed for offering "profane fire." In the wake of that tragedy, God gave clear instructions to Aaron through his brother Moses.

He warned Aaron "not to come at just any time into the Holy Place." Why? Because inside the Most Holy Place was the Ark of the Covenant. On top of the Ark was the mercy seat — the place where the Shekinah glory of God would rest as God visited His people. God's instructions to Aaron were a precautionary warning — He didn't want Aaron to be in the Most Holy Place when He came to rest on the mercy seat. Exposure to the unveiled glory of God would mean certain death to Aaron.

Instead, God let Aaron know he was to come behind the veil only once a year to make atonement for his sins and those of Israel. God also instructed Aaron to make certain preparations — the sacrifices, the blood, the scapegoat, etc. It's clear that Aaron was not to come into God's presence unwanted and unprepared. Think about the preparation you and I make before coming to worship the Lord. Are we coming at "just any time" and any way, or do we carefully consider ourselves and our offerings to God?

## February 24 — Nothing to Fear

*"The Lord is my light and my salvation; whom shall I fear? The Lord is the strength of my life; of whom shall I be afraid?" (Psalm 27:1)*

In his 1933 inaugural address, President Franklin Delano Roosevelt said, "We have nothing to fear but fear itself." In the period between World War I and World War II, and in the wake of the Great Depression, many people were paralyzed with fear because of economic instability. As a result, many Americans started withdrawing their money from the banks, further endangering the American economy. FDR's words were a plea for everyone to set aside their fears and stay the course.

Many Americans could stand to hear the former President's admonition about 100 years later. The folks we encounter are afraid of many things. "Are my children safe when I send them to school? Am I going to have enough money to pay the bills? Will I be able to provide insurance for myself and my family? What happens if my job gets sent to another country?" Unfortunately, we tend to fear the worst, and even if our fears never materialize, the internal damage has already been done.

The psalmist David reminds us that a child of God has nothing to fear. Why? Because "the Lord is my light and my salvation." God Himself lights our way every day and by His grace we are saved, never to be lost again! Furthermore, "the Lord is the strength of my life." He empowers us with everything necessary to resist the devil and draw near to Jesus. Child of God, if you've been living in fear, you have no one but yourself to blame. Place your faith in God and trust Him with the results!

# February 25 — Go and Tell

*"And when He got into the boat, he who had been demon-possessed begged Him that he might be with Him. However, Jesus did not permit him, but said to him, 'Go home to your friends, and tell them what great things the Lord has done for you, and how He has had compassion on you.' And he departed and began to proclaim in Decapolis all that Jesus had done for him; and all marveled." (Mark 5:18-20)*

In Mark 5, we're introduced to one of the most fascinating stories in the Bible. Jesus crossed the Sea of Galilee with the disciples, and when He stepped on the shore, a man who was severely demon-possessed came out to meet Him. Later, when Jesus asked about the demons' identity, they identified themselves as "Legion, for we are many" (Mark 5:9). We can't know for certain how many demons there were, but it took 6,000 soldiers to make a Roman legion. Imagine all those demons!

The demons begged Jesus not to torment them. Why? Because even the devil and every demon of hell know they are on borrowed time. They know it won't be much longer until Jesus banishes them to hell forever. Jesus honored the demons' request and permitted them to enter a herd of swine that was stationed on top of a hill. The swine were so overwhelmed by the demons that they ran into the Sea of Galilee, departing from the man who we call the Gadarenan demoniac.

After the man was set free of the demons, he "begged Him that he might be with Him." I wonder if we're that desperate to spend time with God. Jesus must've loved the man's passion, but He had a different assignment for Him — "Go home to your friends, and tell them what great things the Lord has done for you." The man got the message — he spread the message of Jesus throughout all the Decapolis (ten cities). If Jesus has saved you and set you free, who are you telling? Don't keep the Good News to yourself!

## February 26 – Jesus Is Lord

*"Then He took the child by the hand, and said to her, 'Talitha, cumi' which is translated, 'Little girl, I say to you, arise.' Immediately the girl arose and walked, for she was twelve years of age. And they were overcome with great amazement." (Mark 5:41-42)*

In Mark 4-5, we are presented with four miracles that prove Christ's Lordship over all things. At the end of Mark 4, Jesus proved that He is Lord over disaster by calming a raging storm. In the proceeding verses, Jesus proved He is Lord over demons by exorcising a legion of demons from a man of Gadara. Moving further in Chapter 5, we see that Jesus is Lord over disease, because He healed a woman from a hemorrhage she'd been suffering with for twelve long years!

But Mark saved the best for last. Not only is Jesus Lord over disaster, demons, and disease — He is even Lord over DEATH. A man named Jairus came to ask Jesus to help his twelve-year-old daughter who was dying. On the way to Jairus' house, Jesus was detained by the woman with the issue of blood. Jesus asked, "Who touched me?" because He knew that power had gone out from Him. Jesus assured the woman that she need not fear, because her faith had made her well.

Unfortunately, the time it took for Christ to encounter the woman was all the time it took for Jairus' daughter to die. They said, "It's too late! Why trouble the Master any further?" When Christ arrived, He went into the girl's room, took her hand, and said, "Little girl, I say to you, arise." At that very moment, breath re-entered her body and she rose from the dead. Jesus proved His Lordship over the grave! Clearly, Jesus is Lord of all, but have you acknowledged Him as Lord of your life?

## February 27 – Shaking the Dust from Your Feet

*"And whoever will not receive you nor hear you, when you depart from there, shake off the dust under your feet as a testimony against them. Assuredly, I say to you, it will be more tolerable for Sodom and Gomorrah in the day of judgment than for that city!" (Mark 6:11)*

Have you ever been rejected? No one likes being rejected. Maybe you asked someone out on a date and you were turned down. Maybe you applied for a job you really hoped to get, only to find out the job was given to someone else. Maybe you were applying for a loan to purchase your dream home, only to find out that the bank didn't think you could make the payment. Being rejected hurts, and many people bear the scars of past rejection.

If you've been following Jesus for any amount of time, you're well aware that it's possible for a person to be rejected just because he/she professes to follow Christ. But why would someone reject us on account of Jesus? He went around healing the sick, loving the unloved, and giving hope to the hopeless. Yes, but He also taught things that were hard for some to hear. Some of His truths are still hard for our culture to hear, such as "no one comes to the Father except through Me" (John 14:6).

As a Christian, you're obligated to share the Gospel. Why? Because there is simply no other hope for mankind. And yet, we live in a world that teaches there are many ways of salvation, or that salvation is not necessary at all. If you've made multiple attempts to share the Good News with those who refuse to hear it, Jesus instructs you to "shake the dust from your feet" and move on to those who still haven't heard. Oswald Smith once said, "No one has the right to hear the Gospel twice while there remains someone who has not heard it once."

## February 28 — Listen More, Talk Less

*"In the multitude of words sin is not lacking, but he who restrains his lips is wise." (Proverbs 10:19)*

There's nothing more frustrating than feeling like you aren't being heard. You're trying to make a good point, but it just doesn't seem like anyone is listening. It's important to us that we be heard, and rightfully so. But, sometimes we fail to remember that communication is a two-way street. Do we want to hear the voice of others just as much as we want our voice to be heard? If we're honest, we have to admit that sometimes we talk too much while not listening enough.

A wise person once said, "God gave you two ears to hear and one mouth to speak." The idea is that God designed us to listen just as much, if not more, than we speak. In today's verse, Solomon reminds us that talking too much is a sure path to sin. "In the multitude of words sin is not lacking." We've all been guilty of thinking before speaking, and the sad thing is we can't pull our words back into our mouths once they've hit the air. When it's out there, it's gone for good.

How many times have we hurt ourselves and others with the things we've said? Reflecting on the mischief our words have created, we understand why Solomon said, "He who restrains his lips is wise." Think about it like this — if we don't really need to talk, then maybe we shouldn't. The Bible says that "a gentle and quiet spirit" (1 Peter 3:4) is very precious in the sight of God. So, let's limit the words we say, and when we do speak let's make sure it's for "necessary edification" (Ephesians 4:29).

## February 29 — Truth Trumps Tradition

> *"'For laying aside the commandment of God, you hold the tradition of men — the washing of pitchers and cups, and many other such things you do.' He said to them, 'All too well you reject the commandment of God, that you may keep your tradition.'"* (Mark 7:8-9)

A tradition is defined as "the transmission of customs or beliefs from generation to generation, or the fact of being passed on in this way." All of us are fond of some traditions that are dear to us. For instance, I'm a big Tennessee football fan. Singing Rocky Top when Tennessee scores a touchdown is something I love to do. Watching the Pride of the Southland Band open up the "T" while the team runs out of the north end zone of Neyland Stadium is something I love to witness.

Traditions can be harmless, but they can also become very detrimental — especially when those traditions start to trump the truths God has revealed to us. Today's verses are taken from an occasion where the Pharisees and scribes came to check on the "rabble-rouser" Jesus. They observed Jesus' disciples eating bread with what they called "defiled" (unwashed) hands. That was a big no-no for the Pharisees who were very concerned with washing hands, pitchers, cups, couches, etc.

Jesus rebuked the Pharisees by citing the words of Isaiah the prophet — "in vain they worship Me, teaching as doctrines the commandments of men" (Mark 7:7). Jesus rightfully charged the Pharisees with being more concerned about keeping traditions than obeying commandments. Even in our own day, it's possible for individual Christians and churches to allow their traditions to become more important than God's Word. Let's all be sure to keep our temporary traditions submitted to God's timeless truth.

## March 1 — The Tithe Belongs to God

*"And all the tithe of the land, whether of the seed of the land or of the fruit of the tree, is the Lord's. It is holy to the Lord." (Leviticus 27:30)*

A great preacher once said, "When it comes to tithing, Abraham commenced it, Jacob continued it, Moses commanded it, Malachi confirmed it, Jesus commended it, so who am I to cancel it?" What was the old preacher talking about? A tithe is a gift of 10 percent that is offered to the Lord. In the Old Testament, it could've been 10 percent of a person's harvest, livestock, wealth, etc. Abraham was the first person to give a tithe when he offered 10 percent of all he had to Melchizedek (Genesis 14:20).

And the old preacher was right — Jacob continued the practice of tithing (Genesis 28:22) when he vowed to give back to God 10 percent of all God blessed him with. In today's passage, we find Moses commanding the tithe of the Israelites by the decree of God Himself. The last of the minor prophets, Malachi, also confirmed the tithe when he rebuked his kinsmen for robbing God (Malachi 3:8-10). God said His people were cursed because they had withheld their tithes and offerings.

Some say tithing is an Old Testament practice that has been dismissed in the age of grace, but that doesn't seem quite right. On one occasion, Jesus commended tithing when He rebuked the scribes and Pharisees for failing to fulfill the spirit of the Law (Matthew 23:23). What does all this mean to us? Every Christian should give *at least 10 percent* of their resources back to God's storehouse (the local church) by way of a tithe. Are you faithfully tithing to your local church, or are you robbing God by withholding all that He requires?

## March 2 – Corruption Comes From Within

*"And He said, 'What comes out of a man, that defiles a man. For from within, out of the heart of men, proceed evil thoughts, adulteries, fornications, murders, thefts, covetousness, wickedness, deceit, lewdness, an evil eye, blasphemy, pride, foolishness. All these evil things come from within and defile a man.'" (Mark 7:20-23)*

The Pharisees were very concerned about a person being defiled from things outside the body. For instance, if a person ate a meal with unwashed hands, that meant their food was defiled, and eating defiled foods made a person unclean. The Pharisees were also concerned with eating things sacrificed to idols. They would never have done such a thing, and they would've branded any person "unclean" who dared to do so.

After rebuking the Pharisees, Jesus explained to His disciples that defilement comes from the inside, not the outside. For instance, it's not a pornographic magazine that defiles a man — it's the desire to lust after a woman that causes him to pick it up. It's not a piece of gossip that defiles a woman — it's the desire to malign someone's character by talking behind her back. We are enticed by external factors, but by our own volition we allow those temptations to turn into sin.

James was very clear — "Let no one say when he is tempted, 'I am tempted by God'; for God cannot be tempted by evil, nor does He Himself tempt anyone. But each one is tempted when he is drawn away by his own desires and enticed" (James 1:13-14). Flip Wilson used to say, "The devil made me do it." That's simply not true. If you're living in sin, your corruption lies inside, not outside. I challenge you to examine your heart and let Jesus cleanse you from the inside-out.

## March 3 – The Grace and Mercy of God

*"Sing praise to the LORD, you saints of His, and give thanks at the remembrance of His holy name. For His anger is but for a moment, His favor is for life; weeping may endure for a night, but joy comes in the morning." (Psalm 30:4-5)*

Not everyone agrees on the occasion of Psalm 30, but the superscription says, "A song at the dedication of the house of David." Upon reading the psalm, it's not hard to imagine David saying the words of Psalm 30 upon dedicating his own new residence. By that time, David had been through a great deal — anointed king of Israel, killed Goliath, ran from evil King Saul, hiding in the wilderness, brought back to Israel, and finally crowned the king over the entire nation! All in about a decade of time!

As David reflected on God's grace and mercy, he had to give thanks. "For His anger is but for a moment, His favor is for life." I know we've all experienced God's anger — when we violated His Word, when we failed to pray, etc. We've felt His displeasure burn hot against us at times, but we've also felt the favor that comes with His grace. When we confess our sins and failures, He is faithful and just to forgive our sins and to cleanse us from all unrighteousness (1 John 1:9).

Not only that, but while "weeping may endure for a night … joy comes in the morning." All of us go through extremely difficult times. Some have been diagnosed with cancer, some have lost a spouse or a child, etc. When we go through those times, Satan tempts us to wonder, "Does God really love me?" We discover the answer when our weeping is exchanged for joy — when God's mercy comes pouring in like a flood. How can we help but give thanks to such a gracious, merciful God?

## March 4 — Who Do You Say Jesus Is?

*"He said to them, 'But who do you say that I am?' Peter answered and said to Him, 'You are the Christ.'" (Mark 8:29)*

After Jesus miraculously healed a blind man in Bethsaida, Jesus and His disciples made their way to Caesarea Philippi — not to be confused with Caesarea by the Sea. Caesarea Philippi was basically hewn out of a large rock in Galilee. In Jesus' day, it was a center of pagan worship. Some believed that an entrance to the underworld (Hades) was located in Caesarea Philippi. All sorts of pagan sacrifices and rituals were conducted there.

You might wonder why Jesus would bring His disciples to such a place. It was to teach them a very important truth. He began the lesson with a question — "Who do men say that I am?" The disciples responded with mixed reviews — "some say John the Baptist, some say Elijah, or one of the prophets." But then Jesus turned from public opinion to personal conviction. He asked the twelve, "But who do you say that I am?"

Peter, the unofficial leader of the disciples, was quick to respond — "You are the Christ." Matthew's account adds, "the Son of the living God" (Matthew 16:16). Jesus commended Peter for his accurate response and promised to build His kingdom on the rock of Peter's confession. Did you know the same question remains today? Jesus isn't just concerned with what your friends, family, and neighbors think of Him. He wants to know if you believe He really is the Christ — God's one and only Messiah.

# March 5 — Bring God the Faith You Have

*"Immediately the father of the child cried out and said with tears, 'Lord, I believe; help my unbelief!'" (Mark 9:24)*

Mark tells the story of a man whose son was demon-possessed. On this occasion, the boy's father came to the disciples and asked if they could cast out the demon. If you recall, by this time in Jesus' ministry, Jesus had already empowered His disciples to perform miracles. But the disciples were unable to cast out this demon. Later in the passage, Christ explained that they were unable because some strongholds are broken only by "prayer and fasting" (Mark 9:29).

When the boy's father came to Jesus, he was desperate. After explaining why he wanted Jesus to heal his son, the man heard these words from Christ — "If you can believe, all things are possible to him who believes" (Mark 9:23). It's so good to know that those words are just as true today as they've ever been. Jesus said that even with the faith of a mustard seed, mighty things can happen for the glory of God. Too often, our problem is that we simply don't believe God is able.

The boy's father had a certain measure of faith, but he was honest about his need for more — "Lord, I believe; help my unbelief." I love the simple honesty of that desperate father. He knew his faith wasn't as strong as it needed to be, but he did something we must do — bring the little bit of faith we have to Jesus and trust that He can do great things. God honored the father's faith and blessed him by healing his son. *Bring God the faith you have, and He'll give you the faith you need.*

# March 6 – How We Raise Our Children

*"But whoever causes one of these little ones who believe in Me to stumble, it would be better for him if a millstone were hung around his neck, and he were thrown into the sea." (Mark 9:42)*

The old song says, "Jesus loves the little children, all the children of the world! Red and yellow, black and white — they are precious in His sight. Jesus loves the little children of the world!" We know Jesus had a special love for children because several times during His ministry He used children to demonstrate the truth and bring glory to God. On this occasion, Jesus took some children into the midst of the disciples and helped them understand the importance of discipling our little ones.

Jesus began by talking about the importance of receiving children in a spirit of humility and generosity — "Whoever receives one of these little children in My name receives Me; and whoever receives Me, receives not Me but Him who sent Me" (Mark 9:37). Then Jesus shared the other side of the coin — it's very dangerous to cause an impressionable child to stumble because of our ungodliness. Not only because of what it does to the child, but what it means for the one setting a bad example.

Jesus didn't mince words — "it would be better for him if a millstone were hung around his neck, and he were thrown into the sea." I think what Christ meant is that it would be better for us not to live than to take the opportunity to mislead a child. Why? Because not only will we have to answer for our own sins, but we will have to give an account for theirs as well. Please ask yourself — am I faithfully discipling the little ones in my life, or is my example encouraging them to sin?

## March 7 — The Safety of Wise Counsel

*"Where there is no counsel, the people fall; but in the multitude of counselors there is safety." (Proverbs 11:14)*

You might be old enough to remember the Lone Ranger and his faithful steed Silver. When it was time for the Lone Ranger to ride off into the sunset, he cried out, "Hi-ho, Silver! Away!" All by himself, he blazed a trail into parts unknown, looking for the next adventure. Sadly, some Christians are like that — attempting to navigate the Christian life by themselves when God has called us to strengthen and encourage one another as we do God's will together.

Today's verse calls us to seek counsel from our fellow believers. Why? Because "where there is no counsel, the people fall." It's very foolish for us to think we know everything. Inevitably, there is always someone who knows more about the subject than we do. We cause ourselves a lot of heartache trying to reinvent the wheel when there are many others who've already accomplished what we're trying to do. Our plans often fail because we don't seek the counsel of fellow believers.

Solomon reminds us that "in the multitude of counselors there is safety." When you and I are trying to make decisions, first and foremost we should get alone with God and spend time in prayer. Then, we should ask the Holy Spirit and trusted Christian leaders to guide as we consult the Word of God for answers. And then we should seek the wisdom of fellow believers. Beware of taking counsel from those who don't know Jesus. The safety Solomon describes comes from dialoguing with those who are born-again followers of Christ.

## March 8 — The Voice of Faith

*"Then Caleb quieted the people before Moses, and said, 'Let us go up at once and take possession, for we are well able to overcome it.'" (Numbers 13:30)*

When the children of Israel were delivered from their bondage in Egypt, they took joy in the miracle-working power of God! But it was only a brief matter of time before the Israelites began to complain — not enough food, not enough water, etc. Many of the people actually wanted to return to slavery in Egypt! Suffice it to say that not everything was smooth sailing when God's people began to make their way toward the Promised Land of Canaan.

While the Israelites were stationed on the east side of the Jordan River, God commanded Moses to set aside twelve spies — one from each of the twelve tribes — to confirm the Word of God concerning the Promised Land. A twelve-person committee was probably trouble from the beginning! The delegates snuck into the Promised Land, took a good look around, and even harvested some grapes to bring back to their kinsman. They confirmed that it was indeed a land "flowing with milk and honey."

But there were naysayers. Of the twelve delegates, ten of them said it would be impossible to take residence in the Promised Land because there were too many fortified cities and too many giants. As the cold-water committee demonstrated their lack of faith, Caleb raised his voice — "we are well able to overcome it." He was willing to believe that with God all things are possible. How about you, friend? When the way seems unclear, do you cower down in fear or do you step up in faith? In a world filled with voices of fear, let yours be a voice of faith!

## March 9 — Are You Bearing Any Fruit?

*"Now the next day, when they had come out from Bethany, He was hungry. And seeing from afar a fig tree having leaves, He went to see if perhaps He would find something on it. When He came to it, He found nothing but leaves, for it was not the season for figs. In response Jesus said to it, 'Let no one eat fruit from you ever again.' And His disciples heard it." (Mark 11:12-14)*

The last week of Jesus' life was quite a whirlwind. He went from the highest of highs to the lowest of lows and ended on the highest note of all when He rose from the dead! On the first day of His final week, Jesus entered the city of Jerusalem in the evening and took a tour of the temple. The hour was late, so He left but returned again the next morning. On the way back to Jerusalem, He passed a fig tree — a very common occurrence in the region of Judea.

Mark tells us that it was not the season for figs, but the tree already had its leaves. Of course, Jesus knew it was not the season for figs, but in the presence of the disciples He wanted to make a statement of vital importance. Seeing no figs on the tree, He said, "Let no one eat fruit from you ever again." That might seem a little harsh, especially since it wasn't the season for figs. But we need to understand that Jesus was teaching His disciples a pointed lesson that we must learn as well.

If we've placed our faith in Jesus, God commands us to bear fruit for His glory. Jesus said, "By this My Father is glorified, that you bear much fruit; so you will be My disciples" (John 15:8). If we say we're followers of Christ, then let's prove it! James said, "Show me your faith without your works, and I will show you my faith by my works" (James 2:18). True followers of Jesus don't just talk the talk — they walk the walk. Christ said, "You are My friends if you do whatever I command you" (John 15:14). So how much fruit are you currently bearing for the cause of Christ?

## March 10 – Forgiveness Begins with Forgiving

*"And whenever you stand praying, if you have anything against anyone, forgive him, that your Father in heaven may also forgive you your trespasses. But if you do not forgive, neither will your Father in heaven forgive your trespasses." (Mark 11:25-26)*

In April of 2019, Barna released the results of a survey that asked Christians about forgiveness. The results were enlightening — 76 percent said they've offered unconditional, joyful forgiveness to another person who hurt, upset, or sinned against them (or someone they love). On the other hand, nearly one in six (15 percent) said they've never offered that level of forgiveness. Overall, around one in four practicing Christians (23 percent) has a person in their life who "they just can't forgive."

That's very troubling, especially in light of today's verses. Jesus said that when we pray, we need to forgive those who've sinned against us, "that your Father in heaven may also forgive you your trespasses." Let's be honest — forgiveness isn't always easy, especially when we feel that someone sinned against us in an egregious way. The human tendency is to dwell on our mistreatment while allowing thoughts of bitterness and hate to swell up inside us.

Before you decide not to forgive someone, listen carefully to Jesus — "if you do not forgive, neither will your Father in heaven forgive your trespasses." Perhaps you experienced some horrible things — abuse, rape, or neglect. As awful and inexcusable as those things are, they're no more heinous than your own sins against God. If God willfully forgave ALL your sins, the least you can do is forgive those who've sinned against you. Your own forgiveness is depending on it.

# March 11 — Greed Is the Path to Poverty

*"There is one who scatters, yet increases more; and there is one who withholds more than is right, but it leads to poverty." (Proverbs 11:24)*

Americans are among the most prosperous people on the planet. Many of us have nice homes, dependable cars, and plenty of toys to play with. Worldwide, most Americans would likely fall within the top 10 percent of the world's economic strata. And yet, the average American only gives about 3-5 percent of their income to charitable causes. What's more, the average American church member only gives 2.5 percent of their income to the local church. That percentage is worse than the Great Depression rate (3.3 percent).

One would think that clinging tightly to his/her money would be a sure path to prosperity, but the Word of God tells another story: "There is one who scatters, yet increases more." That doesn't make sense — how can a man grow more prosperous when he's giving so much away? It has to do with the promise of God. To His people Israel, God said, " 'Bring all the tithes into the storehouse, that there may be food in My house, and *try Me now in this*,' says the LORD of hosts" (Malachi 3:10).

God encourages us to prove His faithfulness through our generosity, but those who keep their fists clenched will never know the mighty provision of God. In fact, God says they might very well wind up impoverished — "there is one who withholds more than is right, but it leads to poverty." What kind of person are you? Are you greedy, thinking only of your own needs and neglecting the needs of others? Or are you generous, looking for opportunities to bless others and the local church?

## March 12 – The Nation That Loves the Lord

*"Blessed is the nation whose God is the Lord, the people He has chosen as His own inheritance." (Psalm 33:12)*

Today's verse was written to the nation of Israel — the people God chose to declare His glory among the nations. The God of Israel has always been Jehovah, even in times when they have acted in rebellion against Him. Jehovah made His covenant with Abraham, gave His Law to Moses, directed His people through the prophets, and provided them a Messiah in Jesus Christ. Every person in the world is made in God's image, but the Jews are God's special treasure.

Outside of Judaism, the rest of us are Gentiles. Thankfully, the Bible says we can be grafted into the same grace the Jews experienced through faith in Jesus (Romans 11:17). To that end, it's possible for Jehovah to be the Lord of our nation, and for many years of our country's history our forefathers instilled God right in the middle of our culture. From the Articles of Confederation, to the Declaration of Independence, to the Treaty of Paris, and the Constitution — this nation was established as a Christian nation.

Sadly, it can no longer be said that Jehovah is the Lord of America. In so many places we have exchanged His truth for a lie, and our country is suffering as a result. We can work together to stop the hemorrhaging, but it will begin only when God's people "humble themselves, and pray and seek My face, and turn from their wicked ways" (2 Chronicles 7:14). Only then will God "hear from heaven, and will forgive their sin and heal their land."

# March 13 – God is NOT One of Us

*"God is not a man, that He should lie, nor a son of man, that He should repent. Has He said, and will He not do? Or has He spoken, and will He not make it good?" (Numbers 23:19)*

In 1995, Joan Osborne released a song that asked the question, "What if God was one of us?" The song implied that God might not be some sort of transcendent figure reigning over the affairs of men. Instead, God might be "just a slob like one of us, trying to make his way home." The song did quite well in the public arena, topping out at #4 on the Billboard Hot 100 in the United States. Outside the US, the song reached #1 in several different countries.

It's troubling that a song questioning God's deity and holiness would do so well in our culture, but that explains a lot about our culture. Today's verse takes us back to an amazing story in Scripture. A pagan king named Balak hired a soothsayer named Balaam to curse the nation of Israel. On four separate occasions, Balaam beseeched the Lord to curse the Israelites, but God refused. Today's verse shows one of Balaam's responses to the pagan king.

Essentially, Balaam let the king know that God is NOT one of us. Of course, we know God became flesh during the incarnation through our Messiah Jesus, but that doesn't mean the Lord ceased to be God when Jesus was born. Our God is not a mere human, and He does not lie nor does He need to repent. If God has decreed something, you can take it to the bank because it WILL happen. You can trust in Jesus who is "the same yesterday, today, and forever" (Hebrews 13:8).

## March 14 – The Word of God Will Stand

*"Heaven and earth will pass away, but My words will by no means pass away." (Mark 13:31)*

So many things come and go. For instance, sports dynasties come and go. I'm a basketball fan, so I can remember the Lakers dynasty of the '80s and the Bulls dynasty of the '90s. Sadly, teams that once reigned supreme are now floundering in mediocrity. Fashions come and go all the time. You don't see many folks wearing bell-bottoms and sporting Afros these days. If you don't like the trends of today, just wait because they'll probably be gone by tomorrow.

Living in an ever-changing world can be exciting, but it can also be depressing. Shopping centers once vibrant and full of patrons are now ghost towns. It makes us sad to see once-great institutions now rotting to the ground. In many cases, people come in and out of our lives as well. It's often hard to know exactly who you can trust. Today's verse reminds us that our trust can always be placed in the Word of God, which "will by no means pass away."

While it's possible for us to measure the earth, no man can measure the universe. In fact, they tell us the universe is growing larger all the time. And yet, the heavens and the earth will be destroyed by God Himself to make way for a new heaven and a new earth. Until then, we can trust the Word of God. Centuries of people have mocked it and even tried to destroy it, but the Word still stands though many of them are dead and gone. It will stand forevermore! Study it, trust it, and apply it to your life.

## March 15 – Get a Taste of God's Goodness

*"Oh, taste and see that the Lord is good;*
*blessed is the man who trusts in Him!" (Psalm 34:8)*

I bet you can look back and remember a time when someone begged you to taste something, but you were reluctant to do so. As a child, I remember my mother and my grandmother trying to convince me that skillet fried okra was good. It just didn't look appetizing to me. It was black and it had seeds in it — it just looked yucky. But when they finally convinced me to try some, I loved it! These days, anytime I can get some good home-cooked okra, I scarf it down!

The point is simple — you don't really know if something is good until you try it. The same applies to our relationship with God. No one can know that their Creator is good until they "taste and see." How do we taste and see the Lord's goodness? The verse provides the answer — "blessed is the man who trusts in Him." If you want to experience the goodness of God, you must first place your trust in Him. Specifically, you must place your full faith and trust in Jesus.

Once you place your faith in Jesus, you will undoubtedly experience the goodness of God. Of course, that's not to say that your life will be without trials and adversity. Some have falsely believed that trusting in Christ would remove all their problems. When their problems didn't go away, they lost the faith and returned to an old lifestyle. Those who genuinely place their faith in Jesus will not only experience His goodness on life's mountaintops, but they will feel His goodness in the valley too. What are you currently doing to taste the Lord's goodness on a daily basis?

## March 16 — God Sees and Knows Where You Are

*"The eyes of the Lord are on the righteous,
and His ears are open to their cry." (Psalm 34:15)*

All of us go through the trials of life. It's during those times that we wonder if anyone really knows or cares about all we're going through. Sometimes we even try to express our heartache and disappointment to others, but we get a sense that they're not really listening. It's so frustrating when you feel like no one cares and you're not really being heard. Those thoughts often bring people to a place of despair, and sadly many people have taken their lives because they felt all alone.

One of the many great things about surrendering your life to Christ is that you never have to worry about being alone again. The Bible says when someone is saved, the Holy Spirit takes residence in their heart because they've been adopted into the family of God (Romans 8:15). When a person is truly born again through faith in Jesus, they never have to worry about being disowned, because the Holy Spirit acts as a guarantee of their eternal security (2 Corinthians 5:5, Ephesians 1:14).

What does that mean to us in the here and now? It means that "the eyes of the Lord are on the righteous." If you belong to God, He knows it, and He sees everything you're going through. Not only that, but "His ears are open to their cry." God sees every tear you shed, and He even knows why you're crying. If no one else in the world wants to listen to you, God always wants to hear from you. Dear friend, you can cast all your cares on Him because "He cares for you" (1 Peter 5:7).

## March 17 — The Bible's Definition of Stupid

*"Whoever loves instruction loves knowledge, but he who hates correction is stupid." (Proverbs 12:1)*

There are certain words we teach our children not to say. In our house, one word we've always discouraged our children from using is "stupid." Stupid is defined as "having or showing a great lack of intelligence or common sense." We've always discouraged our kids from using that word because we never wanted them to be tempted to call someone else a stupid person. While we should certainly discourage unwholesome talk, it doesn't negate the fact that some things are downright stupid.

For instance, there are only a small handful of times that the Bible calls something stupid. Today's verse provides one of those occurrences. "Whoever loves instruction loves knowledge." That's the other side of the coin. An intelligent person is someone who loves to learn. The fact is that we will never have everything figured out. Even if you are an expert in your chosen field, there is always someone who knows more than you. We need to remain humble and teachable.

"But he who hates correction is stupid." The Hebrew term used for "stupid" in this verse is *baar*. It is used only five times in the Hebrew Old Testament, and it means "senseless or brutish." Someone who's a brute typically casts wisdom to the wind and often ends up doing some foolish things. Only a fool would despise correction, because it's only by correction that we can learn from our mistakes and make necessary changes. Ask yourself — "How well do I receive instruction and correction?" Pray that the Lord will keep you from stupidly rejecting knowledge and instruction.

## March 18 — Don't Live to Please Others

*"So Pilate, wanting to gratify the crowd, released Barabbas to them; and he delivered Jesus, after he had scourged Him, to be crucified." (Mark 15:15)*

Sometimes it's very tempting to live our lives to please other people. Entire industries are built on the idea of showing everyone else how they ought to live. Just a simple trip to the check-out stand at the grocery store is evidence of that. At the check-out stand, there are magazines that tell women how they ought to look. There are nutrition guides that tell us how we ought to eat. The unwritten goal is to help us conform ourselves to the current standard so we can please everyone around us.

Today's verse takes us back to the occasion when Jesus stood before Pilate. Pilate had the power to release Jesus or the authority to sentence Him to death. The Gospels tell us that Pilate took Jesus aside privately and questioned Him. I think it's clear that Pilate was impressed with Him and even said that he found no fault in Him. But, "wanting to gratify the crowd," he released a criminal (Barabbas) and sentenced Jesus to die like a criminal on the cross.

Had Pilate been led by the truth, he would've surely released Jesus, but he was more concerned with pleasing the crowd. Why? Because he didn't want anything to endanger his privileged position as the Roman leader of Judea. Perhaps you and I succumb to the same temptation. Rather than taking an unpopular stand and living for Christ, we decide to conform to the world and sin against God. Don't live your life to please others — live your life for an audience of One (Galatians 1:10).

# March 19 – God Can Change Anyone

> *"So when the centurion, who stood opposite Him, saw that He cried out like this and breathed His last, he said, 'Truly this Man was the Son of God.'"* (Mark 15:39)

The scene of Christ's crucifixion was horrific. Jesus was flogged by Roman lictors, most likely beaten beyond recognition with a cat-of-nine-tails whip. History tells us there were many criminals who didn't survive the pre-crucifixion beating. Jesus survived the flogging and then was forced to carry His crossbeam outside the city to the place called Golgotha (the place of the skull). It was there He was nailed to a cross and hung between two thieves.

There were several Roman soldiers involved in Christ's crucifixion. They were witnesses to many things that took place on Jesus' crucifixion Friday. They witnessed the agony of Jesus and the criminals. They also must've seen the interaction between Jesus and the criminals and perhaps even the assurance that Jesus gave to one of the dying thieves. They even witnessed the rapid change of weather and the earthquake accompanying Christ's death.

One of the soldiers was a centurion. That simply means he had charge over 100 soldiers. Thus, he was a high-ranking soldier within the Roman army. This man had probably seen many crucifixions throughout his military career, but when he witnessed Jesus on the cross something amazing happened. He cried out, "Truly this Man was the Son of God." The centurion's confession of faith is proof that God can change anyone at any time. All we must do is surrender our lives to Christ through faith in Jesus.

## March 20 — When You Don't Walk in Faith

*"Yet, for all that, you did not believe the Lord your God, who went in the way before you to search out a place for you to pitch your tents, to show you the way you should go, in the fire by night and in the cloud by day." (Deuteronomy 1:32-33)*

The story of the nation of Israel is fascinating. Israel was born with a promise of God to a man named Abram. God promised to make his descendants as numerous as the stars in the heavens and the sand on the shore. "Abraham believed God, and it was accounted to him for righteousness" (Romans 4:3). Taking God at His word, Abram moved his family and possessions to the land of Canaan. His lineage includes Isaac, Jacob (renamed Israel), and Joseph.

You might remember that Joseph found favor with Pharaoh after he was shipped to Egypt, but later something very tragic happened — "there arose a new king over Egypt, who did not know Joseph" (Exodus 1:8). Consequently, the Israelites who lived in Egypt were enslaved for 400 years! And yet God delivered His people from their captivity through a man named Moses. Under Moses' leadership, the Israelites escaped Egypt and made their way to the threshold of the Promised Land.

Standing on the threshold of greatness, the Israelites failed to believe God's promise and refused to obey His command. Today's verses are taken from Deuteronomy — an occasion where Moses reminded the children of Israel of their lack of faith and the consequence of their doubt (wandering the wilderness for forty years). How about you, friend? Do you really believe God is able to deliver on all He's promised you (Ephesians 3:20-21)? Choosing fear over faith will result in disastrous consequences!

## March 21 — Adding to or Taking from the Word

*"You shall not add to the word which I command you, nor take from it, that you may keep the commandments of the LORD your God which I command you." (Deuteronomy 4:2)*

Deuteronomy literally means "second law" — in this case, the second giving of the Law after the children of Israel had wandered in the wilderness for forty years. Moses wanted to remind the children of Israel of the covenant they had previously entered into with the Lord. God's covenant with Israel was governed by commands the Israelites were expected to keep. Throughout their history, God was very clear that failure to adhere to those commands would result in swift retribution.

Moses wanted to make one thing certain — no one was to add to His words or delete any of His comments. Of course, we know Moses was simply repeating the Word God had given him, so in essence Moses was commanding the children of Israel not to add or take anything away from the Word of God. This verse is reminiscent of Revelation 22:18-19 — "If anyone adds to these things, God will add to him the plagues that are written in this book; and if anyone takes away from the words of the book of this prophecy, God shall take away his part from the Book of Life, from the holy city, and from the things which are written in this book."

You might think you've never added anything to Scripture or taken anything away, but we might want to look a little closer. Anytime we've added other books to the Bible, we've added to the Word. Anytime we've minimized the truthfulness of any text, we've taken away from the Scripture. Ask yourself — is it possible that I'm adding to or taking away from the Word? If the answer is yes, do what it takes today to make sure you're clinging only to the Word of God. Only Scripture has the power to make us "complete and thoroughly equipped for every good work" (2 Timothy 3:17).

## March 22 – The Virgin Birth of Jesus

> *"Then Mary said to the angel, 'How can this be, since I do not know a man?' And the angel answered and said to her, 'The Holy Spirit will come upon you, and the power of the Highest will overshadow you; therefore, also, that Holy One who is to be born will be called the Son of God.'" (Luke 1:34-35)*

Ever since the days of Jesus, many people have been skeptical of Christ and the Christian faith. Some of the first skeptics were religious leaders who thought Jesus was a "rabble rouser." Even His own brothers didn't believe He was really the Son of God (John 7:5). For two millennia, skeptics have worked hard to destroy the Christian faith. Many have questioned the element of the miraculous in the Christian faith, and at the heart of the debate is the virgin birth of Jesus.

What is the virgin birth? The doctrine of the virgin birth teaches that Jesus was not conceived the natural way — by a man and a woman. Instead, Jesus was conceived by the Holy Spirit. If that's confusing to you, don't worry because it confused a young Jewish girl named Mary. When she was told she would conceive and have a child, she said, "How can this be, since I do not know a man?" She knew she had been sexually pure so she had no idea how she could become pregnant.

The angel Gabriel answered her question — "the Holy Spirit will come upon you, and the power of the Highest will overshadow you." Consequently, Jesus "will be called the Son of God." Being born of Mary, Jesus was fully man; being conceived of the Holy Spirit, Jesus was fully God. Understand this — the virgin birth is vital to our Christian faith, for without it Jesus is not God, and if He's not God, then He's not able to make atonement for our sins, and we're still bound for hell. We should all thank God that Jesus truly is the virgin-born Son of God and Son of Man.

## March 23 – The First Person to Praise Jesus

*"Now Mary arose in those days and went into the hill country with haste, to a city of Judah, and entered the house of Zacharias and greeted Elizabeth. And it happened, when Elizabeth heard the greeting of Mary, that the babe leaped in her womb; and Elizabeth was filled with the Holy Spirit." (Luke 1:39-41)*

Answer this question — Who was the first person to praise Jesus? What would be your guess? Maybe the shepherds who were keeping watch over their flocks by night? Maybe the wise men who traveled from the East to come and bring their gifts to the Christ child? Maybe even the angels who paused to give glory to God immediately after the birth of Jesus? All those might be pretty good guesses, but they would all be wrong. Someone else beat them to the punch.

You might be surprised to learn that the first person to praise Jesus was prenatal, in utero — in the womb! About six months into her cousin's pregnancy, the recently impregnated Mary went to visit her cousin Elizabeth. It just so happened that Elizabeth was about to give birth to the one who would be named John. We've come to know Elizabeth's son as John the Baptist. God had appointed John to be the forerunner of Christ — to make the people of Israel ready for the coming of their Savior.

On this occasion, God prompted another miracle — He caused the baby in Elizabeth's womb to leap for joy! By the power of God, this pre-born child was the very first to praise our Savior Jesus. I think John's response should teach us at least two things. First, unborn children are human beings that are precious to God. All Christians stand united against abortion. Further, if infants praise our Lord Jesus, then we must do the same. Jesus Christ, the Savior of mankind, is worthy of ALL our praise — from the youngest to the oldest.

## March 24 – What God Deserves and Demands

*"And now, Israel, what does the LORD your God require of you, but to fear the LORD your God, to walk in all His ways and to love Him, to serve the LORD your God with all your heart and with all your soul, and to keep the commandments of the Lord and His statutes which I command you today for your good?" (Deuteronomy 10:12-13)*

Critics have often branded Christianity a religion of do's and don'ts. Some have refused to surrender their lives to Christ because they were afraid of what they'd have to give up. We need to help people understand that Christianity is not about keeping rules. Faith in God is something much deeper, and in today's verses Moses attempted to help his kinsman understand what God really requires. Even though it was written to Israel, we have much to learn from these words.

First, God requires that we "fear the Lord your God." What does that mean? It means we have an understanding and reverence for God's holiness. We acknowledge Him as the awesome Creator of the universe and the Giver and Taker of life. When we have the proper understanding of God's holiness, we will have no problem "walking in all His ways." To put it simply, the fear of the Lord not only involves what we feel, but it also determines what we do and who we serve.

God also requires that we "love Him." Steve Green once sang, "To love the Lord our God, it is the heartbeat of our mission." In other words, all we do should flow out of our abounding love for God. The first and greatest command is to love the Lord with all our heart, soul, mind, and strength (Mark 12:30). It's imperative that we express our love to God, not only with what we say, but much more by what we do — obeying "His statutes," which are "for your good." God deserves and demands our very best!

## March 25 — A Sign to the Shepherds

*"And this will be the sign to you: You will find a Babe wrapped in swaddling cloths, lying in a manger."* (Luke 2:12)

Every Christian loves the beautiful simplicity of the nativity. We all envision Mary and Joseph in a very humble environment with the baby Jesus. But sometimes we don't stop to consider the marvelous way in which God communicated the truth about Jesus to those who were nearby. The Bible says there were shepherds in the fields of Bethlehem keeping watch over their flocks by night when an angel of the Lord stood before them and calmed their fears (Luke 2:8-10).

The angel explained that "a Savior, who is Christ the Lord," had been born in the city of Bethlehem. These shepherds were simple people. If you go to Israel, even today you can see many shepherds in the fields leading a very simple life. The angel gave the shepherds a sign they could not miss — "You will find a Babe wrapped in swaddling cloths, lying in a manger." This was a sign they knew very well as they had seen it many times before as a vital part of their shepherding.

When a new lamb was born, it was the shepherd's responsibility to take it to the basement of "the tower of the flock," wrap it in swaddling cloths (to protect the lamb from injury), and lay it in a manger. These signs communicated a very clear message to the shepherds — the child you seek is the true Lamb of God who takes away the sins of the world. Dear friend, Jesus is the Lamb of God! His blood covers the sins of all those who have placed their faith in Him. Are you trusting in God's perfect Lamb, Jesus?

## March 26 – Being About Our Father's Business

*"And He said to them, 'Why did you seek Me? Did you not know that I must be about My Father's business?'" (Luke 2:49)*

Have you ever been in a public place when you suddenly noticed one of your children was missing? This happened to my wife one time at the grand opening of a Walmart in our community. On the first day the store opened, my wife took our six kids to the store, only for one of our children to wander off into a different part of the store. When my wife notified the manager, the store associates got to practice a lockdown, and thankfully our son was found. Our son was in just a little bit of trouble.

Mary and Joseph went to Jerusalem to celebrate the Passover when Jesus was only 12 years old. After the celebration, they began making their way back toward Nazareth. In those days, travelers often made their trips in groups. It wouldn't have been uncommon for many families to travel together, so it's easy to understand someone getting lost. In this case, Jesus was reported missing one day into the trip, so Mary and Joseph had to return to Jerusalem to find their Son.

After three days of searching, they finally found their Son in the temple dialoguing with the teachers. Mary and Joseph were thankful but appalled all at once. They asked, "Why did you do this to us? We've been searching for you!" Jesus simply responded, "Did you not know that I must be about My Father's business?" Jesus had an urgency about doing God's will at all costs. I wonder if you and I have that same urgency. Today, make a decision that you will be about your Father's business!

## March 27 — The Evidence of Faith

> *"So the people asked him, saying, 'What shall we do then?' He answered and said to them, 'He who has two tunics, let him give to him who has none; and he who has food, let him do likewise.' Then tax collectors also came to be baptized, and said to him, 'Teacher, what shall we do?' And he said to them, 'Collect no more than what is appointed for you.' Likewise the soldiers asked him, saying, 'And what shall we do?' So he said to them, 'Do not intimidate anyone or accuse falsely, and be content with your wages.'"* (Luke 3:10-14)

John the Baptist was the forerunner of our Savior Jesus. God raised Him up to prepare the hearts of the people for the coming of the Messiah. John didn't mince words when he preached — "Brood of vipers! Who warned you to flee from the wrath to come?" Not exactly the feel-good message we hear in so much "Christian" preaching these days, but it was important that the people be confronted with their sins. It's still vitally important that we are confronted with our sins!

The people got the message. Jews from everywhere started coming to John at the Jordan River to be baptized. Keep in mind that John's baptism was one of repentance — a symbol that the people were setting aside their sins and recommitting themselves to holiness. It's a testament to the power of God's Word that people started coming from all walks of life to repent of their sins. Tax collectors, soldiers, sinners — all of them (and all of us) in desperate need of repentance.

What is repentance? Repentance is the act of renouncing one's sins and turning to Jesus in faith and obedience. For the everyday Joe, it meant being generous. For the tax collector, it meant more honest transactions. For the soldier, it meant doing a job without hate and deception. In every case, repentance is the evidence of faith. If a person is not willing to repent of his/her sins, then they're not ready to follow Jesus. Does your life demonstrate the evidence of faith that comes through repentance?

## March 28 – Respect for Spiritual Authority

*"Now the man who acts presumptuously and will not heed the priest who stands to minister there before the LORD your God, or the judge, that man shall die. So you shall put away the evil from Israel." (Deuteronomy 17:12)*

God mercifully allowed His people to enjoy a second giving of the Law after their wilderness wandering and prior to entering the Promised Land. Among many other topics, God addressed the manner in which the Israelites submitted to their God-appointed authorities. Those spiritual authorities included priests, Levites, and judges. When the children of Israel had a dispute they could not resolve, they were to bring it to one of the previously mentioned authorities for a decision.

God was clear with His people — "You shall do according to the sentence which they pronounce upon you in that place which the LORD chooses. And you shall be careful to do according to all that they order you" (Deuteronomy 17:10). Having heard the decision of his spiritual leaders, it was out of the question for an Israelite to reject that leadership and rebel against it. Today's verse says that anyone who acted "presumptuously" by not submitting to authority was to be put to death!

You might say, "That seems too harsh! Why would God order the death penalty for someone who failed to submit?" It was God's desire to "put away the evil from Israel" — taking the life of the offender before his life could infect many others. While we're certainly not Israelites living under the Old Covenant, God has still appointed spiritual leaders for His church. The Bible calls them "shepherds," and we tend to call them pastors. Ask yourself — am I respecting God's appointed leaders and following their counsel?

## March 29 — Anxiety

*"Anxiety in the heart of man causes depression, but a good word makes it glad." (Proverbs 12:25)*

Anxiety disorders are the most common mental illness in the United States, affecting 40 million adults ages eighteen and older, or 18.1 percent of the population annually. Those with an anxiety disorder are three to five times more likely to go to the doctor and six times more likely to be hospitalized for psychiatric disorders. Anxiety disorders are highly treatable, yet only 36.9 percent of those suffering with anxiety receive treatment. Anxiety disorder risk factors include genetics, brain chemistry, personality, and life events.

Of course, a person doesn't have to be diagnosed with a disorder to suffer with anxiety. Anxiety often surfaces in the form of worry, and people tend to worry about a multitude of things. Whether we realize it or not, worry can have devastating effects on our health — high blood pressure, loss of sleep, lack of appetite, etc. Today's verse tells us that anxiety and worry "cause depression." Many times we allow ourselves to become defeated simply by the prospect of what might happen.

There is help for all those who suffer with anxiety. First, there is the encouragement of good friends — "a good word makes it glad." That's all the more reason for us to remain in fellowship with those who love Jesus. Also, God invites us to cast all our anxiety on Him — "casting all your care upon Him, for He cares for you" (1 Peter 5:7). If you know Jesus as your Savior, then you know God as your Father. Stop worrying and start praying! God's got everything under control!

## March 30 – Choose Your Friends Wisely

*"The righteous should choose his friends carefully, for the way of the wicked leads them astray." (Proverbs 12:26)*

Remember the lectures your mom and dad used to give you about choosing the right friends? Why were they so concerned about the company we keep? Because they knew running with the wrong crowd could land us in lots of trouble. You know what? Mom and Dad were right! How many times have we seen a "good kid" get influenced by troublemakers only to reproduce some of the same wicked behaviors they saw in the bad boys — alcohol, drugs, crime, etc.

Today's verse is not just for school-aged kids — it's for every person that longs to live godly in Christ Jesus. "The righteous should choose his friends carefully." Think of it like this — we try to choose carefully when we go to the grocery store. We squeeze the tomatoes to see if they're too soft. We smell the cantaloupes to see if they're ripe. We inspect the bananas to see if they're too brown. Why shouldn't we use even more caution when determining our circle of friends?

Solomon reminds us that "the way of the wicked leads them astray." Paul said something similar to the church at Corinth — "Do not be deceived: 'Evil company corrupts good habits' " (1 Corinthians 15:33). Don't surround yourself with people who discourage your walk with God and try to get you back into old habits. Align yourself with those who love the Lord and encourage others to follow Christ. Together, you can join forces to reach those who still need Jesus.

## March 31 — Dust in the Wind

*"Certainly every man at his best state is but vapor." (Psalm 39:5)*

Growing up, I was introduced to a band named Kansas. Seems I had an affinity for bands named after places — Boston, Chicago, etc. Many years ago, Kansas released a song called "Dust in the Wind." The song was about the frailty of life and the brevity of the human experience. One of the song's lines says, "Don't hang on, nothing lasts forever but the earth and sky. It slips away and all your money won't another minute buy." Seventy or eighty years is just a blip on the radar of human history and eternity.

The psalmist David used the analogy of a vapor — "man at his best state is but vapor." A vapor is defined as "a substance diffused or suspended in the air, especially one normally liquid or solid." In essence, a vapor is a fleeting state of matter between two different states. It's here today and gone tomorrow. If you talk to many senior adults, they'll tell you that life has flown by. No matter what we do to slow the aging process, inevitably we all have an appointment with death.

That being the case, we should all be motivated to use the time we have remaining for the glory of God. Most of us probably expect to live about eighty years, but the fact is that we're not promised tomorrow. Any of us could be taken instantly with a massive heart attack, a car accident, etc. We don't have time to waste! A good pastor friend used to tell me, "Only one life and it soon shall pass, only that which is done for Jesus is that which will last." Make the most of your time today and every day!

## April 1 — The Necessity of Prayer

*"Now it came to pass in those days that He went out to the mountain to pray, and continued all night in prayer to God." (Luke 6:12)*

When it comes to Jesus, we tend to focus on the miraculous — the blind eyes, mute mouths, and deaf ears that were opened, the lepers that were cleansed, the dead that were raised to life, etc. It's good to focus on those supernatural occurrences because each of them proves that Jesus is the Messiah. What we don't spend near enough time considering is the amount of time Jesus spent in prayer. Today's verse finds Jesus praying through the entire night!

More than any other Gospel writer, Luke does a great job chronicling some of the times that Jesus prayed. Many of those times were prior to major events in His ministry (see also 3:21, 5:16, 9:18, 28-29, 11:1, 22:32, 40-46). Jesus was completely and fully God, and there's no doubt about that. But, in the incarnation, He elected to empty Himself of some of His divine privileges (Philippians 2:6ff). I take that to mean that Jesus had an even greater need for His Father while He was on the earth.

Has it ever occurred to us that perhaps part of the reason for Jesus' miracle-working is that He was empowered through prayer? And not only that, in Luke 6 He was preparing to make a vitally important decision about which twelve men He would select as disciples — a decision that kept Him up praying all night. If Jesus needed to be empowered through prayer and equipped with the wisdom He needed to make godly decisions, don't you think prayer is even more vitally important for us?

## April 2 – Before I Correct Someone Else

*"First remove the plank from your own eye, and then you will see clearly to remove the speck that is in your brother's eye." (Luke 6:42)*

There's an old Southern saying — "Those who live in glass houses shouldn't throw stones." It's our own way of saying that you shouldn't get too busy correcting someone else when you haven't taken the time to correct yourself. Jesus used a different analogy. Essentially, He said we shouldn't worry about the speck of sawdust in our brother's eye until we have taken care of the plank in our own. To employ another analogy — "Sweep your own doorstep before worrying about someone else's."

Why are we so good at picking on everyone else's faults when we have so many of our own? I think it's a diversion — if we focus on the shortcomings of others, then we don't have to consider our own. If we have a problem with bad language, we'd rather focus on someone else's alcohol problem. If we have a problem with pornography, we'd rather focus on someone else's homosexuality. We often justify our self-righteousness by saying, "Well, at least my sins aren't as bad as his."

As Christians, we have been called to correct one another. For example, Paul confronted Peter when he was wrong about avoiding the Gentiles in certain company (Galatians 2:11-12). That said, it's not wrong to confront a fellow believer with his sin, but we need to make sure we're not being hypocrites. Before confronting a brother or sister about his/her shortcomings, we need to ask God to forgive our own and take the needed steps to repent. Then we will be in a position to help others with their sins.

## April 3 — The Grave Robber

*"And when He came near the gate of the city, behold, a dead man was being carried out, the only son of his mother; and she was a widow. And a large crowd from the city was with her. When the Lord saw her, He had compassion on her and said to her, 'Do not weep.' Then He came and touched the open coffin, and those who carried him stood still. And He said, 'Young man, I say to you, arise.' So he who was dead sat up and began to speak. And He presented him to his mother." (Luke 7:12-15)*

When someone mentions a grave robber, it usually doesn't bring to mind any good thoughts. I know it used to make my granny furious when she would go to put flowers on her son's grave, only to come back days later and find them gone. No one likes a grave robber, unless of course you're talking about Jesus. I don't know if you've ever thought about it, but Jesus is the best grave robber of all. He robbed three graves during His ministry and even one following His death!

During His ministry, Jesus robbed the grave *before* burial (Jairus' daughter) and once *after* a man's burial (Lazarus). Today's verses are taken from the occasion when Jesus robbed a grave *during* burial. Luke tells us about a poor widow in the city of Nain who lost her only son. Can you imagine the devastation that poor woman must've felt? Not only had she lost her husband, but now she's lost her son! During the funeral procession, the Bible says Jesus "had compassion on her."

He told the poor widow not to cry and instructed her son's dead carcass to "arise." At that very moment, "he who was dead sat up and began to speak." And then there was the sweetest part of all — "He presented him to his mother." What an awesome Savior and an amazing Grave Robber! And yet, Christ's greatest grave robbery took place in another man's tomb when He rolled the stone away and presented Himself alive on the third day. Our grave-robbing Savior is alive and well today!

## April 4 – Only Faith Can Save You

*"Then He said to the woman, 'Your faith has saved you. Go in peace.'" (Luke 7:50)*

From the beginning of His ministry, the religious establishment criticized Jesus. The Pharisees were one of the main culprits. Today's verse records an occasion when one of the Pharisees (Simon) wanted to get a closer look at Jesus, so he invited Him over for a meal. As they were reclining at the table, "a woman in the city who was a sinner" (Luke 7:37) came and knelt down behind Jesus. Her actions must've been shocking to Simon because women typically never approached men in ancient culture.

Not only did she kneel behind Jesus, but the Bible says she touched Him. Specifically, her tears began to fall on the feet of Jesus, so she wiped His feet dry with her own hair. Not only that, Luke tells us she even kissed His feet and anointed them with some fragrant oil. Keep in mind that feet were typically the dirtiest part of the body because the ancients used to travel barefoot or with only sandals on their feet. And who would think of taking costly oil and placing it on someone's feet?

The woman took a great risk touching Jesus, but she felt her worship was worth the risk. When the encounter was almost over, Jesus turned to the sinful woman and said, "Your faith has saved you. Go in peace." It wasn't her humility or her costly oil that saved her — it was her faith in Jesus. Two thousand years later, one thing hasn't changed — it's only through faith in Jesus that you can be saved. All the money in the world can't buy your salvation. Make certain you've placed your faith in Jesus and encourage all those around you to do the same!

## April 5 — The Man God Buried

*"So Moses the servant of the Lord died there in the land of Moab, according to the word of the Lord. And He buried him in a valley in the land of Moab, opposite Beth Peor; but no one knows his grave to this day." (Deuteronomy 34:5-6)*

Moses turned out to be an amazing man of God, but he was originally groomed for something much different. I'm sure you remember that Moses's mother instructed his sister (Miriam) to place her little brother in the Nile River in a small ark she had prepared for him. By God's providence, Pharaoh's daughter discovered Moses and consequently raised him in a house of Egyptian royalty. There, Moses doubtless enjoyed every pleasure of life for a good number of years.

As a young Egyptian noble, Moses saw one of his fellow Jews being beaten by an Egyptian taskmaster. Anger overtook him, and he killed the Egyptian. Knowing he couldn't stay in Egypt, Moses fled to the back of the desert where he was a keeper of sheep. While minding his own business among the flock, Moses saw a bush that was on fire but not being consumed. After he drew a little closer, he heard the Angel of the Lord calling him to his life's assignment — leading the Jews out of captivity and into the Promised Land.

Through Moses's leadership, the children of Israel were liberated from their captivity only to be enslaved by fear. Their fear cost them a shot at the Promised Land, and Moses himself made a critical mistake by failing to believe God and hallowing His name among the people. For that reason, Moses was not permitted to enter the Promised Land — only to see it from Mount Nebo. There God took Moses's soul to heaven and buried his body in the ground. Thus, he will always be remembered as the only man buried by God Himself — a high honor for a holy man. His legacy inspires us to live each day for the glory of the Lord.

## April 6 — God's Idea of Success

*"This Book of the Law shall not depart from your mouth, but you shall meditate in it day and night, that you may observe to do according to all that is written in it. For then you will make your way prosperous, and then you will have good success." (Joshua 1:8)*

After the death of Moses, the nation took time to grieve the loss of a great man of God. And yet, God didn't allow them to look backward for too long — "arise, go over this Jordan" (Joshua 1:2). God gave Joshua clear instructions on how he and the rest of the people were to make their voyage into the Promised Land. Several times, God instructed the people to "be strong and of good courage" (Joshua 1:6-7, 9). In order for them to fulfill their destiny, they had to trust the Lord.

In the midst of God's call for strength, He provided the instruction we're considering today. "This Book of the Law shall not depart from your mouth." The Book of the Law was the written Word of God given to Israel through God's servant Moses. The precepts of the Law were not to depart from Joshua's mouth, nor were they to depart from his mind — "meditate in it day and night." Why? "That you may observe to do according to all that is written in it." Not just for information, but for application and transformation!

In speaking, thinking, and obeying the Word, God assured Joshua that only then would the way for Israel be made prosperous. We know God blessed Israel with great prosperity in their own land — a prosperity that climaxed under the reign of King Solomon. God also said it was only through obedience that Joshua and Israel would be a true "success." So then, success is not really about the materials you own or the riches you possess — it's really about the Word of God that you know and obey.

## April 7 — Desperate for God

*"As the deer pants for the water brooks, so pants my soul for You, O God." (Psalm 42:1)*

Seems that Americans are becoming more health conscious, and that's led to an increase in cardiovascular activity. A favorite form of exercise for many is running or walking. Both can be relaxing once a person is in good shape, but those preliminary workouts are tough. And even after your body is conditioned, there's really nothing very easy about a two-mile run or a four-mile walk. Hot days are the worst! Those are the times when your tongue clings to the roof of your mouth.

When an arduous run or walk gives us a good case of cottonmouth, there's nothing we want more than a cold bottle of water. It relieves every part of a parched throat on a hot day. If you're a person who saves your water for the end of your workout, you yearn for it more and more with each passing step — much like a thirsty deer pants for a cold-water brook. There's a desperation and urgency that simply can't be satisfied until it's quenched with liquid refreshment.

The sons of Korah (writers of this psalm) used the words of this verse to express the heart of a believer that yearns to be with God. The psalmists were referring to a desperation to be in God's presence in heaven, but I think the words can certainly be a beautiful picture of a believer that's desperate for more of God. As John the Baptist said, "He must increase, and I must decrease" (John 3:30). Are you more desperate for God than anything else in your life? Not sure? Ask your calendar and your bank account — they'll tell you how desperate you are for Christ.

## April 8 — The Cost of Discipleship

*"Then He said to them all, 'If anyone desires to come after Me, let him deny himself, and take up his cross daily, and follow Me.'" (Luke 9:23)*

We hear the word "disciple" thrown around quite a bit in the world today, especially in the sports world. Some say that Bill Belichick was a Bill Parcells disciple, emulating many of the defensive principles he learned from Parcells. I've watched a documentary on those two. Belichick was the defensive coordinator when Parcells was coach of the New York Giants. Though Belichick was well-paid, coaching under Parcells still came at a price — a lot of yelling, harassing, second-guessing, etc.

No matter the cost Belichick had to pay, it's nothing in comparison to what a disciple of Jesus must pay in order to enjoy the privilege of following Christ. Jesus didn't mince words — "If anyone desires to come after Me" — that is, to be my disciple. "Let him deny himself." If you want to follow Jesus, the first thing you must do is deny yourself. By signing on as a disciple of Christ, you are relinquishing all control of your life. It's no longer about you — it's all about Him!

Next, a disciple must "take up his cross daily." What does that mean? Let's think about that — a cross was an instrument of death. So then, Jesus was saying that a Christ-follower must die to himself every day and willfully take up the burdens that come with following Jesus. And of course, a disciple must "follow Me" — he must follow in the footsteps of Christ. I heard a preacher summarize it as denying, dying, and devoting ourselves to Jesus. Can those three words be used to describe your pursuit of Christ?

## April 9 – Don't Look Back!

*"But Jesus said to him, 'No one, having put his hand to the plow, and looking back, is fit for the kingdom of God.'" (Luke 9:62)*

I grew up listening to rock music, and that's not always a good thing. Being raised in a Christian home, my parents made sure that our song selections never got too far out of control. That said, I tried to stick with bands that weren't associated with devil worship or drugs. I liked bands named after places — Chicago, Kansas, America, etc. And my favorite childhood band was Boston. I distinctly remember getting a CD player one year for Christmas, and Boston's first album was my first CD.

I wore that CD out, and it wasn't long before I was looking for their second album. It was entitled "Don't Look Back," based on the title track from that album. The song says, "Don't look back! A new day is breaking." It's just a simple anthem about pressing forward, and perhaps it could be the soundtrack for today's verse. When a potential Christ-follower wanted to go home and say goodbye to his family before following Jesus, he probably wasn't prepared for Christ's response.

Jesus said, "No one, having put his hand to the plow, and looking back, is fit for the kingdom of God." Seems a little harsh to tell a potential disciple that he can't say goodbye to his family, but Jesus was making a point we need to understand — you can't move forward if you're looking back. When you sign up to follow Jesus, He is your highest allegiance, and you don't need to spend time longing for the things of your past. Don't look back! Keep your eyes fixed on Jesus (Hebrews 12:1-2).

## April 10 – Getting Ahead of the Lord

*"Then the men of Israel took some of their provisions; but they did not ask counsel of the Lord." (Joshua 9:14)*

Have you ever committed to do something and regretted it later? Maybe you signed a contract and got stuck with some recurring payments you couldn't get out of. Maybe you bought a car without really considering the full impact of the payment terms on your budget. Unfortunately, we often tend to make quick decisions, and those decisions can often be bad ones. We have an example of a quick, bad decision by Joshua and the leadership of Israel in today's verse.

When the Israelites crossed over into the Promised Land, God clearly commanded them to remove all the inhabitants of the land. The command was non-negotiable and purposeful — God did not want His children influenced by the worship of pagan gods the natives worshiped. Initially, Joshua and the Israelites did what God commanded, annihilating cities like Jericho. But, today's verse points us to an occasion when the Jews were snookered by the Gibeonites.

The Gibeonites sent leaders to Joshua who posed as inhabitants of a far country, rather than natives of the Promised Land. After a brief inquisition, Joshua accepted the terms of a treaty because "they did not ask counsel of the Lord." Joshua made a mistake because he didn't seek God first. You and I will make the same mistakes if we start running ahead of God. Before making decisions, we should always go to God first. Seeking Him above all others will keep us from making some critical mistakes.

## April 11 – Being a Mary in a Martha World

*"And Jesus answered and said to her, 'Martha, Martha, you are worried and troubled about many things. But one thing is needed, and Mary has chosen that good part, which will not be taken away from her.'" (Luke 10:41-42)*

It seems that Americans are busier than we've ever been. Our days are filled with all sorts of activity — work, school, exercise, etc. Long gone are the days when parents sat and read the evening paper while the kids road bikes outside until dusk. Now the kids have practice and games to attend while Mom and Dad act as taxi drivers. Practices that used to be only one night a week happen nearly every night of the week, not to mention weekends that are spent traveling to games — for little league!

One of the best things we could do is eliminate unnecessary activities from our schedule. But no matter how hard we try, there will always be an abundance of things for us to deal with. Even though life was simpler in the 1st century, there were still burdens to bear. Today's passage takes us back to an occasion where Jesus met two sisters — Martha and Mary. You could say that Martha was a worker bee, making preparations for guests, while Mary was willing to leave the work and sit at Jesus' feet.

Martha wasn't happy about being left by her sister to make the preparations alone, and she asked Jesus to make her return to the work. Jesus refused to make Mary go to the kitchen by saying that she "has chosen that good part." We need to learn from that. In a world filled with all sorts of Martha activity, we need to learn to take time to sit at the feet of Jesus. As the old preacher used to say, "We need to come apart before we come apart." Guard your time at Jesus' feet — take time to be Mary in a Martha world.

## April 12 – The Blessing of Hearing and Obeying the Word

> *"And it happened, as He spoke these things, that a certain woman from the crowd raised her voice and said to Him, 'Blessed is the womb that bore You, and the breasts which nursed You!' But He said, 'More than that, blessed are those who hear the word of God and keep it!'"* (Luke 11:27-28)

It's one thing to listen, but it's another thing to act on what you've heard. For instance, you can hear someone say "the building is on fire," but if you don't get up and exit the building, then you're destined to go down in flames. You can hear a nurse call your name in a waiting room, but if you don't get up from your seat you won't see the doctor. This principle holds true for our Christian faith. It's one thing to hear the Word, but obeying its counsel is another matter altogether.

After Jesus exorcised demons from a possessed man, a woman from the crowd cried out, "Blessed is the womb that bore You, and the breasts which nursed You!" Clearly, the woman was trying to worship our Savior, but Jesus used her praise as an opportunity for truth. "More than that, blessed are those who hear the word of God and keep it!" That's quite a statement! The virgin Mary was blessed indeed, but no more blessed than those who believe and obey the Word of God.

Clearly, it is a blessing to hear the Word of God. There aren't too many things I love more than hearing the Bible read publicly or listening to a biblical message. But if the blessing stops there, we won't receive all God intends for us to have. James said, "Be doers of the word, and not hearers only, deceiving yourselves" (James 1:22). You're lying to yourself if you think you'll experience the favor of God without obedience to His Word. Today, be a hearer AND a doer of the Word. You won't regret it!

## April 13 – Let Your Light Shine

*"No one, when he has lit a lamp, puts it in a secret place or under a basket, but on a lampstand, that those who come in may see the light." (Luke 11:33)*

As kids we were taught to sing, "This little light of mine, I'm going to let it shine!" Makes sense doesn't it? We have lights in our houses for a purpose — we expect them to shine and give light to the rest of home. We have lights in our workplaces for a reason — it's hard to get much done in the dark. Think of how absurd it would be for a homeowner or business owner to go to all the expense of installing lights, but then refusing to turn them on. A light that doesn't shine is no light at all.

Jesus made that point very plain in today's verse. The ancients didn't have bright LED lights and light switches in their homes. Instead, they had oil-driven lamps that provided light to the house. It's unthinkable that someone would ignite the home's only means of illumination and then hide it "in a secret place or under a basket." Absolutely not! The light was placed "on a lampstand, that those who come in may see the light." To do otherwise would've been unthinkable.

The point is clear — if you know Jesus as Savior, His light radiates in your soul. Rather than taking that light and hiding from others, we should let His glory illuminate the darkness so that others might see. In the parallel passage to this verse, Jesus said, "Let your light so shine before men, that they may see your good works and glorify your Father in heaven" (Matthew 5:16). We don't live to put on a show, but we do live to point others to Christ. Ask yourself — how bright is my light shining for Jesus?

# April 14 — When Being Rich Is a Problem

*"So is he who lays up treasure for himself, and is not rich toward God." (Luke 12:21)*

You can't deny that Americans have been very blessed. Per capita, Americans are some of the richest people on the planet, and the competition isn't even close. The only country that outpaces America in per capita wealth is Switzerland. That's probably why we hear so much about Swiss bank accounts! Americans spend their money on so many things — houses, cars, clothes, food, toys, etc. Let's be honest — many countries would love to have the food we waste every day.

While Americans have done very well and many could even be considered rich, their wealth doesn't correspond to their giving. In fact, only about half of Americans give to charitable causes, and those that do only give about $5,500 of their income to charity annually. When it comes to how much Americans "give back to God," the numbers get even worse. Only about 10-25 percent of church members tithe biblically, and the average church member only gives 2.5 percent of his/her income to the local church.

"Houston, we have a problem." The problem is that Americans have no problem pampering themselves, but they have a much harder time being generous to the work of our Lord. Jesus told a story about a man who tore down his barns to build bigger barns, rather than giving his prosperity to others. It's not ungodly to be rich or to have a large bank account. It's "the love of money" that is the root of all sorts of evil (1 Timothy 6:10). Your wealth becomes a problem only when you choose to enrich yourself without giving sacrificially to the work of the Lord. How much are you currently sacrificing for the glory of God?

## April 15 – Where Is Your Treasure?

*"For where your treasure is, there your heart will be also." (Luke 12:34)*

What comes to mind when you hear the word "treasure"? Maybe you think about Treasure Island or Indiana Jones on one of his treasure-hunting adventures. It's not a word we use very much, but it used to be a general reference to money. Churches and many other organizations still have "treasurers" who assist with the oversight of finances. When Jesus mentioned the word "treasure," He was talking about money and possessions rather than something buried in the ground or lost at sea.

Jesus instructed His disciples to lead very simple lives and trust God to provide all their needs. He warned against the accumulation of wealth and material possessions by using a very simple principle — "where your treasure is, there your heart will be also." What did Jesus mean? To use a modern analogy, open the banking app on your mobile device. Take a look at your expenses over the course of the past few months. It's very likely you are passionate about the things you're spending money on.

I don't know about you, but my monthly bills include a mortgage because I'm passionate about providing a home for my family. I also pay a monthly premium for medical insurance because I'm also passionate about my family's health. And my monthly expenses also include a tithe to the local church because I'm passionate about Jesus. In fact, He should be the first and greatest passion of our lives! So, when you follow your money, what does it say about the greatest priorities of your life?

## April 16 – Be Still and Know

*"Be still, and know that I am God; I will be exalted among the nations, I will be exalted in the earth!" (Psalm 46:10)*

I've got six kids, so I don't have much time to "be still." Our kids are involved in sports, band, and a host of other activities. My wife and I have a good time running around and supporting all their interests, but it doesn't leave much room for "being still." And yet, the psalmist encourages us to be still in today's verse. Psalm 46 is a beautiful passage that inspired Martin Luther to write "A Mighty Fortress Is Our God." The first half of the psalm praises God for His ever-present watch care over Israel.

The second half of the psalm shifts toward a future perspective. The psalmist praises God because He causes desolations in the earth and He also brings wars to an end (Psalm 46:8-9). When will those things happen? The Apostle John answers that question for us in the Revelation. At the end of time, Jesus will return to make war against the Beast, the False Prophet, and Satan. It's no surprise that Jesus will be victorious and will then establish a kingdom of peace on the earth (Revelation 20:1-3).

The psalmist invites us to "be still and know" for a purpose — to remember God is going to be exalted among the nations and all over the earth. Why would a Christian in the 21st century need to be still and consider the coming kingdom of Jesus? Because the devil is currently having his way in our fallen world. We see murder, violence, and rampant immorality on every side. Every day we need to be still and remember that this world is not our home. Jesus Christ is returning to make all things new!

# April 17 — The Free Will of Man

*"O Jerusalem, Jerusalem, the one who kills the prophets and stones those who are sent to her! How often I wanted to gather your children together, as a hen gathers her brood under her wings, but you were not willing!" (Luke 13:34)*

I'm sure it comes as no surprise to you that Jesus was Jewish. His followers were Jewish. Their Scripture originated with the Jews. Their customs and religious practices were all Jewish. In fact, early in His ministry Jesus said, "Do not go into the way of the Gentiles ... but go rather to the lost sheep of the house of Israel" (Matthew 10:5-6). We know that Jesus extended His mission to reach everyone — Jew or Gentile — but today's verse demonstrates that Jesus yearned for the salvation of His own people.

Even though the Jews are the chosen people of God, the Lord never forced them to place their faith in Him. Throughout the ages, God has given the Jews chance after chance to come to Christ, and they have often refused it. Why is that? It's something called the free will of man. Even though God is sovereign, He has still granted the Jews the capacity to receive or reject His grace. That same free will belongs to every other human being — each of us can either accept or reject Jesus Christ.

The Bible is very clear — God "desires all men to be saved and to come to the knowledge of the truth" (1 Timothy 2:4). And yet, not everyone is saved. Jesus said the majority of people are headed to hell (Matthew 7:13-14). Is God responsible for the fact that many people will suffer in hell? Absolutely not! Each man chooses what he will do with Christ, and based upon that choice each man is responsible for his own eternal destiny. Have you exercised your free will by placing your faith in Jesus?

## April 18 – Don't Believe Everything You Hear

*"The simple believes every word, but the prudent considers well his steps." (Proverbs 14:15)*

Have you ever known someone that's gullible? Gullible is defined as "easily persuaded to believe something." There are some people willing to believe anything you tell them, sometimes no matter how ridiculous. And to be honest, each of us is probably a little more gullible than we want to believe. When a juicy piece of gossip comes our way, we're quick to believe what we hear because the details are just too tantalizing to resist.

Believing everything you hear is not only gullible, it's very dangerous. For example, let's say a coworker comes to you and reports that one of your friends is stealing money from the company. Your coworker even provides an elaborate explanation of how the theft is occurring. Not only that, she informs you that many others in the office are aware of the theft. Based on the nature of the allegation, the accompanying story, and the number of those who believe it, you're tempted to buy in too.

When things like that happen, we must resist the temptation to automatically affirm what we've heard. We should stop and think about the people that will be hurt if we perpetuate what we've been told. When you hear a rumor, you should treat someone else like you want to be treated. Go to the person directly, ask him if what you've heard is true, and, if it is, then do all you can to assist him/her with repentance. If what you've heard is not true, you should confront those who are perpetuating a lie and encourage them to seek forgiveness from the one they've lied about.

## April 19 – God Will Put Your Faith to the Test

*"And they were left, that He might test Israel by them, to know whether they would obey the commandments of the LORD, which He had commanded their fathers by the hand of Moses." (Judges 3:4)*

All of us have been put to the test. In my lifetime, I've been blessed to graduate high school, college, and seminary (twice). If I had a $20 bill for every test I've taken, I'd be a wealthy man by now! Have you ever wondered why a teacher would administer a test? Just to punish the class? Because the school board says so? Of course not. A teacher issues a test to gauge the student's understanding of the subject matter. A test is designed to separate those who know from those who don't.

The Bible tells us that teachers are not the only ones who issue tests. When the children of Israel took possession of the Promised Land, they were not able to drive out all the inhabitants of the land. The Word says, "These are the nations which the LORD left, that He might test Israel by them" (Judges 3:1). Why would God want to test His own people? "To know whether they would obey the commandments of the LORD." God wanted to know if His people would stand up or fold up.

In the process of time, Israel folded like a lawn chair. They started intermarrying the natives and worshiping their pagan gods. Time and again God judged them for failing the test. Likewise, God will test your faith. He will test you by allowing the devil to tempt you, placing you in the fire of adversity, etc. Every time God tests your faith, He's doing it for one reason — to see if you will continue to glorify Him. In the process of every test, He'll make your faith stronger if you'll simply trust in Him.

## April 20 — Cause a Celebration in Heaven

*"I say to you that likewise there will be more joy in heaven over one sinner who repents than over ninety-nine just persons who need no repentance." (Luke 15:7)*

Luke 15 is one of the most beloved chapters in all of the Bible. In it, we read stories about a lost sheep, a lost coin, and a lost son. Today's verse is taken from a parable Jesus told after the Pharisees condemned Him for associating with "tax collectors and sinners" (Luke 15:1). Jesus didn't associate with the wicked to participate in their activities. Rather, He befriended the wicked in order to reach them with God's grace. Today's parable demonstrates that Jesus wants everyone to be born again.

Jesus said there was a man who had 100 sheep, and while ninety-nine of them were accounted for, one of them went missing. The owner of the sheep was willing to leave the ninety-nine in order to find the absent one. Having found the lost sheep, he threw a party with friends and neighbors because the one that was lost had been found. Jesus said, "Likewise there will be more joy in heaven over one sinner who repents than over ninety-nine just persons who need no repentance."

Was Jesus trying to say that some people are so good they don't need to repent? Clearly not! Just two chapters earlier, Luke recorded these words of Jesus — "unless you repent you will all likewise perish" (Luke 13:3). Every human is a wicked sinner in desperate need of Jesus, but sadly some are too proud to realize it. The story reminds us that the self-righteous will not experience God's grace, but those willing to turn to God will cause heaven to break out in celebration every time!

## April 21 — Celebrating the Repentance of Others

*"It was right that we should make merry and be glad, for your brother was dead and is alive again, and was lost and is found." (Luke 15:32)*

Somewhere along the way, I bet you've heard the story of the prodigal son. That's what we typically call the story found in Luke 15:11-32. As amazing as the prodigal's repentance is, he's really not the point of the story. As unbelievable as the father's love is, not even he is the real story. The focus of the story is the older brother. While the first two parables in this chapter (lost sheep and lost coin) focus on the Finder of lost things, the last story focuses on those who were never "lost" to begin with.

Consider the context — Jesus was accosted by the Pharisees because He was willing to associate with tax collectors and sinners. In what I call "the parable of the older brother," Jesus wanted the Pharisees to see that the lost son represented the sinners He associated with. He wanted them to understand that the Father represented Almighty God — longsuffering and not willing that any should perish. That leaves the older brother, upset that his father threw a party when his prodigal brother returned home.

Today's verse is the voice of the father, and clearly these words were directed at the Pharisees who were acting like an angry older brother, despising the repentance of sinners. The Pharisees should've been celebrating that so many were drawn to Christ and being saved, but instead they were unhappy. Why? Because the focus was on Jesus and not them. How about you? Do you rejoice over the salvation of the lost, or have you been despising what you should be celebrating and encouraging?

## April 22 – A Reversal of Fortunes

*"There was a certain rich man who was clothed in purple and fine linen and fared sumptuously every day. But there was a certain beggar named Lazarus, full of sores, who was laid at his gate, desiring to be fed with the crumbs which fell from the rich man's table. Moreover the dogs came and licked his sores." (Luke 16:19-21)*

The human experience is a story of haves and have-nots. There are those who are wealthy and don't seem to have a care in the world, while others struggle even to keep clothes on their backs and food in their stomachs. The disparity between rich and poor is nothing new — it's as old as time itself. Jesus highlighted that disparity when He was talking to the Pharisees. Luke tells us that the Pharisees "were lovers of money," so Jesus shared a parable directed right at them.

There was a rich man who fared well every day, but laid at his gate each morning was a poor man named Lazarus who desired to eat the crumbs that fell from the rich man's table. Apparently, the rich man had grown accustomed to ignoring Lazarus, but all that changed when both men died and passed into the afterlife. From there, Lazarus could be seen in "Abraham's bosom" in heaven, while the rich man was in torment in hell. He begged for comfort but found no way out of hell.

The rich man even begged Father Abraham to send someone to witness to his five brothers, but Abraham reminded the rich man that his brothers had the Law and the Prophets. The story very vividly explains there is going to be a great reversal of fortunes at the end of time. Those who have trusted in their riches will be banished to hell, while those who have trusted in Christ will experience something far beyond their wildest dreams. Ask yourself — am I trusting in my riches, or am I trusting in Jesus?

## April 23 — Giving Thanks to God

*"And one of them, when he saw that he was healed, returned, and with a loud voice glorified God, and fell down on his face at His feet, giving Him thanks. And he was a Samaritan." (Luke 17:15-16)*

We should all live with an attitude of gratitude, but if we're honest, we have to admit that sometimes we struggle with thanksgiving. Sometimes we get so fixed on what we want that we forget to give thanks for all we have. What do we have to be thankful for? The blessings are too many to mention — the running water in our homes, the food in our pantries, the clothes in our closet, etc. Every day we take for granted the necessities of life, not to mention our amazing salvation!

Luke tells the story of an occasion when Christ and the disciples were headed to Jerusalem, and along the way they passed through Galilee and Samaria. In a certain village, there were ten lepers who stood far off and cried out to Jesus. Leprosy was a horrible disease in the ancient world, and those who suffered from it were forced to live on the edge of civilization so that no one else would contract their disease. The life of a leper was a lonely, miserable life filled with heartache and adversity.

When these ten lepers called on Jesus, He mercifully healed each one of them. After they saw that they'd been healed, one of the ten lepers came back to Jesus to give thanks. Luke tells us he was a Samaritan. You would've expected one of Christ's fellow Jews to return and say thank you, but not a single one did. Would you say that you're more like the ungrateful nine or the thankful one? God has done great things for all of us! The very least we can do is take time to thank Him today and every day!

## April 24 — His Name Is Wonderful

> *"Then Manoah said to the Angel of the* Lord, *'What is Your name, that when Your words come to pass we may honor You?' And the Angel of the* Lord *said to him, 'Why do you ask My name, seeing it is wonderful?'" (Judges 13:17-18)*

Maybe you've heard the story of Samson — the guy with the really long hair who was one of the strongest men to ever live. Samson's story is like a roller coaster — he experienced some amazing highs and some really bad lows. While you may be familiar with Samson, you might not know much about his parents. Manoah (Samson's father) and his wife (unnamed in Scripture) were both very sad because they were not able to have children. That's when the Angel of the Lord showed up.

The Angel of the Lord visited Manoah's wife to let her know she would conceive and have a son who would deliver Israel. Unfortunately, Manoah was not present when the Angel appeared to his wife, so he prayed that God would resend the Angel to him. God answered his prayer, and when the Angel made another appearance, Manoah heard the good news for himself. Before the Angel departed, he asked Him for His name, something you rarely see in the Word of God.

Today's verse provides the Angel's response — "Why do you ask My name, seeing it is wonderful?" The word translated "wonderful" is *pilee*, and it describes something that is "incomprehensible or extraordinary." Most evangelicals believe the Angel of the Lord is an Old Testament appearance of Jesus Christ. That explains the Angel's response! When it comes to Jesus, the old hymn says, "His Name is Wonderful." JESUS is the most wonderful name ever given to mankind!

# April 25 – Asking God for Forgiveness

*"Have mercy upon me, O God, according to Your lovingkindness; according to the multitude of Your tender mercies, blot out my transgressions." (Psalm 51:1)*

If you were to ask most Christians to identify three biblical stories, I'm guessing the story of David and Goliath would come up again and again. In his battle with the giant Goliath, David set himself apart as a great man of faith. Years later, after the death of Saul, God raised David up to be the king of Israel. Under David's leadership, Israel reached heights it had never before seen. David built his palace in the city of Jerusalem, and he began to make preparations for a future temple.

Yet, in spite of all David's successes he made a critical mistake. At a time when he should've been out to war with his troops, he stayed home in his palace. Being where he shouldn't have been, he started doing things he shouldn't have done. He allowed a look to turn into lust, and his sin finally led him to murder Bathsheba's husband. Not long after the incident, the prophet Nathan confronted David with his sin, and the king was brokenhearted by the conviction of the Holy Spirit.

That story is the background for today's verse in Psalm 51. The superscription of the psalm even says, "A Psalm of David when Nathan the prophet went to him, after he had gone into Bathsheba." It is a cry for forgiveness that also serves as a model for us. Every one of us makes mistakes that displease the Lord (Romans 3:23). When we sin, we've got a choice — we can wallow in guilt and self-pity, or we can confess our sins and begin the process of repentance. Today, make certain that you choose the path of forgiveness and repentance. Start now by confessing your sins to God and receiving His tender mercies.

## April 26 – What Makes A Nation Great

*"Righteousness exalts a nation, but sin is
a reproach to any people." (Proverbs 14:34)*

In 1980, presidential hopeful Ronald Reagan and his team used the slogan, "Let's Make America Great Again." The slogan resonated with the American people and Mr. Reagan became President Reagan by an electoral vote of 489-49. The Clintons even utilized the slogan for President Clinton's 1992 campaign and again for Hillary's 2008 presidential primary campaign. And of course, President Donald Trump utilized the slogan before and after his election to office.

It's an idea that's easy for Americans to buy in to — we all want to see our nation succeed and do well. But how do you really measure a nation's greatness? Is it by its expansive roads and infrastructure? Is it by its world-class military? Is it by its record-breaking economy? According to the Scripture, a nation can have all those things and still not be great in the sight of God. The Lord doesn't measure greatness by *riches*. Rather, He measures a nation's greatness by *righteousness*.

"Righteousness exalts a nation" — just look what holiness did for Israel when they pursued the Lord. Look back and consider how God has blessed the United States on those occasions when we have magnified the name of Jesus. "But sin is a reproach to any people" — rampant sin has wreaked havoc on Israel, America, and every other nation that forgot the Lord. As a nation we have a choice to make — either we can submit to God and be exalted, or we can reject Him and be disgraced.

# April 27 — Doing What's Right in Our Own Eyes

*"In those days there was no king in Israel; everyone did what was right in his own eyes." (Judges 17:6, 21:25)*

Four times the Book of Judges tells us there was no king in Israel during those days (17:6, 18:1, 19:1, 21:25). Two of those occurrences also add that "everyone did what was right in his own eyes." We need to think back and remember that by this time, Israel had been led by Moses and Joshua among others. They had also been given the written Law of God by the finger of God Himself. Clearly, the children of Israel had every opportunity to know right from wrong.

Instead of obeying God's commands after they settled the Promised Land, the Bible says they turned to sin over and over again. And because we serve a merciful God, each time the Israelites cried out to God, He raised up a "judge" that delivered them from their enemies. But sadly, the Jews had short memories — just as soon as God spared the Jews from their adversaries, they turned right back to the sins that got them in a mess in the first place.

The culmination of Israel's sin is that "everyone did what was right in his own eyes." Rather than doing what was right in the eyes of God, they chose to do what seemed best to themselves. That's a sure-fire recipe for disaster and one we seem to be following quite well in the United States. Sometimes even our "churches" tend to follow their own desires rather than God's will. Today I encourage you to discover what God desires for your life and do what's right in HIS eyes.

## April 28 – Don't Make the Stones Cry Out

*"And some of the Pharisees called to Him from the crowd, 'Teacher, rebuke Your disciples.' But He answered and said to them, 'I tell you that if these should keep silent, the stones would immediately cry out.'" (Luke 19:39-40)*

On the first day of the last week of His life, Jesus came riding into Jerusalem on the back of a colt. The Scripture says the people were totally enamored with Jesus, and they began to cast their clothes and palm branches on the ground before Him as a symbol of worship. It's no secret the Pharisees hated Jesus and wanted Him dead. They commanded Jesus to instruct His followers to be quiet. The response that Jesus gave tells us a great deal about the glory of God.

Christ replied, "If these (people) should keep silent, the stones would immediately cry out." Wow! The Bible tells us that creation declares the glory of God (Psalm 19:1), but we don't usually hear their praise in an audible voice. In this case, Jesus said even the stones would cry out in praise on the occasion of His triumphal entrance into Jerusalem. Thankfully, the stones didn't have to make a sound because the crowds kept singing "Hosanna" to Jesus their Messiah.

The praise of creation is wonderful, but it's not the same as the praise of humans. Why? Because humans have a soul that's been made in the image of God. Creation has no choice but to praise the Lord, but we do. If we refuse to praise the Lord, God is able to cause stones to break out in praise! I don't know about you, but I don't want any stones out-praising me! After all, a stone has never experienced the saving power of grace. Today, let's keep the stones silent by lifting our praises to God!

## April 29 – Falling on Jesus

*"Then He looked at them and said, 'What then is this that is written: "The stone which the builders rejected has become the chief cornerstone"? Whoever falls on that stone will be broken; but on whomever it falls, it will grind him to powder.'" (Luke 20:17-18)*

Today we're looking at a powerful passage from the Word of God. These words of Jesus were directed at the Pharisees, but they're applicable to all of us. Jesus quoted Psalm 118 — "The stone which the builders rejected has become the chief cornerstone." You and I know that Jesus is that chief cornerstone, but unfortunately, He has been rejected by Jews and Gentiles alike. The Pharisees were certainly a part of that — they rejected Jesus when they should have received Him.

We need to pay close attention to the next words of Jesus — "Whoever falls on that stone will be broken." In other words, if you surrender your life to God through faith in Jesus, you WILL be broken. But how? God will break you of your pride, and He will also break you through the convicting power of the Holy Spirit. Let me be clear — it's not a bad thing to be broken by God. It is only in being broken by God that He can rebuild you into the image of His Son. God breaks the old and re-creates us new.

The alternative is much worse — "but on whomever it falls, it will grind him to powder." So we have a choice — we can either be broken by falling on Jesus, or we can be pounded to dust for failing to surrender our lives to Him. The obstinate Pharisees refused to fall on Jesus, so they will be pounded by His wrath at the judgment seat of Christ. How about you, friend? Have you allowed God to break you by placing your faith in Jesus? Take heart in knowing that God always rebuilds every person that He breaks.

## April 30 – Pouring Out Your Soul to God

*"But Hannah answered and said, 'No, my lord, I am a woman of sorrowful spirit. I have drunk neither wine nor intoxicating drink, but have poured out my soul before the Lord.'" (1 Samuel 1:15)*

Have you ever "borne your soul" to someone else? Have you ever been so overcome with emotion that you desperately needed to get some things off your chest? Maybe you sat with a friend and cried and prayed and cried some more. Maybe you had a heart-to-heart conversation with your significant other. Sometimes people pour out their soul when they're trying to unload some hurt from their past. Those times are often very difficult, but they can also be very cathartic.

Today's verse is taken from the life of a woman named Hannah. She was married to a man named Elkanah who had two wives. His first wife was able to have children, but sadly Hannah's womb remained closed. Year after year, they made their way to the tabernacle to worship at Shiloh. On one occasion, Hannah could no longer take the misery, so she decided to go to the tabernacle by herself. From there, she sat at the door and poured her soul out to the Lord.

Hannah was so overcome with emotion that the High Priest (Eli) thought she was intoxicated. He said, "How long will you be drunk? Put your wine away from you!" Hannah responded with the beautiful words of today's verse. Upon hearing her heart, Eli prayed that God would grant her petition for a child, and about a year later He did. Her child (Samuel) became a great man of God, and it all started with a woman's prayer. Maybe you should take time to pour out your soul to God today.

## May 1 — Sacrificial Giving

*"And He looked up and saw the rich putting their gifts into the treasury, and He saw also a certain poor widow putting in two mites. So He said, 'Truly I say to you that this poor widow has put in more than all; for all these out of their abundance have put in offerings for God, but she out of her poverty put in all the livelihood that she had.'" (Luke 21:1-4)*

Some people have no trouble giving lots of money to charitable causes. It's no secret some people make millions of dollars each year, so giving a few thousand dollars to charity is no real sacrifice. Of course, not everyone is quite so blessed. Many people live from paycheck to paycheck, so giving any of their income for needs outside their own home is sacrificial. It's truly awe-inspiring to see a person give to someone else when they barely have enough resources to meet their own needs.

Today's verses come from an account that Luke recorded in the Word of God. Jesus was standing by the temple treasury as folks were coming to bring their gifts to the Lord. To use our modern currency, I'm sure some gave $10, $100, and maybe even $1,000 or more. But there was "a certain poor widow" who placed two mites into the treasury. Two mites valued one Roman lepton — about six minutes of one day's wage. So then, the poor widow literally gave only pennies to the Lord.

The undiscerning might expect Jesus to be enraged with such a small gift, but Jesus saw beyond the woman's gift directly into her soul. He knew she was giving the very best gift she could bring — "all the livelihood that she had." For that reason, Jesus said "this poor widow has put in more than all." You see, it's not about equal giving, but equal sacrifice. Every one of us should be giving sacrificially to the work of the Lord. Are you cheerfully "giving 'til it hurts"?

## May 2 – Take Heed to Yourself

*"But take heed to yourselves, lest your hearts be weighed down with carousing, drunkenness, and cares of this life, and that Day come on you unexpectedly." (Luke 21:34)*

To "take heed" is to pay attention to. We pay attention to lots of things, don't we? We pay attention to how well our favorite football team plays and the recruits that are coming in next year. We pay attention to advertisements so we can find out when our favorite brand names are going on sale. Sometimes we fail to pay attention like we should. Many people who've received a speeding ticket wish they could go back and pay attention to how fast they were going.

In today's verse, Jesus commands us to pay attention to ourselves. What does He mean? I think He's saying we need to pay attention to our hearts and minds. If we're not careful, we can get busy with "carousing, drunkenness, and the cares of this life." In other words, human tendency tempts us to walk down the paths of sin as we fix our attention on temporary things. Paying attention to who we associate with, what we put in our bodies, etc., would save us all from many heartaches in life.

Instead, Jesus emphatically states that our focus needs to be on Him and "that Day" when all men "will see the Son of Man coming in a cloud with power and great glory" (Luke 21:27). We need to pay attention to what we believe and what we do because when Jesus comes back, it will be too late to change our hearts. As you look over the course of your life, how are you doing? Are you carelessly and recklessly living for yourself, or are you focusing your time and energy on living for Jesus?

## May 3 — When God Gives You What You Want

*"Nevertheless the people refused to obey the voice of Samuel; and they said, 'No, but we will have a king over us, that we also may be like all the nations, and that our king may judge us and go out before us and fight our battles.'" (1 Samuel 8:19-20)*

Have your kids ever begged you for something that you knew they wouldn't like? Maybe it was a gigantic sucker shaped like Spongebob Squarepants. You warned your kids that while the sucker might look really cool, it probably tastes bad. They weren't deterred. Instead, they were determined to find out what Spongebob tastes like. When you finally caved in and bought the sucker, they quickly took their first lick — only to discover that Spongebob tastes like some old wax from China.

You knew your kids would be much happier with some M&Ms, but they simply had to find out the hard way. Today's verses come from a story much like that. Throughout their history to this point, Israel never had a king. Instead, God raised up great leaders for them like Abraham, Isaac, Jacob, Moses, and Joshua. But no matter their leader, Israel always had Jehovah for their King. But after the period of the judges, the Israelites decided they wanted to trade their heavenly King for an earthly king.

Samuel warned them that their desire for an earthly king would lead to disaster — forced labor, taxation, etc. But the Israelites were not deterred by Samuel's warning. God gave the children of Israel what they wanted, and they eventually ended up with a coward for a king (Saul). A few generations later, King Rehoboam divided the nation, and thereafter the northern kingdom never had a godly king. The lesson is simple — be careful what you wish for. God might just give you what you want.

## May 4 — Jesus Knows All About You

> *"And the Lord said, 'Simon, Simon! Indeed, Satan has asked for you, that he may sift you as wheat. But I have prayed for you, that your faith should not fail; and when you have returned to Me, strengthen your brethren.'" (Luke 22:31-32)*

We have lots of acquaintances, but there are very few people who know us really well. We draw near to people like parents, siblings, children, and best friends. But even as much as those people might love us, there are things about us that even our closest loved ones don't know. Let's be honest — we'd probably be embarrassed for another human being to know everything about us. While it's true that no other human knows all our secrets, it's also true that Jesus does.

Just before His arrest, Jesus predicted that Peter would deny Him. How did Jesus know that? It's simple — because Jesus was, and is, completely and fully God. He is all-powerful, all-present, and all-knowing. He knew Peter would act like a coward on the night of His arrest, leaving Jesus to fend for Himself. Peter tried to deny that any such betrayal could ever happen, but Jesus told Peter he would deny Him three times before the crowing of the morning rooster.

Here's the awesome part — knowing Peter would deny Him, Jesus loved and prayed for him anyway. He knew Peter would return to Him after his original act of cowardice, and Jesus prayed he would strengthen the rest of the disciples upon his return. We can sing "Jesus loves me" all day long, but we really don't understand the magnitude of those words until we stop to consider that He loves us in spite of all our imperfections. He knows all about you, and He loves you anyway.

## May 5 — When I Am Afraid

*"Whenever I am afraid, I will trust in You. In God (I will praise His word), in God I have put my trust; I will not fear. What can flesh do to me?" (Psalm 56:3-4)*

Unfortunately, it seems fear is a significant part of the human experience. People are afraid of so many things — getting sick, inability to pay bills, tragedy to a child, etc. Being afraid does not do one thing to improve our situation — in fact, it only makes things worse. But that doesn't keep us from working ourselves all up into a fear-induced tizzy about things that are usually beyond our control. Even the most faithful among us would have to confess there are times we battle with Freddy Fear.

What are we supposed to do when we are tempted to live in fear? David provides us a wonderful answer. On the occasion of Psalm 56, he had been captured by the Philistine king and was in jeopardy for his life. It just so happened that God spared his life, but David was initially afraid because he did not know what the outcome would be. He said, "Whenever I am afraid, I will trust in You." Trust in who? "In God … in God I have put my trust." David said the antidote for fear is faith in God!

David also gives us a key parenthetical point — "I will praise His word." In the midst of his captivity, David was able to look back on the Word of God and know the Lord had promised to make him king of Israel. Placing his confidence in God and His Word, David overcame his fear and made this awesome declaration — "What can flesh do to me?" Amen! Fear is the absence of faith. If you are living in fear, it's time for you to renew your faith in God and trust in the promises of His Word!

## May 6 — Obedience Is Better Than Sacrifice

*"Has the Lord as great delight in burnt offerings and sacrifices, as in obeying the voice of the Lord? Behold, to obey is better than sacrifice, and to heed than the fat of rams." (1 Samuel 15:22)*

The Israelites were a people of sacrifices. Throughout the year, God's people were commanded to come to the place of worship and offer their sacrifices to God. There were all sorts of sacrifices, and in every case the people were commanded to bring their very best. You may know that the sacrificial process was committed to the priests and Levites. And yet, after a battle with the Amalekites, King Saul thought it was his place to disobey God for the sake of sacrifice.

God clearly commanded Saul and his army to utterly destroy the Amalekites, keeping nothing alive so they could no longer be a thorn in their side. When the people came upon the spoils of war, they decided to keep the best of the animals alive, blatantly disobeying God's command. For that reason, God sent Samuel to rebuke cowardly King Saul. Today's verse is that rebuke, and it makes a very clear statement — "to obey is better than sacrifice, and to heed than the fat of rams."

God was simply saying you can prepare all the sacrifices you want, but if you're not obedient to God it's all for nothing. The same is true in the 21st century — we can go through all the ritual and tradition of our worship, but if we're not living in humble obedience to God, then our ceremonies mean nothing. You may attend church weekly, put on your Sunday best, and open your Bible when the pastor preaches — but if you're not living in obedience to God, then you're missing the mark.

## May 7 – Don't Judge a Book by Its Cover

*"But the Lord said to Samuel, 'Do not look at his appearance or at his physical stature, because I have refused him. For the LORD does not see as man sees; for man looks at the outward appearance, but the LORD looks at the heart.'" (1 Samuel 16:7)*

After the Lord rejected Saul as king over Israel because of his disobedience, the Lord instructed Samuel to go to the house of a man named Jesse in Bethlehem. Jesse had eight sons, and the Lord told Samuel he would show him which one of those sons he was to anoint as the next king over Israel. When Samuel arrived, Jesse sent his oldest son (Eliab) to stand before Samuel. As the oldest, he must've been impressive, and Samuel was convinced he would be Israel's next king.

The Lord let Samuel know that Jesse's oldest son would not be the next king, and He gave Samuel a very important lesson — "man looks at the outward appearance, but the LORD looks at the heart." After God instructed Samuel, Jesse's next six sons came to stand before him, but in each case the Lord did not select any of them to be king. That left just one son — the youngest — whom Jesse did not even bother to call in from the pasture. Samuel said they would not eat until the youngest was called in.

A ruddy, handsome young man came walking up to the prophet. God let Samuel know that the ruddy, young shepherd boy standing in front of him would be Israel's next king. That young man was David. When others looked at him they simply saw a shepherd, but looking into his soul God saw a king. That's a great lesson for us. We're so tempted to judge a book by its cover, but we need to start seeing people as God sees them. Let's look beyond the surface and to the heart of those around us.

## May 8 – Preaching Through the Scriptures

*"And beginning at Moses and all the Prophets, He expounded to them in all the Scriptures the things concerning Himself." (Luke 24:27)*

On the same day that Jesus rose from the dead, two of his followers decided to make the seven-mile journey from Jerusalem to Emmaus. Along the way, a gentleman approached them and began a conversation. It's no surprise that the two men were talking about Jesus and all that had happened to Him over the last few days of His life. The two men had no idea that Jesus was risen from the dead, and they also did not know the identity of the man who began to travel with them.

The man asked them to explain the things that happened to Jesus in Jerusalem, and so the two men obliged. After they explained that Christ's tomb was now empty, the man began to do some talking himself. He began by rebuking the two men for their biblical ignorance, then "beginning at Moses and all the Prophets, He expounded to them in all the Scriptures the things concerning Himself." Of course, the third Traveler was Jesus, and He began to preach through the Word.

The two men's eyes were finally opened, and they said, "Did not our heart burn within us while He talked with us on the road, and while He opened the Scriptures to us?" (Luke 24:32). The holy heartburn the two men felt was clearly because of Jesus, and yet we have much to learn from Christ's approach. He started at the beginning of the Scripture and worked His way through to demonstrate that the Scripture points to Jesus. All pastors and teachers should take note and "preach the Word" (2 Timothy 4:2)!

## May 9 – Life Until Jesus Comes Back

*"And they worshiped Him, and returned to Jerusalem with great joy, and were continually in the temple praising and blessing God." (Luke 24:52-53)*

After Jesus rose from the dead, He presented Himself alive to at least several hundred people mentioned in the Word of God. Among those were the disciples, to whom He presented Himself on multiple occasions. When the time came for Christ to ascend to heaven, He led the disciples up the Mount of Olives as far as Bethany. From there He ascended into heaven, where He is now seated at the right hand of God. One day, we know Jesus will come back to take His children home to heaven!

But how should we be living until Jesus comes back? We should follow the example of the disciples. First, the Bible says they "worshiped Him." The highest work we have as followers of Christ is to worship God. All our obedience to His commands flows out of our desire to bring Him glory! Also, Luke says they "returned to Jerusalem." Perhaps they were tempted to stay on the Mount of Ascension, but they knew their missionary work was calling them back to the city, and it calls us as well.

Scripture also says they returned to Jerusalem "with great joy." In other words, the disciples were overcome with happiness because they knew that Jesus is Lord. If anyone should be happy, it should be those of us who know our sins have been forgiven! And finally, Luke says the disciples "were continually in the temple praising and blessing God." We should remain in close fellowship with the church until Jesus returns. May God help every one of us to live each day like Jesus is alive and coming back!

# May 10 – Jesus, the Living Word

*"In the beginning was the Word, and the Word was with God, and the Word was God ... and the Word became flesh and dwelt among us." (John 1:1, 14)*

One of the most pivotal portions of the New Testament is the prologue to John's Gospel. John was most likely the youngest of the apostles, and church history says that he outlived them all. During the latter part of his life, he had a significant ministry in Ephesus where he wrote to churches throughout Asia Minor. First, Second and Third John are those letters, and together they emphasize the full humanity of Christ. John wrote his Gospel about a decade later and in it he emphasized the full deity of Christ.

The first eighteen verses of John make up the Gospel's prologue. With his very first words, John's emphasis is unmistakable — "In the beginning was the Word." These words are much like Genesis 1:1, but there is a marked difference. Genesis 1:1 starts with creation and looks down through the rest of human history. John 1:1 starts with creation and looks back into eternity. That's where John lets us know Jesus existed when nothing else did. Through Him all things were made (Colossians 1:16).

Also, "the Word was with God" — Jesus, the Father, and the Holy Spirit had perfect fellowship before humans ever existed. *"The Word was God"* — the Greek NT actually reads, "God was the Word." John was very clear — Jesus is completely and fully God. And the great news is, "the Word became flesh and dwelt among us." The One who is completely God took on human flesh and became fully man. Being fully God and fully man, He is fully able to deliver us from our sins. He alone is the Living Word!

## May 11 – A Simple Plan for Success

*"Commit your works to the Lord, and your thoughts will be established." (Proverbs 16:3)*

Everyone is guilty of getting the cart in front of the horse from time to time. For instance, we start planning vacations before we've determined how to pay for them. We start thinking of all we'll do upon graduation without making sure that every assignment is complete. In regard to today's verse, we often like to define our own version of success while creating a plan to get us there. But sadly, we put the cart in front of the horse by laying out a host of plans before seeking the will of God.

King Solomon wants to help get our priorities right. Everyone desires to be "successful," but we need to start with the right definition of success. If your idea of success only includes material, financial, vocational, or relational prosperity, then you're already off on the wrong foot. Solomon invites you to "commit your works to the Lord." In other words, we need to start with God rather than ending with Him. But let's be honest — too often we're guilty of creating a mess and then asking God to bless our mess.

"Commit your works to the Lord" — that means start with prayer, Bible study, and seeking the counsel of godly men and women in your church who can direct you to seek the Lord. Once you've dedicated yourself to honor God in all you do, then true success is inevitable. "Your thoughts will be established" — as you fall in love with God, His plans will become your plans, and we know God is going to accomplish His will. As Jesus said, "Seek FIRST the kingdom of God and His righteousness, and all these things shall be added to you" (Matthew 6:33).

# May 12 — The First Miracle

*"This beginning of signs Jesus did in Cana of Galilee, and manifested His glory; and His disciples believed in Him." (John 2:11)*

Depending on how you count the miracles of Jesus, there are about forty recorded miracles of Christ in the New Testament — seven of them included in John's Gospel. The first miracle takes us back to an occasion when Christ and the disciples had been invited to a wedding. Weddings are important in the 21st century, but they were even more important to the ancients. They were village-wide events that were often seen as pinnacle experiences. Each family wanted to put their best foot forward.

Upon arriving at the party in Cana, something embarrassing happened — the host ran out of wine. I'm sure Mary didn't want her friend to be embarrassed, so she confronted Jesus with the problem and instructed the servants to do whatever Christ told them. He commanded them to fill six large water pots, each one with a capacity of twenty-thirty gallons, meaning that they probably retrieved about 150 gallons of water! Seemed like a crazy idea, but God loves to do miracles in the midst of crazy.

Miraculously, the water was transformed from water to wine, and the master of ceremonies confirmed it himself, supposing the groom had saved the best wine for last! What are we to make of this miracle? That Jesus likes for people to get drunk and use alcohol? Clearly not! The point of the miracle is that Jesus is the new and living wine. All who came before Him were inferior, but He is the One sent by God to make a new and living way of salvation.

## May 13 — Born of Water and the Spirit

*"Jesus answered, 'Most assuredly, I say to you, unless one is born of water and the Spirit, he cannot enter the kingdom of God.'" (John 3:5)*

John gives us glimpses into the life of Jesus that are not provided by the Synoptic Gospel writers. One of those glimpses is John 3 — Christ's encounter with a truth-seeking Pharisee named Nicodemus. The Bible doesn't tell us much about him — simply that he was "a ruler of the Jews" and that "this man came to Jesus by night." A Pharisee like Nicodemus could not afford to be seen with Jesus during the day, for fear of what his peers might say, so he approached Jesus under the veil of darkness.

Nicodemus began his encounter with Jesus by applauding His amazing signs and wonders. Jesus did not mince words when He responded, "Unless one is born again, he cannot see the kingdom of God" (John 3:3). Nicodemus was immediately confounded, knowing it's totally impossible for a human to re-enter the womb after birth. Seeing he was confused, Jesus helped him understand — "unless one is born of water and the Spirit, he cannot enter the kingdom of God."

When Jesus spoke of being "born of water," He was talking about natural birth. Every human has experienced a natural birth, but not everyone experiences re-birth. That's what it means to be born of "the Spirit." Simply put — a natural birth is not enough to save you. Each of us must be born again by the regenerating power of the Holy Spirit. How is a person "born of the Spirit"? By placing his/her faith in Jesus Christ. You've experienced a natural birth, but have you been born again by the power of the Spirit through faith in Jesus?

## May 14 — More of Him and Less of Me

*"He must increase, but I must decrease." (John 3:30)*

John the Baptist was a fascinating man. God set him apart to be the forerunner of Jesus. By all human standards, we would say he was a little unorthodox. Scripture tells us his diet consisted of locusts and wild honey, and he chose to wear camel's hair. I imagine he spent much of his time in seclusion and prayer, but he also spent a good deal of time preaching repentance and baptizing his Jewish peers in the Jordan River. He was preparing the nation for the coming of Jesus.

After Christ's ministry began, people were immediately attracted to Jesus. People that would've typically been baptized by John started coming to Jesus, and those who followed John weren't happy about it. John responded to his followers with a beautiful analogy about being the "best man," and then he gave us these amazing words — "He must increase, but I must decrease." In other words, John was saying, "The world needs to see much more of Jesus and much less of me."

The same is still true today — the world needs to see much more of Jesus and much less of us. How can we apply this principle to our lives? How about starting with the things we say? Do our words point others to Jesus? How about the way we live? Do our actions point others to Christ? We can spend our lives living for our own pleasure, just as John the Baptist could've held on to his influence over the nation, but instead he pointed the masses to Jesus. Will others be pointed to Christ because of you?

## May 15 – The Urgency of Evangelism

*"But He needed to go through Samaria." (John 4:4)*

Some time after Christ's encounter with Nicodemus, He made the decision to leave Judea and head north toward Galilee. Between Judea in the south and Galilee in the north, there is a small section of Israel known as Samaria. Samaria was an area heavily influenced by the Babylonians. When the Babylonians captured Israel, they repatriated the land with some of their own men who remarried the native Jewish women. Their offspring became known as Samaritans.

The Jews looked down on Samaritans because they felt they were "half-breeds." The Samaritans even adopted their own places and customs of worship in an attempt to set themselves apart from the Jews. The Jews showed contempt for the Samaritans by crossing the Jordan River to avoid going through Samaria on their way to or from Judea. Jesus knew all about the history and racism, but the Scripture says, "He needed to go through Samaria." But why?

There was a woman in Samaria who needed to be saved. She was a woman with a bad reputation, and that's why she was at the well during the middle of the day when Jesus stopped to rest. She attempted to conceal her sin, but Jesus knew all about her five husbands and the live-in boyfriend she was currently with. The woman placed her faith in Jesus and the rest is history. Jesus exemplified the urgency of evangelism — going to places and talking to people that everyone else had cast aside. I wonder if you and I exemplify that same kind of passion and urgency to see others won to Christ?

## May 16 – My Priorities

*"Jesus said to them, 'My food is to do the will of Him who sent Me, and to finish His work. Do you not say, "There are still four months and then comes the harvest?" Behold, I say to you, lift up your eyes and look at the fields, for they are already white for harvest!'" (John 4:34-35)*

If someone asked you to rank your priorities in order, how would you list them? Many people would include spouse, children, other family, work, hobbies, etc. Some people might even include God and the church. If we're honest, we'll admit that we let our priorities get out of whack. There are times when we get more passionate about temporary things than eternal ones. For example, sometimes we spend more money on ballgames and movies than we do the church and missions.

After Christ's encounter with the woman at the well, the disciples urged Jesus to eat some lunch. After all, it was the middle of the day. Jesus said, "I have food to eat of which you do not know." The disciples did not know He was attempting to lead a village woman to the Lord, nor did they know that through her the entire village would hear about Jesus. He helped the disciples understand — "My food is to do the will of Him who sent Me and to finish His work."

When you think about it, eating is high on our list of priorities, right along with breathing, drinking, etc. And yet, just as important as food is, Jesus wanted us to know that salvation is even more important than our daily necessities. Imagine what it would be like if we were just as concerned about seeing others saved as we are about securing our next meal. The Gospel would be shared much more, many more would be convicted of their sins, and we would experience a harvest like we've never known!

## May 17 — Worshiping for the Lord

*"So David said to Michal, 'It was before the Lord, who chose me instead of your father and all his house, to appoint me ruler over the people of the Lord, over Israel. Therefore I will play music before the Lord. And I will be even more undignified than this, and will be humble in my own sight.'" (2 Samuel 6:21-22)*

King David had an amazing rise to the throne of Israel. It all started when he was a young shepherd boy who was not afraid to fight the Philistine giant Goliath. After his amazing victory, David had to wait several years until evil King Saul was out of the picture. After the passing of Saul, the entire nation coronated David as king over Israel. Not long after he became king, he desired to bring the Ark of the Covenant back to the tabernacle in Jerusalem.

As the Ark drew near to Jerusalem, David began worshiping the Lord demonstratively. The Bible says he started "leaping and whirling before the Lord" (2 Samuel 6:16). His wife, Michal — Saul's daughter — was looking down on the procession from her window and was not pleased. Scripture says, "She despised him in her heart." When he returned home, she made fun of him for worshiping like "one of the base fellows (who) shamelessly uncovers himself" (2 Samuel 6:20).

David let his wife know quickly he wasn't worshiping for her — "it was before the Lord." He went a step further and let her know, "I will be even more undignified than this." In other words, David didn't care what anyone else thought about his worship because he wasn't worshiping for anyone else — he was worshiping for an Audience of One. How about you? Do you let others keep you from following the leadership of the Holy Spirit in worship? Remember, you're worshiping God and no one else.

## May 18 – The Davidic Covenant

*"And your house and your kingdom shall be established forever before you. Your throne shall be established forever." (2 Samuel 7:16)*

After the Ark was moved to Jerusalem, the Bible says, "The LORD had given him (David) rest from all his enemies all around" (2 Samuel 7:1). David was situated very comfortably in his palace, but his heart was still not satisfied. It was his heart's desire to build a house of worship for the Lord, and the prophet Nathan initially added his blessing to David's desire. I'm sure the prophet was impressed with a king who still had a heart for God when so many others would've been concerned only about themselves.

God let the prophet know the Lord had not appointed David to build a house of worship. Instead, it was God's desire to establish David's throne. God let the king know that He would be with his son (Solomon) and that His mercy would rest on him even in the midst of his mistakes. Then God went a step further — He looked beyond David's son (Solomon) to One that would come through his son in the proceeding generations. In other words, God made a promise to David concerning Jesus.

God established His covenant with David — "your house and your kingdom shall be established forever … your throne shall be established forever." God was not simply talking about David's throne as king over modern-day Israel. God was talking about the everlasting kingdom of our Savior Jesus Christ. Isaiah said, "Of the increase of His government and peace there will be no end, upon the throne of David and over His kingdom" (Isaiah 9:7). Jesus, the son of David, is King of kings forevermore!

## May 19 – A More-Than-Enough God

*"Therefore they gathered them up, and filled twelve baskets with the fragments of the five barley loaves which were left over by those who had eaten." (John 6:13)*

The masses were incredibly attracted to Jesus. On one occasion, many people came to follow Jesus, so He sat on the side of a mountain and began teaching. About lunchtime, Jesus asked Philip where they could turn to provide food for such a large crowd. John tells us that Jesus inquired of Philip, not because He didn't know what to do, but to test his faith. Philip simply replied that 200 denarii (200 days' wages) would not be enough to feed such a crowd.

Andrew, Peter's brother, was able to find one small boy who had five loaves and two fish, but he asked, "What are they among so many?" (John 6:9). Jesus told the disciples to make the people sit down, and then He did something miraculous — He gave thanks and started passing out the five loaves and two fish. Keep in mind, John tells us there were 5,000 men in attendance, not including their wives and children. And yet, when the meal was done, there were 12 basketfuls left over!

Why did Jesus perform such an extraordinary miracle? I think He wanted His fellow Jews to know He is the long-awaited Messiah who had come to save each member of the 12 tribes. The miracle also proves we serve a God who is more than enough. The people only needed lunch, but Jesus provided much more. Paul said Christ is "able to do exceedingly abundantly above all that we ask or think" (Ephesians 3:20). You can trust that He is always more than enough and everything you need.

## May 20 – When God Corrects You

*"So David arose from the ground, washed and anointed himself, and changed his clothes; and he went into the house of the LORD and worshiped. Then he went to his own house; and when he requested, they set food before him, and he ate." (2 Samuel 12:20)*

Let's be honest — none of us really enjoys correction. On one hand, sometimes we're the ones being corrected. We've all been punished as children, and even as adults we've been corrected by employers, friends, etc. Correction is something we don't enjoy because it often damages our pride and can be quite painful. On the other hand, sometimes we're the ones doing the correcting. If you're a parent or a boss, you know what that's all about. Often, it's harder to correct than to be corrected.

If we're children of God, we're going to be corrected by Him from time to time. The author of Hebrews said, "whom the LORD loves He chastens, and scourges every son whom He receives" (Hebrews 12:6). We discipline our children because we love them, not because we hate them. So it is with God — He lovingly corrects us so we can be further conformed to the image of His Son Jesus. In those times God chooses to correct us, we need to carefully consider how we're going to respond.

God corrected David severely for his sin with Bathsheba. One of the ultimate punishments came in the death of his son. For seven days, David prayed and fasted that God would not take his son's life, but on the seventh day God took David's son to heaven. David responded by getting up, cleaning up, and going up to God's house for worship. He continued to press forward in his service to God. Has God been correcting you? If so, how will you respond? May it be with worship, perseverance, and thanksgiving.

## May 21 – Nowhere Else to Turn

*"Simon Peter answered Him, 'Lord, to whom shall we go? You have the words of eternal life. Also we have come to believe and know that You are the Christ, the Son of the living God.'"* (John 6:68-69)

Jesus fed many people when He gave thanks and passed out the five loaves and two fish. Our Lord probably fed around 20,000 people on that occasion, and those who ate stuck around to hear Christ teach. Jesus delivered a message many were not prepared to hear — He spoke of His followers partaking of His body and blood. The message was offensive to the multitudes, and many of those who received a free lunch decided they didn't want anything further from Christ.

As the multitudes walked away, Christ turned to His disciples and asked, "Do you also want to go away?" (John 6:67). Peter wasn't a perfect man, but on this occasion he got his answer exactly right — "To whom shall we go? You have the words of eternal life." Peter and the disciples realized salvation is found in no one other than Christ (Acts 4:12). You can search for eternal life through Allah, Krishna, Buddha, and many others, but you'll only find it by coming to Christ.

Furthermore, Peter said, "We have come to believe and know that You are the Christ, the Son of the Living God." What an amazing confession of faith! Peter affirmed that Jesus is "the Christ" — God's only Messiah. He also affirmed Jesus is the eternal Son of "the Living God" — Jehovah. That being the case, there is nowhere else we can possibly turn for salvation. Sadly, many people will continue to turn to drugs, alcohol, pornography, etc., but the only place to find true satisfaction is in Jesus.

## May 22 – Pot-Stirrer or Peacemaker?

*"An ungodly man digs up evil, and it is on his lips like a burning fire. A perverse man sows strife, and a whisperer separates the best of friends." (Proverbs 16:27-28)*

Some people like to stir the pot, while others prefer to keep the peace. Why would someone want to keep things stirred up? I'm sure there are a variety of reasons. Sometimes people want to give the impression they've got the inside scoop. Sometimes they want to intentionally inflict damage on someone they're at odds with. How do they do it? Solomon tells us "an ungodly man digs up evil." Some people take joy in trying to dig up and dish out the dirt on others.

The evil that a pot-stirrer digs up "is on his lips like a burning fire." In other words, the gossip is so hot, he can't keep it to himself. Contrast this with the fire shut up inside the bones of the prophet Jeremiah (Jeremiah 20:9). Jeremiah's words were hot because they came from God, and he could not keep from sharing them. In the case of a gossip, their words are motivated by the devil, and the fire they spread doesn't help anyone draw closer to Christ. Their gossip actually destroys lives.

Furthermore, a pot-stirrer "sows strife" — so much that he even "separates the best of friends." A gossip doesn't care about who he hurts or what he destroys. On the other hand, Jesus said, "Blessed are the peacemakers" (Matthew 5:9). A peacemaker is someone who attempts to put out the fires started by others. As you live your life, you have a choice — you can be like the perverse man who digs up evil and spreads strife, or you can be the person who speaks life and causes strife to cease. Be a peacemaker!

## May 23 – When Gray Hair is Glorious

*"The silver-haired head is a crown of glory, if it is found in the way of righteousness." (Proverbs 16:31)*

Gray hair gets a bad rap in our culture, doesn't it? Don't believe me? Just take a stroll down to your local store and look at the amount of hair-coloring products on the shelves. American consumers spend millions of dollars annually on hair care products, and there's no doubt a hefty percentage of that money is spent on hair dye. Men and women color their hair for a variety of reasons, but most would probably say they choose to do so because they don't want to look older than they really are.

Some people choose to embrace their gray hair, and today's verse provides us a good reason why — "The silver-haired head is a crown of glory." It's a wonderful thing for a person to live long enough to have gray hair. Even if a person begins to go gray early in life, they've still outlived many people who didn't make it to their 21st birthday. Rather than bemoaning the symptoms that come with advanced age, we should thank God that He has allowed us to experience another day.

This truth is conditional — "if it is found in the way of righteousness." Sometimes we tend to think that a person is wise just because they're old. That's like assuming someone is uninformed just because they're young. Being old and having gray hair is glorious only if we are dedicating our lives to God. A senior saint can look back on life and see where God used him/her for His glory. When your hair turns gray (or turns loose), will you be found in the way of righteousness or foolishness?

# May 24 — Go and Sin No More

*"When Jesus had raised Himself up and saw no one but the woman, He said to her, 'Woman, where are those accusers of yours? Has no one condemned you?' She said, 'No one, Lord.' And Jesus said to her, 'Neither do I condemn you; go and sin no more.'" (John 8:10-11)*

If you were to ask the American public what they believe about God, those who affirm His existence would probably tell you about His love and kindness. As evidence of His great love, I'm sure many would talk about the forgiveness He's provided for their sins. All of us have good reason to praise God for His love and mercy. It's a wonderful thing to know all your sins have been forgiven — past, present, and future. That assurance belongs to every person who has placed his/her faith in Jesus.

And yet, in all our discussion of God's love, mercy, and forgiveness, we often fail to emphasize His holiness and our need of repentance. Today's verses illustrate that very well — they are taken from the occasion when the Pharisees cast a woman at Jesus' feet whom they said was caught in the act of adultery. The Pharisees were ready to stone her to death, but in that heated moment Jesus stooped down to write on the ground. We don't know what Jesus wrote, but everyone got the message.

The Bible says each of the Pharisees — from the oldest to the youngest — dropped their stones and walked away. The woman realized no one was left to condemn her to death, and Jesus said, "Neither do I condemn you." We like to stop at that point when we tell the story, but we must not leave out the next words — "go and sin no more." When Jesus forgave your sins, it was with the expectation that you would turn from your sins and live for Him! So, are you daily repenting of your sins as you seek to live for Christ?

# May 25 – The Lord Knows Your Heart

*"The refining pot is for silver and the furnace for gold,
but the Lord tests the hearts." (Proverbs 17:3)*

Some people prefer the clean, simple look of silver, while others prefer the time-tested appearance of gold. Both are precious metals, and both are quite valuable. As of 2019, silver was valued at $17/ounce, while gold was valued at a staggering $1,500/ounce! If you ever want to test the integrity of your silver or gold, all you need to do is put it in the fire. By means of a "refining pot" or "the furnace," you can heat your precious metals, and if there are any impurities, they will rise to the top.

While a refining pot and furnace can tell you what lies at the core of your metals, they can't tell you what lies inside the human heart. There's no test we can run to tell us what really rests within the heart of man — no MRI, no X-ray, nothing. The only One who can really know what rests inside each person's heart is God. That's one of the reasons Jesus commanded us, "Judge not, that you be not judged" (Matthew 7:1). While we can examine someone's work, only God knows what's truly in a person's heart.

Today's verse helps us understand why the Apostle John wrote that the eyes of Jesus were "like a flame of fire" (Revelation 1:14). That means His eyes can see right through us as He distinguishes the good from the evil. You can hide your true emotions, thoughts, and intentions from everyone else, but you'll never hide them from God. That can be disconcerting and comforting all at once. The good news is that He knows your heart better than anyone, and yet He loves you anyway. What an amazing God!

## May 26 – The Urgency of Our Savior

*"I must work the works of Him who sent Me while it is day; the night is coming when no one can work." (John 9:4)*

These words of Jesus are so simple and yet very profound. The analogy is easy to understand — you don't see folks mowing their yards in the middle of the night. We don't want to wake our neighbors up, but more importantly we can't see what we're doing in the darkness of night. Can you imagine a farmer attempting to harvest his crops at midnight? We choose to work during the heat of the day — not because we enjoy sweating, but because the work we need to do can't be done in the darkness of night.

Throughout the Word of God, the second coming of Jesus is called "the Day of the Lord." Think of the present as being "the day before" the Day of the Lord. Right now we await the time when Jesus will rapture the church and usher in the end of time (1 Thessalonians 4:13-18). You could say we are in "the 11th hour" of human history. The signs of the times are all around us (Matthew 24:3-14, 2 Timothy 3:1-5). When Jesus comes back to establish His kingdom on earth, the time to work will be complete.

Jesus had an urgency to use every moment for the glory of His Heavenly Father, knowing His days on earth were numbered. As Christians, you and I should live with the constant realization that our days are also numbered, not to mention that Jesus could return at any moment! Knowing we have precious little time left, we need to use all the remaining days of our lives to bring glory to God — loving others, making disciples, etc. Live today and every day with Christ's sense of urgency!

# May 27 – 'Twas Blind, But Now I See

*"He answered and said, 'Whether He is a sinner or not I do not know. One thing I know: that though I was blind, now I see.'" (John 9:25)*

The Gospel of John includes seven miracles that point to the full deity of Christ, while demonstrating that He alone is God's Messiah. One of those miracles is found in John 9 where Jesus healed a young man born blind. In ancient Jewish culture, the prevailing wisdom said that if some horrible tragedy happened to you, it must've been a result of your sin or perhaps that of your parents. That thinking was wrong 2,000 years ago, and it's still wrong today.

The truth is that bad things happen to everyone simply because we live in a fallen world. Jesus helped His disciples understand that God permitted the young man to be born blind so the Lord could be glorified through His life (John 9:3). Jesus commanded the young man to wash in the pool of Siloam, and when he did his eyes were miraculously opened by God. Being the devout Jews they were, the bystanders brought the gentleman to the Pharisees who could declare him healed.

The Pharisees began to question the young man, and when he mentioned the miracle-working power of Jesus, they denied the miracle and said that Jesus was a sinner. The former blind beggar simply responded, "Whether He is a sinner or not I do not know. One thing I know: that though I was blind, now I see." That's all that needed to be said. Even today, people will doubt and mock the Christ who saved you. Just let them know He's opened your eyes and now you can see that He's the Light of the world (John 8:12).

## May 28 – If You Had One Wish

*" 'Therefore give to Your servant an understanding heart to judge Your people, that I may discern between good and evil. For who is able to judge this great people of Yours?' The speech pleased the Lord, that Solomon had asked this thing." (1 Kings 3:9-10)*

From our childhood we remember stories about those who found magic lamps. When they rubbed the lamp, a genie popped out and granted them three wishes. In the world of make-believe, let's imagine you were the one who found the lamp, and when the genie popped out he was prepared to give you only one wish. What would you wish for? A bigger house? A nicer car? More money in the bank? Better health for family and friends? There's a lot of things you could wish for!

Of course, God is no genie, but there was an occasion in the Word of God when He granted the desire of young King Solomon. Having just been coronated as king, Solomon wanted to kick his kingdom off on the right foot. For that reason, he went to Gibeon to sacrifice to the Lord. When his worship was all said and done, Solomon offered one thousand burnt offerings on the altar (1 Kings 3:4). God chose to bless Solomon for his sacrificial worship. He said, "Ask! What shall I give you?" (1 Kings 3:5).

Solomon could've asked for wealth, land, prestige, or any number of things. Yet, instead of asking for something that would've been for his own welfare, he asked for something to bring glory to God — "an understanding heart to judge Your people." Not only did God make Solomon the wisest man on earth, but He also blessed Him with riches and honor. We need to be reminded that if each of us will seek first the kingdom of God and His righteousness, He'll take care of everything else we need (Matthew 6:33).

## May 29 — Nip It in the Bud

*"The beginning of strife is like releasing water; therefore stop contention before a quarrel starts." (Proverbs 17:14)*

Some things were a constant in the house I grew up in. For instance, we went to church every Lord's Day. When Sunday morning rolled around, we didn't even have to ask, "Are we going to church today?" The answer was always YES. In the Stinnett household, we also ate our fair share of beans and cornbread. When it came to television, the Andy Griffith Show was on just about every day. Who could help but fall in love with the loveable cast of characters from Mayberry, North Carolina?

Deputy Barney Fife is one of the most memorable characters in American television history. Barney is remembered as a know-it-all with a knack for getting himself and others in a jam. He was also high-strung — it didn't take much to get him going. And there was one phrase he often used when attempting to advise Andy — "nip it in the bud." In other words, you need to get something stopped before it ever gets started. "Nip it in the bud" is a very accurate summary of today's verse.

"The beginning of strife is like releasing water" — it starts with a drip, then a steady pour, and before you know it the floodgates have opened! For that reason, it's much better for us to "stop contention before a quarrel starts." When we're in a disagreement with someone, we should work diligently to resolve our differences before the disagreement leads to something much worse. Are you currently at odds with someone? If so, what are you going to do about it? Don't wait too late — ask the Lord to help you nip it in the bud today!

## May 30 – The Resurrection and the Life

*"Jesus said to her, 'I am the resurrection and the life. He who believes in Me, though he may die, he shall live. And whoever lives and believes in Me shall never die. Do you believe this?'" (John 11:25-26)*

The Gospel of John is like none other, and it contains seven "I AM" statements from the lips of Jesus. For instance, Jesus said, "I am the Bread of life ... the Light of the world ... the Door of the sheep ... the Good Shepherd," etc. John 11 takes us to the occasion when Jesus' dear friend, Lazarus, was on death's doorstep. When Jesus learned Lazarus was near death, He decided to stay where He was another two days. That sounds very callous, but Jesus knew what was about to occur.

After two days, Jesus and the disciples returned to Bethany. When they arrived, Martha (Lazarus' sister) ran out to meet Him. She said, "If You had been here, my brother would not have died" (John 11:21). She thought it was too late — Lazarus was dead and there was nothing that could be done about it. Jesus comforted Martha — "Your brother will rise again" (John 11:23). Martha thought Jesus was talking about "the resurrection at the last day" (John 11:24).

Jesus made another I AM statement — "I am the resurrection and the life." Those words tell us that eternal hope can only be found in Jesus. Furthermore, "He who believes in Me, though he may die, he shall live." Every person that has ever died in Christ will be resurrected at the end of time (1 Thessalonians 4:13-18). Not only that, but "whoever lives and believes in Me shall never die." Upon his/her last breath, every Christ-follower is ushered into the presence of Jesus in paradise. Why? To be absent from the body is to be present with the Lord (2 Corinthians 5:8).

## May 31 — When Jesus Wept

*"Jesus wept." (John 11:35)*

Have you ever made a commitment to memorize more of God's Word? If so, how are things going? If your answer is, "Not so good," then I suggest you start with today's verse. As you may know, this is the shortest verse in the Word of God. Though it is very brief, entire sermons and volumes have been written about its meaning. This verse is inserted by John just prior to Lazarus' resurrection from the dead. When Jesus saw the family and the crowds weeping, the Bible says He joined them.

That begs the question — why was Jesus crying? The obvious answer is that Jesus was crying because Lazarus was dead. Yet, that answer doesn't make much sense. Because Jesus was completely and fully God, He knew everything — including the fact that He was about to resurrect His friend from the dead. To suggest Jesus was mourning the death of His soon-to-be-raised friend doesn't make much sense. So, if Jesus wasn't crying for His friend, who was He crying for?

While John doesn't answer that question, I think Jesus wept because of the horrific effects of sin on the human race. Prior to sin, there was no such thing as sickness or suffering. Only after Adam and Eve's fall in the Garden of Eden did men begin to suffer and die. And sin didn't just affect us — it touched the whole of creation (Romans 8:19-21)! It's good to know our Savior Jesus, while He is fully God, is also fully man. Being our compassionate High Priest, Jesus can "sympathize with our weaknesses" (Hebrews 4:15). He knows how to dry our tears because He's shed tears Himself.

## June 1 — When Intermarriage Is Wrong

*"'You shall not intermarry with them, nor they with you. Surely they will turn away your hearts after their gods.' Solomon clung to these in love." (1 Kings 11:2)*

When you read the term "intermarriage," what comes to mind? In our culture, most people would probably think about a person of one race marrying a person of a different race. You might be surprised to know that interracial marriage was not legalized throughout the entire United States until 1967. At that time, only 3 percent of Americans were involved in an interracial marriage. As of 2015, that percentage had risen to 17 percent — nearly a 500 percent increase in just fifty years.

Since the civil rights movement of the '60s, some people — especially Southerners — have had a difficult time accepting mixed-race marriages. Perhaps you've never heard that Miriam had the same problem when her brother (Moses) married an Ethiopian woman (Numbers 12). God judged Miriam for her opposition by striking her with leprosy. Moses interceded on her behalf, and God mercifully removed her leprosy after only seven days. That said, there is no biblical reason that two people of different races can't have a relationship with one another.

And yet, there is a time when intermarriage — or "inter-relationships" — are wrong. Not when they involve two people of different races, but when they involve two people who serve a different God/gods. God strictly commanded His people not to intermarry the natives of the Promised Land — not because they were a different color, but because they served different gods. That said, the person you marry/date doesn't have to be the same race, but they must serve the same God (2 Corinthians 6:14). Anything else is sin, and sadly Solomon found out the hard way.

## June 2 — Man-Pleasers and God-Pleasers

*"Nevertheless even among the rulers many believed in Him, but because of the Pharisees they did not confess Him, lest they should be put out of the synagogue; for they loved the praise of men more than the praise of God." (John 12:42-43)*

When you get right down to it, there are two kinds of people in the world — man-pleasers and God-pleasers. Let's start with man-pleasers — they're the people who are primarily interested in pleasing themselves and others. Sadly, politicians get thrown into this category, but some of them have earned the reputation. Think about it — when do we hear from most of our elected representatives? Usually when it's time for re-election. At that time, they work hard to please their constituents.

Politicians are not the only ones who live for the approval of others. If we'll be honest, we'd have to admit we're all tempted to live for the affirmation of others, and sadly we often succumb to the temptation. For example, we know we shouldn't participate in the office gossip, but we run our mouths anyway because we want to be accepted by the group. Or, we know we shouldn't lie, but we think of how happy others will be if we tell them what they want to hear.

In Christ's day, there were some local rulers who believed Jesus was the Christ, but they were not willing to confess Him as Lord because "they loved the praise of men more than the praise of God." They yearned for the approval of the Pharisees more than the approval of God. My friend, ask yourself — "Who am I living for?" If the answer is anyone other than "God Almighty," you're living for the wrong person. Today and every day, yearn for God's approval rather than that of men.

## June 3 – Washing One Another's Feet

*"Jesus, knowing that the Father had given all things into His hands, and that He had come from God and was going to God, rose from supper and laid aside His garments, took a towel and girded Himself. After that, He poured water into a basin and began to wash the disciples' feet, and to wipe them with the towel with which He was girded." (John 13:3-5)*

We live in a day filled with many modern conveniences. Among them are paved roads and nice shoes. If we want to take a stroll, there's a good chance we can walk down a smooth road in our favorite pair of tennis shoes. The ancients were not so lucky — if they wanted to take a trip, they were often forced to walk down roads and trails that were dusty or muddy. And while most probably owned a good pair of sandals, it was not uncommon for a person's feet to get quite dirty.

That's why washing the feet of house guests was a job reserved for servants. After all, who wants to touch someone else's nasty, smelly feet? Yet, when Christ came to His last night with the disciples, He did something they never would've expected. Leaving the Passover table, He girded Himself with a towel, filled a basin with water, and began to wash the disciples' feet. Why would the King of glory do such a thing? He was setting an example for the disciples and for us.

Jesus said, "You also ought to wash one another's feet. For I have given you an example, that you should do as I have done to you" (John 3:14-15). I've participated in "foot-washing services," and those have been some powerful times. But I don't think we actually have to wash someone else's feet to fulfill the spirit of Christ's command. All we need to do is serve one another. Rather than looking for ways to be first, let's place others before ourselves and look for ways to serve them in Jesus' name.

## June 4 — The One True God

*"'Then you call on the name of your gods, and I will call on the name of the LORD; and the God who answers by fire, He is God.' ... Then the fire of the LORD fell and consumed the burnt sacrifice, and the wood and the stones and the dust, and it licked up the water that was in the trench." (1 Kings 18:24, 38)*

Since the beginning of time, men have been fashioning other gods in their quest for the divine. Today's verses come from an occasion when the prophet Elijah was surrounded by hundreds of people who served other gods. We need to be clear — the other "gods" they were serving were not really gods at all. Their names were Baal and Asherah, and they were simply figments of the pagan imagination. And yet, that didn't keep them from believing their gods were real.

At the height of Israel's ungodliness, Elijah offered wicked King Ahab a proposition — "you call on the name of your gods, and I will call on the name of the LORD; and the God who answers by fire, He is God." Ahab and his wicked prophets consented. Keep in mind, there were 450 prophets of Baal in Israel along with 400 prophets of Asherah. If my math is correct, Elijah was outnumbered by a margin of 850-1. And yet, Elijah proved that a man is always in the majority when he stands with God.

You know the rest of the story — the wicked prophets of Baal and Asherah cried out and cut themselves from dawn till dusk, but their gods never answered. Then Elijah stepped up and told those standing by to pour a massive amount of water over the sacrifice and the altar — so much that it filled a trench dug around the altar. Elijah called on the Lord and the Lord answered by fire, proving once and for all that the God of Abraham, Isaac, and Jacob is the one and only true God. Is He the Lord of your life?

## June 5 — The Way, the Truth, and the Life

*"Jesus said to him, 'I am the way, the truth, and the life.
No one comes to the Father except through Me.'" (John 14:6)*

The Gospel of John gives us a very special glimpse into the final hours of Jesus on this earth. John Chapters 13-21 focus on the final twenty-four hours of Christ's life. Jesus celebrated the Passover with His disciples, washed their feet, then proceeded to give them some final instructions that would carry them well beyond His resurrection from the dead. At the end of Chapter 13, Jesus let His disciples know He was about to be taken from them — even predicting Peter's denial following His arrest.

Those words must've been devastating to Peter. I'm sure he couldn't imagine denying the Lord three times prior to sunrise, but that's just what happened. And yet in the midst of that devastating news, Jesus gave Peter and the rest of the disciples the best news of all — "I go to prepare a place for you" (John 14:2). Better still, Jesus said His disciples knew the way to that special place (John 14:4). Thomas responded with doubt — "Lord, we do not know where You are going, and how can we know the way?" (John 14:5).

Jesus responded with some of the most familiar words in the Christian faith. First, He said, "I am the way" — the only way of salvation for lost and sinful men. He also declared, "I am the truth" — the One from whom all truth proceeds. Finally, He said, "I am the life" — because abundant life and eternal life are found only in Christ. And just so no one could confuse His statements, Jesus added, "No one comes to the Father except through Me." All those who come to God must come through Jesus Christ.

## June 6 — The Greatest Love of All

*"Greater love has no one than this, than to lay down one's life for his friends." (John 15:13)*

The use of the word "love" has become pretty trivial in our English language. Don't get me wrong — sometimes it is used to express deep-seated emotion that can't be adequately expressed with words. At other times, it is used in reference to trivial things. We say, "I love pizza," "I love seashells," or "I love my new notebook." If someone is truly in love with pizza, shells, or office supplies, they probably need to talk to a counselor. We use the word "love" where it would be better to say "like."

Throughout the Gospels, Jesus never misused the word "love." When we come to John 15, He told us what love is really all about — "Greater love has no one that this, than to lay down one's life for his friends." We have many modern examples of this highest and greatest form of love. For instance, between 2006 and 2018, nearly 17,000 active military personnel lost their lives while defending our freedom — a good number of them in active combat. They willingly laid down their lives for us and others!

We learn a lesson on love by looking at our soldiers, but we can learn the greatest example of love by looking at Jesus. When Jesus spoke of one willing to lay down his life for his friends, clearly He was speaking of Himself. There really is no greater love — the One who was totally God took on our corruptible human flesh and walked this earth with sinners and finally died on an old rugged cross for our sins. If that isn't love, I don't know what is! It's not just any love — it's the greatest love of all!

# June 7 — Cheer Up!

*"These things I have spoken to you, that in Me you may have peace. In the world you will have tribulation; but be of good cheer, I have overcome the world."* (John 16:33)

The World Health Organization (WHO) estimates that more than 300 million people worldwide suffer from depression. It's also the world's leading cause of disability. That said, there are many forms of depression — ranging from mild forms (seasonal depression) to more severe types (psychotic depression). Some people have clinical depression due to physiological reasons that require the care of a physician. Many others are just "down in the dumps" because life has not unfolded as planned.

In some of His final words to the disciples, Jesus let them know He had spent His time teaching them so they might "have peace." And yet, He didn't sugarcoat the truth about their future — "In the world you will have tribulation." You can mark it down — if you are a follower of Jesus Christ, you are not going to walk through this world unscathed. The disciples proved the words of Jesus — each of them was harassed throughout the rest of their lives, and all died a martyr's death.

And yet there was good news — "Be of good cheer, I have overcome the world." The disciples could rejoice in knowing that even death could not separate them from the love of God (Romans 8:38-39). Likewise, when we're going through the trials and adversities of life, we need to pause and remember that our trials are only temporary because Jesus has overcome the world. As Paul said, "I consider that the sufferings of this present time are not worthy to be compared with the glory which shall be revealed in us" (Romans 8:18). Cheer up — God is in control!

## June 8 – The Heart of a Senior Saint

*"Now also when I am old and grayheaded, O God, do not forsake me, until I declare Your strength to this generation, Your power to everyone who is to come."* (Psalm 71:18)

We go through many stages in life — infant, toddler, child, youth, adult, and finally senior adult. Maybe you're already a senior citizen, or perhaps you're making plans for the time when you'll reach advanced age and retire. Either way, the goal for our "golden years" should be the same — to declare God's power to coming generations. Why would senior saints be well-suited for such a task? Because they've lived a good number of years and seen God do a great many things.

For starters, senior adults have lots of life experiences. They can talk about all the ways God "showed up and showed out" in their lives. In addition, seniors should have a better knowledge of the Word because they've been studying it for so long. When a senior's children or grandchildren come seeking counsel, they should be able to provide a voice of wisdom from the Word of God. Seniors can point to passages such as Psalm 136 that highlight the power of God.

Why is it so important that all of us take this seriously? Because there is a generation coming up that has not experienced the power of God. Why? Because many of those in Generation Z have never darkened the door of a church. If current trends remain unchanged, nine of every ten youngsters in Generation Z will grow up and die lost apart from Jesus. As a seasoned child of God, you are well-positioned to share the power of the Gospel with a generation that hasn't heard. Will you do it?

## June 9 — A Place of Protection

*"The name of the* LORD *is a strong tower; the righteous run to it and are safe." (Proverbs 18:10)*

In the city I live in, there is an old fort called James White's Fort. I can remember taking field trips there as a child. From our studies in school, we learned that a fort is a place of protection. As a youngster, I can remember standing outside the walls of the fort and thinking of how hard it would be for an invader to get inside. That's because the walls of the fort are made of long, individual posts that have been cut down to a sharp point at the end. No one would attempt to cross the wall.

Today's verse tells us that God is like that old fort — only much better. "The name of the LORD is a strong tower." The very name of God itself is a refuge for the children of God. When we're in the midst of despair and tempted to be afraid, we can call on the name of Jesus and find the help we need. This verse reminds us that God is our protection. He is forever a strong tower we can run to when we need to seek refuge from our enemies and from our main adversary the devil.

When others are spreading rumors and lying about your integrity, run to God and He will protect you from the verbal assaults. When sickness and disease ravage your body, run to God and you'll find He is the Great Physician. When family or friends betray your confidence, run to God and discover He's a friend that sticks closer than a brother (Proverbs 18:24). This life is spiritual warfare. Don't fight by yourself — find refuge in the very name and presence of your Protector.

## June 10 — Listen Before You Speak

*"He who answers a matter before he hears it,*
*it is folly and shame to him." (Proverbs 18:13)*

Have you ever noticed how we don't like to be interrupted, but we don't seem to mind interrupting others? Why is that? We all think that what we've got to say is of great value and deserves a hearing. For some reason, we don't place as much value on what others have to say. That being the case, we're tempted to answer a matter before we've given it a full hearing. Having only a fraction of the story, we think we've got more than enough information to make a statement.

How many times have you put your foot in your mouth by doing this? When I was in 8th grade, I remember my teacher showing me a picture of her children. I'm sure she was about to tell me they were her children, their names, their interests, etc. Before she had a chance to explain those things, I interrupted, "Are those your grandchildren?" She said, "No — they're my children." Her late '80s frosted hair threw me off, and I embarrassed myself because I spoke when I should've been listening.

How many times have you pre-judged someone when you only heard half the story? I'm ashamed to admit that I've not only misjudged innocent people, I've even perpetuated the half-story I was told. In doing so, I brought shame to myself and others. We need to remember God gave us two ears to hear and one mouth to speak. When we hear something, we need to make sure we have all the details before we respond. If not, it's only a matter of time before we wind up looking foolish.

# June 11 — Behold the Man

*"Then Jesus came out, wearing the crown of thorns and the purple robe. And Pilate said to them, 'Behold the Man!'" (John 19:5)*

The word "behold" is a transliteration of an old English word *bihaldan* — "bi" means "thoroughly," and "haldan" means "to hold." In other words, to behold something is to fix your attention on it for the purpose of thorough examination. In his attempts to appease the Jewish leaders, Pilate commanded that Jesus be scourged. Following the severe beating, Pilate instructed the crowds to behold Jesus — not so they could worship Him but so they could see how thoroughly He was beaten.

It would do you and I some good to behold Jesus right now. Look at the crown of thorns thrust down onto His head. The thorns are about one to two inches long, and as they dig down into His scalp and forehead, the blood flows into His eyes. Look at the bare spots in His beard where the hair was plucked from His face. See the bruises on His cheeks where He was beaten with a rod and with soldiers' fists. Look at the purple robe they placed on Jesus in an attempt to mock Him as a fallen king.

Look a little closer and see deep lacerations all over His body — the result of the chords of a whip driving into His skin time and again, then ripping away the flesh as they were pulled out. Behold the man Jesus! Stop and fix your gaze on Christ! This is what Jesus was willing to go through to secure your pardon and mine. Let's make a commitment to behold Jesus like this much more often. In beholding the broken and battered Jesus, we will never forget all He endured to secure our salvation.

## June 12 – Faith Will Change Your Life

*"And Nicodemus, who at first came to Jesus by night, also came, bringing a mixture of myrrh and aloes, about a hundred pounds.'"* (John 19:39)

Nothing has the power to take a person from cowardice to courage better than faith. Just consider the example of Nicodemus. We're introduced to Nicodemus in John 3. There we're told that he was "a man of the Pharisees" and "a ruler of the Jews." That means he was wealthy, educated, and powerful. Nicodemus is not the sort of man that would've shown any interest in a messiah-type figure, but when Jesus began His ministry, something inside of Nicodemus was intrigued to find out more.

For that reason, the Bible says "this man came to Jesus by night" to ask him some questions that were on his heart. If you wonder why Nicodemus chose to approach Jesus at night rather than during the day, it's because he couldn't afford to be publicly associated with a "rabble-rouser" like Jesus. Christ proceeded to tell him that a person must be born again to enter the kingdom of heaven. When Nicodemus left the encounter with Jesus, he still had questions but he was intrigued to learn more.

Fast forward to Nicodemus' second appearance in John 7. There he was willing to defend Jesus to his fellow Pharisees, saying that no man should be condemned before he's had a full hearing. That took boldness, but it took even more courage for him to do what he did in John 19. There, he came to bury Jesus in the heat of the day (instead of night), bringing with him very expensive supplies for burial. What made the difference for Nicodemus? Only one thing — faith that Jesus Christ is Lord! God will change your life if you're willing to believe He's everything He said He is.

# June 13 – The Purpose of the Gospels

*"And truly Jesus did many other signs in the presence of His disciples, which are not written in this book; but these are written that you may believe that Jesus is the Christ, the Son of God, and that believing you may have life in His name." (John 20:30-31)*

From an early age, you probably learned that the four Gospels are Matthew, Mark, Luke, and John — the first four books of the New Testament. Each one of them has their own uniqueness. Matthew's Gospel was written to a primarily Jewish audience, Mark is a condensed version covering Peter's testimony, and Luke was written to a Gentile audience — these three are the Synoptic Gospels. John's Gospel is in a category all by itself, as it was the last one written and very theological.

At the end of his book, John placed a good summary on the purpose of all the Gospels. While there are many more things the Gospel writers could've shared, the things that were included "are written that you may believe." Believe what? "That Jesus is the Christ." The Gospels were written to show us that Jesus is God's only Messiah — the Anointed One of God. Also, they tell us that Jesus is "the Son of God" — conceived of the Holy Spirit and born to the virgin Mary. He is the Son of God and the Son of Man.

Not only did John write so that others might believe, but "that believing you may have life in His name." John didn't just write for the sake of information — he wrote for transformation. It was his desire that every person who read his Gospel would have their life transformed through faith in Jesus. All those who trust in Christ "have life in His name." That means abundant life on this earth (John 10:10), and eternal life in heaven (John 3:16). Thankfully, the purpose of the Gospels is salvation.

## June 14 – The Power of the Tongue

*"Death and life are in the power of the tongue,
and those who love it will eat its fruit." (Proverbs 18:21)*

It's amazing how something can be used to do so much good, and yet the very same thing can be used to do so much evil. For instance, money can be used to feed the hungry or to purchase drugs and alcohol. The internet can be used to do research on a school project, or it can be used to solicit sex acts from a child. In both cases, the user is the one who determines if his resources will be used for good or evil. We all need to understand that the tongue falls into this category.

Solomon tells us that "death and life are in the power of the tongue." Does he mean we have the power to give birth to someone or kill someone just by saying a few words? No — what he means is that our words will either bring life to ourselves and others, or they can be used as instruments of destruction and death. For instance, if you know someone struggling with sin, you can talk behind their back (death), or you can lovingly confront them and encourage them to change (life).

Think about the ramifications of this verse — with every word you say, you are either giving life or taking life from someone else. I don't know about you, but I want to be counted among those breathing life into people — the kind of person that someone doesn't want to avoid when they see me coming. And be warned — "those who love it will eat its fruit." In other words, if you love to talk, you need to be prepared to live with the consequences of your words. Let's all choose to speak life!

## June 15 – A Friend Closer Than a Brother

*"A man who has friends must himself be friendly, but there is a friend who sticks closer than a brother." (Proverbs 18:24)*

The Proverbs are wisdom literature that provide us general guidelines for living. In this case, Solomon wants us to understand that a man with many friends may have lots of companions, but he may not have many true friends. The NIV translates this verse, "A man of many companions may come to ruin." Just because a person has a lot of friends doesn't mean he is destined for success. Have you ever known someone with tons of friends? It can be like a full-time job keeping them all satisfied.

Solomon wants us to understand it would probably be better for us to have fewer, truer friends than to have a bunch of half-hearted acquaintances who won't be there to stand with us when the going gets tough. "There is a friend who sticks closer than a brother." That said, we shouldn't be using our time trying to "win friends and influence people." While it's perfectly fine to be winsome and personable, we should focus on trying to find friends that truly love the Lord and truly love us.

There is an application of this verse that goes well beyond any human friend you can find. Even the best and most loyal of friends you have is a fallen sinner. He/she could betray you at any moment, but there is a Friend who will never betray us. Jesus said, "I will never leave you nor forsake you" (Hebrews 13:5). If you are a Christ-follower, the Friend who sticks closer than any brother is Jesus. Though every other person in the world may turn their back on you, Jesus will remain faithful and true. You can always trust in Him!

## June 16 – When Poverty Is Better

*"Better is the poor who walks in his integrity than one who is perverse in his lips, and is a fool." (Proverbs 19:1)*

I think everyone yearns for what we call "a better life." What does a better life look like? It depends on who you ask. If you ask magazines, TV commercials, and social media ads, they'll tell you that a better life is a bigger home, a nicer car, and designer clothes. They say it includes physical fitness, a large bank account, and the acclamation of others. Yet, it's entirely possible for a person to have all these things and still be "perverse in his lips" and foolish. It takes more than money to fix a fool.

If you look to the Bible for a definition of "better life," you might be surprised to know it has very little to do with cash, cars, and clothes. Instead, it has much more to do with holiness and love. A better life is probably best defined in Galatians 5:22-23 in what we call the fruit of the Spirit — "love, joy, peace, etc." In other words, the Bible's definition of better living is a life of integrity. You may not have much money in the bank, but if you live with integrity before God, you are very rich indeed.

Understand this — it's better for you to be poor and holy than rich and wicked. A person's riches bring them great pleasure in this life, but what happens when this life ends? Those material things that brought us so much joy on earth won't do one thing for us in the hereafter. Take comfort in this — you may not have everything you want, but if you have Jesus, you've got everything you need. Don't worry about someone else's possessions — concern yourself with your own integrity and pursuit of the Lord.

## June 17 – Marks of a True Church

*"So continuing daily with one accord in the temple, and breaking bread from house to house, they ate their food with gladness and simplicity of heart, praising God and having favor with all the people. And the Lord added to the church daily those who were being saved. (Acts 2:46-47)*

It's very sad that the church of the 21st century does not more closely resemble the early church of the 1st century. If it did, we would see many more people transformed for the glory of God. Let's look at just a few of the things that made the early church so special. First, the Scripture says they were unified — "continuing daily with one accord." If a church has no unity, it will not accomplish great things for God. Also, they maintained consistent fellowship with one another — "from house to house."

Further, these verses tell us they "ate their food with gladness." The joy of the Lord was evident in their midst and noticeable by others. They were also a simple people, living with "simplicity of heart." They were not overwhelmed with many of the modern distractions that have hampered the church today. Furthermore, they spent their time "praising God." When a group of believers fails to worship, they have ceased to be the church. Glorifying God is our highest goal!

Finally, Scripture tells us the Lord caused the church to have favor with all people. In other words, the Lord blessed them to find good graces even with those outside the church — true evidence of revival and awakening! And what was the result of a church on fire for Christ? "The Lord added to the church daily those who were being saved." Contrast that with churches across our country who may not baptize one person all year long. May God help us not to simply "come to church," but to be the church!

# June 18 – The Lord Is Near

*"We give thanks to You, O God, we give thanks! For Your wondrous works declare that Your name is near." (Psalm 75:1)*

We have so many reasons to give thanks to God. Just a quick consideration of His attributes should cause us to rejoice forever. A theologian once explained to me that all the attributes of God flow out of His two main attributes — holiness and love. Holy means "set apart," so we give thanks to God because He is exalted high above our wickedness. Theologically, this is called the transcendence of God. When Isaiah got his own glimpse of the Lord, he witnessed God's holiness firsthand (Isaiah 6:3).

And yet, today's verse emphasizes the love of God in that He is near to all of us. The "nearness" of the Lord is what theologians call the imminence of God. The psalmist said, "Your wondrous works declare that Your name is near." What works of God is Asaph talking about? Creation proves we serve a God who is near. The fact that there is intricate design in creation and that it is all held together by a higher power proves God is near. The fact that you are breathing proves God is near!

Think of the wonderful comfort this verse provides! We don't serve an ivory tower god that refuses to look on the affairs of man. We don't serve a god that wound up the world and is now allowing it to spin out of control. We serve a God who is intimately involved in every detail of His creation. He even allows blessings to come to the holy and the unholy (Matthew 5:45). And never forget that God is only a prayer away if you've placed your faith in Jesus. You and I should draw nearer to Him because He's promised to draw near to us (James 4:8).

## June 19 – Have You Been With Jesus?

*"Now when they saw the boldness of Peter and John, and perceived that they were uneducated and untrained men, they marveled. And they realized that they had been with Jesus." (Acts 4:13)*

Sometimes the evidence of our activity is simply too hard to deny. If your clothes smell sugary-sweet, then you've been around the donuts at Krispy Kreme. A temporary inability to talk properly might indicate your mouth has not recovered from the numbing medication at the dentist. At times, we're tempted to be less than forthcoming about our recent activity, but other times we're proud of it. Such was the case for Peter and John — they had been with someone they could not deny.

Let's consider the context of today's verse. In Acts 3, the disciples were making their way to the temple when they came to the Beautiful Gate. There they found a man who had sat there many times before, begging alms from those who came to worship. Peter and John didn't have any "silver or gold" to give the man, but they gave him what they had — the miracle-working power of Jesus. The lame man jumped up immediately — walking and leaping and praising God! He let everyone know he was healed!

Not everyone was happy about the miracle. The religious leaders questioned Peter and John about the power that provided the miracle, and of course they said it was Jesus. When the religious leaders saw their boldness, even though Peter and John were uneducated fishermen, they "realized that they had been with Jesus." What a testimony! I wonder if others can tell that we've been Jesus when they encounter us? Don't let the busyness of life keep you from spending precious time with Christ!

## June 20 — The Power of Prayer

*"And when they had prayed, the place where they were assembled together was shaken; and they were all filled with the Holy Spirit, and they spoke the word of God with boldness." (Acts 4:31)*

After the religious leaders released Peter and John from their temporary incarceration, they went right back to the church and reported the things they had experienced. When the church heard their report, they gave praise to God and lifted their voices in prayer. With their prayer, they praised God as the Creator, reflected on the Word of God, lifted up the name of Jesus, and even asked that God would give them more boldness by performing more signs and wonders.

Verse 31 is the result of their prayers. First, "the place where they were assembled together was shaken." God answered their prayers for more miracles immediately by superseding the laws of nature and shaking the room they were gathered in. In addition, "they were all filled with the Holy Spirit." That should be a challenge to every one of us. If we've placed our faith in Jesus, we are inhabited by the Holy Spirit, but it should be our goal daily to be filled with His power (Ephesians 5:18).

Furthermore, "they spoke the word of God." The same Holy Spirit who authored Scripture filled their mouths with His own words. Being Spirit-filled and Word-focused, the church was blessed "with boldness." Notice the progression — prayer led to a miracle, then the Holy Spirit's presence, then sharing the Word with boldness. If God was able to accomplish those mighty things when His church prayed, He's able to do the same today. Let's spend much more time on our knees seeking the power of heaven in prayer!

# June 21 — Slow to Anger

*"The discretion of a man makes him slow to anger, and his glory is to overlook a transgression." (Proverbs 19:11)*

One of the many amazing things about God is that He is "slow to anger and abounding in mercy" (Psalm 103:8). Though He certainly deserves to be enraged with us over our sin, He mercifully sets aside His anger as He awaits our confession and repentance. Though God is slow to anger, unfortunately, the same often can't be said of us. When someone offends us, or gossips about us, or simply beats us to the punch on something, we allow our emotions to get the best of us by lashing out in anger.

Solomon has a lesson for us today — "the discretion of a man makes him slow to anger." One man defined discretion as "the quality of behaving or speaking in such a way as to avoid causing offense." The word is often interchangeable with "wisdom." In this case, wisdom says it's much better to avoid anger than be overcome with rage. Why? Because we can say things and do things that can never be taken back. No amount of apologies can take back many things we later regret.

We need to understand that "his glory is to overlook a transgression." Let's be honest — this is something we ALL struggle with. When someone mistreats us, our natural inclination is to retaliate with something similar or worse than what they did to us. Even though we don't want to, we need to suppress the desire for revenge and learn to overlook things that have no eternal significance. Is there someone you're currently at odds with? Perhaps it's time for you to forgive and put away the anger.

# June 22 – Rejoicing Over Suffering

*"So they departed from the presence of the council, rejoicing that they were counted worthy to suffer shame for His name." (Acts 5:41)*

There are many things in life that cause us to rejoice and celebrate. We rejoice when two people marry. We rejoice when a sweet little baby is born. We rejoice when a child graduates from school. We even celebrate trivial matters — when our team wins the game, when our favorite pizza is on sale, etc. Of all the things you could celebrate, there's probably one that's not on your list — suffering. No one wants to suffer for any reason, and we certainly don't see it as a reason to rejoice.

And yet, today's passage reminds us of an occasion when the apostles actually celebrated over their suffering. Acts 5 tells us the apostles were arrested because they continued to preach the Gospel of Christ, even after they had been warned by Jewish leaders not to do so. After they were incarcerated, a miracle occurred — "an angel of the Lord opened the prison doors and brought them out" (Acts 5:19). They were instructed to go back and start preaching again, and that's just what they did.

The religious leaders apprehended them once more, and after they questioned them, they released them. But the apostles were not released until they had been thoroughly beaten. How did the apostles respond to their suffering? "Rejoicing that they were counted worthy to suffer shame for His name." If you are suffering for the cause of Christ, you shouldn't let it discourage you. Instead, you should wear it as a badge of honor and thank the Lord that He's using you for His glory!

## June 23 – What Is a Deacon?

*"Then the twelve summoned the multitude of the disciples and said, 'It is not desirable that we should leave the word of God and serve tables.'" (Acts 6:2)*

The early church did a great job of sharing the Gospel and reaching many people for Christ, both Jews and Greeks. All those new converts presented a challenge to the church — how are we going to effectively minister to all those that God has entrusted to our care? Initially, the church didn't do such a great job because the Greek widows were being overlooked in the daily distribution of resources. I'm sure the leaders of the church must've felt like something needed to be done quickly to avoid a conflict.

For that reason, they said, "It is not desirable that we should leave the Word of God and serve tables." The apostles sympathized with the Greek-speaking widows, but God did not call them to serve tables — He called them to preach the Gospel. So God granted them a wonderful idea — select able-bodied men out of the church who can serve the material needs of the congregation. That way, the apostles would be able to dedicate themselves to "prayer and to the ministry of the Word" (Acts 6:4).

The church set aside seven men to meet the needs. The seven men (Acts 6:5) are called *deacons*. The word "deacon" comes from the Greek *diakonos*, which literally means "through the dust." Just picture a person kicking up the dust by rushing around from person to person. God has blessed the church with deacons who are supposed to minister to the needs of the congregation so that pastors and ministers can fulfill the calling God has placed on their lives. When deacons serve the church faithfully, they are a tremendous blessing to the Body of Christ! Please pray for the deacons in your local church.

# June 24 — Lending to the Lord

*"He who has pity on the poor lends to the LORD,
and He will pay back what he has given." (Proverbs 19:17)*

In a house of eight people, we borrow things from one another all the time. If my son can't find his jacket, his brother lends him his. If my girls can't find their hairdryer, my wife lends them hers. Like all parents, we teach our children to share. When we think about the Lord, we "borrow" things from Him all the time, except they're really gifts because we have no way of returning them. I'm talking about things like the air we breathe, the blood that runs through our veins, etc. God is generous to us!

You might be surprised to know that there's actually a way you can lend something to God. Solomon said, "He who has pity on the poor lends to the LORD." That's an amazing statement. Of course, we know God doesn't need anything we have. Here, Solomon uses a human concept to help us understand the way God repays generosity to those in need. When we give to the poor, we're not just doing it for their sake. Ultimately, we're doing it for the glory of God.

Solomon said, "He (the Lord) will pay back what he has given." The old saying is that "you can't out-give God." In my own experience, I've found that to be very true. There have been times when God has prompted me to give away resources I needed for myself. In those times that I was willing to give toward others in faith, I can say that God repaid me many times over. Getting should never be our motivation for giving, but when we lend to the Lord we should always expect a return.

# June 25 – The Only Plan That Matters

*"There are many plans in a man's heart, nevertheless the Lord's counsel — that will stand." (Proverbs 19:21)*

We make all sorts of plans for all sorts of reasons. If we want to go on a vacation, we plan where we will go, stay, eat, visit, etc. If we want to get an education, we plan what school to attend and what program of study to pursue. Sometimes our plans go incredibly well, and other times they fail miserably. Sometimes the failure is not our fault, but other times the failure is a direct result of a bad plan. Being fallen humans, it's often hard for us to discern whether a plan is good or bad.

Solomon accurately depicts the human condition — "there are many plans in a man's heart." No matter the situation, we're often tempted to think we've got an answer among all our internal plans. When we attempt to execute a plan that didn't begin with the Lord, we can find ourselves embarrassed and ashamed. Rather than concocting our own plans, it would be much better for us to seek "the Lord's counsel." God's primary counsel comes through the Word of God.

Though our schemes often falter, we can be confident that the Lord's counsel "will stand." It will stand against the onslaught of deceitfulness and the attacks of the devil. All of us go through the storms of life, much like ships get caught in bad weather. When a ship is being tossed to and fro, it's nice to know that it won't be destroyed because the anchor is secure. As you plan all the remaining days of your life, anchor yourself to the Word of God and your plans will be established.

## June 26 — The Day Jesus Stood

> *"But he, being full of the Holy Spirit, gazed into heaven and saw the glory of God, and Jesus standing at the right hand of God, and said, 'Look! I see the heavens opened and the Son of Man standing at the right hand of God!'" (Acts 7:55-56)*

We're all well-acquainted with the story of Jesus — born of a virgin, raised by a carpenter, ministering to all, dying for our sins, buried in another man's tomb, raising back to life, etc. The last time we saw Jesus on earth, He was gathered with His disciples and then He ascended to heaven (Acts 1). The author of Hebrews tells us that Jesus sat down at the right hand of God (Hebrews 10:12). So, the last mention we have about Jesus' location is seated at God's right hand — the place of privilege.

And yet, when Stephen (one of the first deacons) was bold enough to preach the resurrection to the same Jews who crucified Jesus, something amazing happened. The Jews "were cut to the heart, and they gnashed at him with their teeth" (Acts 7:54). That kind of reception would've been enough to silence some preachers, but not Stephen. "He, being full of the Holy Spirit, gazed into heaven and saw the glory of God, and Jesus standing at the right hand of God." What an amazing sight!

After Jesus presented His own precious blood to the Father, He sat down at the right hand of God because His atoning work was done. Yet, when Stephen was martyred, Jesus stood up — not because He needed to sacrifice, but because He was about to welcome one who had sacrificed himself for God. What an amazing reception into heaven! If you have placed your faith in Jesus, you will also be welcomed into the presence of God when your life is through. What a day that will be!

# June 27 — Adversity Is Opportunity

> *"At that time a great persecution arose against the church which was at Jerusalem; and they were all scattered throughout the regions of Judea and Samaria ... Therefore those who were scattered went everywhere preaching the word." (Acts 8:1, 4)*

No one enjoys the trials of life, but all of us experience them. I once heard a man say, "You're either going into a storm, you're in the midst of a storm, or you're coming out of a storm." I think there is a lot of truth in that statement. Sometimes we wish we had a crystal ball to see what lies ahead, but it's probably a good thing we don't know the future because it would surely scare us to death. When we go through hard times, we're tempted to ask, "Why me, God?" as we question the Lord's plan.

We need to start seeing adversity as an opportunity for God to do great things in and through us. Today's verses provide a great example. After the stoning of Stephen (Acts 7), "a great persecution arose against the church which was at Jerusalem." The assault was led by a man named Saul, whom you and I have come to know as the Apostle Paul. This is Saul before he was converted on the road to Damascus (Acts 9). Consequently, the persecuted church was scattered throughout Judea and Samaria.

Most anyone would've seen that as a terrible tragedy, but the early church didn't see it that way. They saw their adversity as an opportunity to reach more people with the Gospel. As a result of their expulsion from Jerusalem, the Gospel began to spread north to Samaria and beyond. If God had not permitted the church's persecution, the Gospel wouldn't have spread. What are you going through right now? Whatever it is, trust that God can take it and use it for your good and His glory!

## June 28 – The One Requirement for Baptism

*"Now as they went down the road, they came to some water. And the eunuch said, 'See, here is water. What hinders me from being baptized?' Then Philip said, 'If you believe with all your heart, you may.' And he answered and said, 'I believe that Jesus Christ is the Son of God.' So he commanded the chariot to stand still. And both Philip and the eunuch went down into the water, and he baptized him." (Acts 8:36-38)*

In Acts 8, we find the amazing story of Philip's encounter with the Ethiopian eunuch. Philip was one of the first deacons selected by the early church to serve the needs of the congregation (Acts 6:5-6). In addition to serving tables, he also did the work of an evangelist. The Bible tells us that "an angel of the Lord spoke to Philip" and instructed him to travel down the road that runs between Jerusalem and Gaza (modern-day Egypt). Philip obeyed the instruction, and thereafter he had a divine appointment.

A eunuch was someone who had been castrated, usually so they could work in service to kings and queens. This particular eunuch served the queen of Ethiopia, and he was returning to his country after worshiping in Jerusalem. When Philip encountered the eunuch, he was reading the Scripture and he had just come to the Suffering Servant passage in Isaiah 52-53. When the eunuch asked Philip about the identity of the man Isaiah wrote about, Philip was happy to explain that Jesus was the man.

As Philip continued to preach to the eunuch, he came under conviction and placed his faith in Jesus. The eunuch was ready to declare his faith publicly — "What hinders me from being baptized?" While there are many different ideas about baptism, Philip set the record straight — the only requirement for Christian baptism is faith in Jesus Christ. The eunuch believed, and so he was baptized. That's why it's called "believer's baptism." Do you believe in Jesus? Have you publicly declared your faith through Christian baptism?

## June 29 – What Is Alcohol?

*"Wine is a mocker, strong drink is a brawler, and whoever is led astray by it is not wise." (Proverbs 20:1)*

According to the 2015 National Survey on Drug Use and Health (NSDUH), 86.4 percent of people ages eighteen or older reported they drank alcohol at some point in their lifetime; 70.1 percent reported they drank in the past year; 56.0 percent reported they drank in the past month. That being the case, it's safe to say about half of American adults drink alcohol on a regular basis. And though the legal drinking age is twenty-one years old, a good number of young people use alcohol as well.

As a pastor, I've heard all the reasons alcohol use should be considered acceptable. Some say, "The Bible doesn't say, 'Thou shalt not drink.'" That's a true statement, but it doesn't tell the whole story. There are many verses that discourage the use and abuse of alcohol, and today's verse is one of them. Solomon tells us that "wine is a mocker." The Hebrew term translated "mocker" carries the idea of scorn, so Solomon is saying that the use of wine can turn your life into mockery and shame.

He also tells us that "strong drink is a brawler." To the ancients, "strong drink" would've been wine allowed to ferment for a longer period of time, thus increasing the alcoholic content. Those who've had too much booze are infamous for becoming combative and fighting. Solomon leaves us with a word of wisdom — "whoever is led astray by it is not wise." In my opinion, the best way to never be led astray by alcohol is to abstain from using it. Remember, every alcoholic started with his first drink. Rather, let's be filled with the Holy Spirit (Ephesians 5:18)!

## June 30 – Putting God in a Box

> *"How often they provoked Him in the wilderness, and grieved Him in the desert! Yes, again and again they tempted God, and limited the Holy One of Israel."* (Psalm 78:40-41)

If you've ever owned a pet and some sort of cage, then you probably have a good idea what this verse is about. If you own a dog, there might be times when you need to put him in a kennel — so he won't destroy the house, use the bathroom on the carpet, etc. That said, a kennel is a temporary solution to a temporary problem, but it's not intended to be a long-term home for your dog. Why? If a dog lives his entire life in a kennel, he will never develop completely and reach his full potential.

I guess you could call that "keeping a dog in a box," and we would say it is inhumane to keep a dog locked in a box all the time. And yet, we often seem to have no problem putting God in a box. Of course, none of us can physically capture the Lord and confine Him to a box, nor would we want to. Putting God in a box means that we limit the miracle-working power of God because we refuse to believe He is able to deliver. "Again and again, they tempted God, and limited the Holy One of Israel."

When the psalmist says the Israelites "limited the Holy One of Israel," he means that God refused to do greater works in their midst because of their lack of faith. Did you know the church of the 21st century still has the same problem? We look at the reasons God can't or won't do something instead of believing He can. As a result, we rob ourselves of some tremendous blessings. How about you? Are you putting God in a box, or are you putting Him on display by taking Him at His Word?

## July 1 — The Gospel Is for Everyone

*"And a voice spoke to him again the second time, 'What God has cleansed you must not call common.'" (Acts 10:15)*

The early church grew exponentially, even after the martyrdom of Stephen. But the growth was contained primarily to Judea and Samaria. By Acts Chapter 10, it was time for the Gospel to move beyond just the Jews. Remember, when Jesus ascended to heaven, He said, "You shall be witnesses to Me in Jerusalem, and in all Judea and Samaria, and to the end of the earth" (Acts 1:8). The early church did an outstanding job with Judea and Samaria, but now it was time to go to the end of the earth.

Taking the Gospel to all the nations meant that the Gospel would have to go beyond the Jews. Acts 10 is the story of God initiating the advancement of the Gospel to the nations (Gentiles). There we find the story of a devout soldier named Cornelius. The Bible says he "feared God with all his household" and "gave alms generously to the people and prayed to God always." As holy as Cornelius was, he still had a problem — he had not received God's grace through faith in Jesus Christ.

God enlisted Peter to lead Cornelius to Christ, but before he sent him away God gave him an object lesson — a sheet descending from heaven and filled with unclean animals. When God commanded him to "kill and eat" (Acts 10:13), Peter objected because he didn't eat things that were forbidden by God. God used the vision to help Peter understand that just as Jesus fulfilled the Law, those people that were previously seen as unclean were now being invited to receive God's grace. The good news is that the Gospel is for everyone — even sinners like you and me.

## July 2 — Finding a Faithful Man

*"Most men will proclaim each his own goodness, but who can find a faithful man?" (Proverbs 20:6)*

Did you ever hear of the man who was proud of his humility? Even when we try to be humble, sometimes we just can't help but toot our own horn. Some people come right out and tell you how great they think they are — how much money they make, how many miles they can run, etc. Most of us know it's improper to brag too much, so we find ways to veil our self-praise. For instance, we're guilty of telling stories that are supposed to be about something else but end up focusing on us.

Though "most men will proclaim each his own goodness," it's hard to find someone whose walk is as good as their talk. We should all take this as a personal challenge. Rather than talking about how good we are, we should demonstrate our goodness to others through the way we live our lives. Where do we begin? We need to start with the first and greatest command — love the Lord your God with all your heart, soul, mind, and strength (Mark 12:30). Our lives should be an offering of love to God.

Loving God means we will also dedicate ourselves to the second greatest command — love your neighbor as yourself (Mark 12:31). Loving others means you won't serve others to be recognized. Instead, you'll selflessly give of yourself because you're living for Jesus, and thus you won't need any recognition. This world is filled with people who need to be recognized. In a world of vanity and pride, commit yourself to being that rare faithful man that Solomon wrote about 3,000 years ago.

## July 3 — The Origin of 'Christian'

*"The disciples were first called Christians in Antioch." (Acts 11:26)*

For two millennia, all over the world, followers of Jesus Christ have been identified as Christians. What does it mean and where did it begin? The meaning is simple — a Christian is someone who has placed his/her faith in Jesus and is now following in the footsteps of the Savior. "Christian" was first applied to the believers in Antioch. Ancient Antioch was located at one of the southernmost parts of what we now call Turkey, at the northeast corner of the Mediterranean — a vitally important ancient city.

After Stephen was stoned to death, God providentially caused the first Christians to scatter from Jerusalem. Some went south and west, as far as Cyrene (modern-day Libya). Others traveled north through Samaria, then on to the Mediterranean coast, and even to the island nation of Cyprus. What made the Antioch group of believers so special? The Bible leads us to believe it was the presence of two men — Barnabas and Saul. The encourager Barnabas sent for the teacher Saul, and the rest is history.

The Bible says the dynamic duo stayed in Antioch for one year where "they assembled with the church and taught a great many people" (Acts 11:26). Though Saul probably provided a great deal of instruction, there's no doubt Barnabas did his part exemplifying the Christian life. "He was a good man, full of the Holy Spirit and of faith" (Acts 11:24). You may know what "Christian" means and where it began, but can others tell what a Christian looks like when they evaluate your life?

## July 4 – Pride Precedes Punishment

*"Then immediately an angel of the Lord struck him, because he did not give glory to God. And he was eaten by worms and died." (Acts 12:23)*

Most people would not call this one of the most pleasant verses in the Bible, but Christians can actually take comfort in this passage. It starts with a man named Herod. History tells us that Herod (the grandson of Herod the Great) had run up quite a few debts in Rome, so he fled to Palestine. Once the Emperor Tiberius passed away, Herod was released from his imprisonment and made ruler over northern Palestine. From there, he persecuted many Christians in an attempt to appease the Jews.

Acts 12 tells us Herod was displeased with the people of Tyre and Sidon, residents in his jurisdiction living on the Mediterranean coast. The residents of Tyre and Sidon acted very shrewdly — they befriended Herod's personal aide. Through their strategic connection, they were able to talk Herod into a celebration in the Emperor's honor. The historian Josephus tells us that Herod was arrayed in a robe of pure silver when he arrived at the celebration and that he gave a moving oration (Acts 12:21).

In their attempts to butter Herod up, the crowds cried out, "The voice of a god and not of a man!" Herod had two choices — he could rebuke their cries of deity, or he could soak it up like a sponge. To his demise, he chose the latter and suffered the judgment of God "because he did not give glory to God." He went from wowing the crowds to feeding the worms in almost no time. The lesson is clear — it is dangerous for us to rob God of His glory. It's our privilege and duty to deflect all praise and point it to the Lord.

## July 5 – Buyers Are Liars

> *"'It is good for nothing,' cries the buyer; but when he has gone his way, then he boasts." (Proverbs 20:14)*

Sellers often get a bad rap for lying. For instance, car salesmen have an infamous reputation for being less than forthright when selling a car. We really shouldn't generalize salesmen or any other group of people, especially since it's usually a few bad apples that spoil the bunch. Nevertheless, some car salesmen have used some sleazy tactics to get buyers to sign on the dotted line. With the advent of marketplace exchanges on social media, the days of the lying salesmen are in full swing.

But Solomon wants us to know it's not just sellers who are dishonest — buyers are liars too. For example, how many people have agreed to buy something only to discover they couldn't pay. In essence, they lied about their income in order to manipulate the seller. And let's be honest — lying is not just something that touches buyers and sellers. Deceitfulness is something that touches the entire human race. In fact, lying seems to be added to the list of things that used to be wrong.

While God freed His people from the obligation of the ceremonial and civil laws of the Old Testament, God's moral law has never changed. When God said, "You shall not bear false witness against your neighbor" (Exodus 20:16), He meant that dishonesty is universally wrong in every age. That being the case, take a good, long look at your life. Can you honestly say all your dealings with others are truthful? Are you living a life of deception? If so, God can help you exchange your lies for His truth.

## July 6 — Shaking the Dust from Your Feet

*"But the Jews stirred up the devout and prominent women and the chief men of the city, raised up persecution against Paul and Barnabas, and expelled them from their region. But they shook off the dust from their feet against them, and came to Iconium." (Acts 13:50-51)*

Throughout our lives, we're encouraged to never give up. I'm sure you'll agree that's a good thing. It doesn't matter if you're studying to pass a test, if you're entering the last phase of your workout, or if you're getting close to clocking out — we reap wonderful rewards when we refuse to give up. And yet, there are times we need to realize that expending any additional effort on some projects would not be helpful. It's in those moments we need the wisdom to wrap things up and move on.

Today's verses come from the missionary journey of Barnabas and Paul. Traveling through Asia Minor, they came to the lesser known Antioch in Pisidia. Upon arriving, they entered the synagogue and began to preach Jesus. The Jews were not thrilled to hear about Jesus, but the Gentiles were eager to hear more about the grace of God. On the next Sabbath, "the whole city came together to hear the Word of God" (Acts 13:44). The Jews were overtaken with jealousy and began to contradict them.

Even in spite of the Jewish resistance, "the word of the Lord was being spread throughout all the region" (Acts 13:49). Yet, the Jews were able to expel Barnabas and Paul from the region. The Bible says, "They shook off the dust from their feet against them." This was a symbolic action that meant they were finished and moving on. That said, you and I should do all we can to reach everyone for Christ, but if there are some who refuse to listen, we need to move on to others that still have not heard.

## July 7 – Through Many Tribulations

*"We must through many tribulations
enter the kingdom of God." (Acts 14:22)*

There is a very bad misconception that needs to be addressed. Some well-meaning people have been given the impression that all their problems will go away once they place their faith in Jesus. The good news is that our greatest problems do go away when we trust in Jesus. We don't have to worry about going to hell, we don't have to live in fear, and we can trust that the One living in us is greater than the one living in the world (1 John 4:4). Praise the Lord, Jesus took care of our greatest needs!

And yet, coming to Jesus doesn't mean we're immune from adversity. The Christian life is not a cake walk — it is filled with trials and tribulations that we must endure until Jesus returns. Today's verse is taken from the lips of the Apostle Paul. After he and Barnabas had been forcibly removed from Antioch, Iconium, and Lystra, the Bible says they re-entered those towns after a period of time in order to strengthen the disciples. Even after Paul had been nearly stoned to death (Acts 14:19), he kept going.

Because they refused to give up, the churches in those hostile regions were strengthened and leaders for each church were appointed. What trials and tribulations are you currently experiencing? Have you felt like throwing in the towel? I encourage you to remember that many great men and women of God have gone through much worse than what you're experiencing. And remember this — if you refuse to give up in the midst of your trial, God will bless you immensely on the other side (Galatians 6:9).

## July 8 – Grace Comes Through Faith Alone

*"But we believe that through the grace of the Lord Jesus Christ we shall be saved in the same manner as they." (Acts 15:11)*

How can a person know for sure that they are saved? Depends on who you ask. Some people will tell you there's no way you can know for sure that you're saved and going to heaven. Others believe it is possible for you to be saved and lose your salvation. The majority of people will tell you that you've got to do something in order to be saved. The list of things is long and varied — you've got to go to church, say your Hail Marys, be a good person, walk little old ladies across the street, etc.

Because of persecution in Judea, the early church sent missionaries to Samaria and far beyond that into Asia Minor. When the Gentiles began to hear the Gospel, many of them were saved through faith in Jesus. Yet, when news got back to Jerusalem that Gentiles had received the Holy Spirit, a group of believing Pharisees said, "It is necessary to circumcise them and to command them to keep the Law of Moses." In other words, they said faith in Jesus is not enough — you must follow all the rules as well.

Just then, Peter stepped up and addressed what has come to be known as the Jerusalem Council. Speaking of the Gentiles, he said that God had "purified their hearts by faith" (Acts 15:9). He affirmed once and for all "that through the grace of the Lord Jesus Christ we shall be saved in the same manner as they." That said, it doesn't matter who you are or where you're from — the only way you can be saved is through faith alone in Christ alone. Anything more than faith in Jesus is a works salvation that will send you to hell. Have you trusted in Christ alone for your salvation?

## July 9 — Disagreeing Without Derailing

*"Then the contention became so sharp that they parted from one another. And so Barnabas took Mark and sailed to Cyprus; but Paul chose Silas and departed, being commended by the brethren to the grace of God." (Acts 15:39-40)*

After the church's victory over false doctrine at the Jerusalem Council, Paul desired to go back and revisit the churches he and Barnabas established on their first missionary journey around AD 48. It had been three years since they had last visited with their brothers and sisters in Christ. When Paul indicated his desire to Barnabas, he was also eager to return, but with one stipulation: Barnabas wanted to "take with them John called Mark" (Acts 15:37).

The Bible identifies John Mark as the cousin of Barnabas (Colossians 4:10) and, traditionally, he is also seen as the man who penned the Gospel of Mark. It's understandable why Barnabas would want to take his cousin on a second missionary journey, but there was a problem. John Mark had abandoned Paul and Barnabas on their first journey and returned to Jerusalem. The Bible doesn't tell us exactly why John Mark left the disciples — only that he left them both "high and dry."

"Paul insisted that they should not take with them the one who had departed from them" (v. 38). The contention became so sharp that they parted company — Paul carried on with Silas, and Barnabas took off with John Mark. But the good news is that they disagreed without derailing the mission of the church. Disagreement is part of the human experience, even in the church! But our disagreements should never keep us from seeking reconciliation and continuing the work of the Gospel. Because Paul and Barnabas disagreed like brothers in Christ, the Gospel spread even further than before.

## July 10 – Serving God Is No Bed of Roses

*"But when her masters saw that their hope of profit was gone, they seized Paul and Silas and dragged them into the marketplace to the authorities." (Acts 16:19)*

I bet you're familiar with the story of Paul and Silas. Both of them were men who loved the Lord and joined forces to spread the Gospel and plant churches. One of their missionary journeys brought them to the city of Philippi. After ministering in the city for many days, they became annoyed by a young lady who kept following them and proclaiming, "These men are servants of the Most High God" (Acts 16:17). Her words were true, but they were coming from a demon spirit inhabiting her.

The Scripture says that Paul became increasingly annoyed with her loud proclamations and turned and rebuked the demon spirit. The Bible says the young girl was freed from her demon spirit that very same hour. You would think everyone would be elated by the girl's exorcism, but sadly that was not the case. The Bible tells us that her masters were not pleased when they saw that their possibility of profit was gone. They had been exploiting the young lady for their own gain.

Paul and Silas ended up being beaten with rods and they were locked away with the dregs of society in an inner prison cell. Why would God allow Paul and Silas to be punished so severely when they were serving Him? In case we didn't get the memo, serving God is no bed of roses. We are not immune from life's trials just because we're born again — in fact, it's our salvation that puts us right in Satan's crosshairs. And yet, we should not lose heart as we serve the Lord. Jesus promised us many trials, but He also promised to see us through each one. Keep pressing forward with Christ!

## July 11 — Sold Out to Jesus

*"And Micaiah said, 'As the Lord lives, whatever my God says, that I will speak.'" (2 Chronicles 18:13)*

Micaiah is one of my favorite biblical characters that you've probably never heard of. His story should inspire any of us to keep serving Christ, no matter how perilous the circumstances around us might become. When I was pastoring Grace Baptist Church in Morristown, Tennessee, I actually went to a local sign company and had this verse placed on a small plaque. I brought the plaque back to the church and affixed it to the pulpit as a constant reminder to preach only God's Word to God's people.

Micaiah had a reputation for being a true prophet of the Lord. When evil King Ahab was trying to convince good King Jehoshaphat to go to war with him, he called for many false prophets to forecast their war efforts. Not surprisingly, the false prophets came back with nothing but good news. Jehoshaphat was not persuaded by false prophets, so he sought the services of a true prophet of the Lord. That's when Micaiah was called in to bring a genuine word from the Lord.

King Ahab hated Micaiah because he knew he was sold out to Jehovah and could not be bought at any price. Regardless, when the messengers came to retrieve Micaiah, they warned him to prophesy only good things. Micaiah responded with these iconic words — "whatever my God says, that I will speak." Wow! If only that resolve were found in every one of us! When others want you to be quiet or compromise, make your stand with Christ and leave the results with God. Be sold out to Jesus!

## July 12 – Filter Everything Through Scripture

*"These were more fair-minded than those in Thessalonica, in that they received the word with all readiness, and searched the Scriptures daily to find out whether these things were so." (Acts 17:11)*

The missionary journey of Paul and Silas eventually brought them to the city of Berea. Upon their arrival, they did what they were prone to do — they went to the synagogue in an attempt to share the good news about Jesus. Scripture tells us the Jews in Berea "were more fair-minded than those in Thessalonica." The Thessalonians had just recently attempted to seize Paul and Silas, but when they could not find them, they concentrated their persecution on their friend, Jason.

Though Paul and Silas received a poor reception from many in Thessalonica, they were received more fairly in Berea. The Bereans "received the word with all readiness." In other words, they were willing to listen as Paul and Silas shared the truth about Jesus. But the Bereans didn't just take the missionaries' word for it — instead they "searched the Scriptures daily to find out whether these things were so." They took it upon themselves to find out if their words matched those of Scripture.

Have you ever heard someone say, "Believe half of what you see and none of what you hear?" Unfortunately, that's not terribly bad advice. Why? Because many things we see and hear are not true. Before we automatically affirm what we've been told, we need to run it through the filter of the Bible. If what we've heard passes the test of Scripture, then we can stake our lives on it. If not, then we must cast it aside as falsehood. Don't be gullible or naïve — filter everything through the Word of God.

## July 13 – The Sovereign Over All Sovereigns

*"The king's heart is in the hand of the Lord, like the rivers of water; He turns it wherever He wishes." (Proverbs 21:1)*

This world has its share of leaders. We've got everything from kings and queens, presidents and prime ministers, and even tyrants and dictators. Some leaders are elected, and some are unelected. Some arrive to their position by the will of the people, while others come to power through coercion and military might. Some leaders are entrusted with final and absolute power, and in such cases we call them "sovereigns." They are free to exercise complete control over the kingdom.

Regardless of who is in power, we need to understand there is a Higher Power over all earthly powers. There is a King above all kings — a Ruler who is exalted over all the rulers of the earth. To demonstrate that point, Solomon (a king himself) was inspired to say that "the king's heart is in the hand of the Lord." In other words, though rulers might think they have complete control and are accountable to no one else, each of them was appointed to their position by God Himself (Romans 13:1).

That being the case, God has the power to turn the heart of a king "like the rivers of water." As the Sovereign above all sovereigns, "He turns it (the king's heart) wherever He wishes." Of course, we know God has given us free will. Rulers can and often do make terrible decisions — just think of Hitler, Stalin, etc. And yet, at any time the King of kings can turn the heart of any king any way He desires. May we never forget that Christ is still in complete control as King of kings and Lord of lords.

## July 14 – Righteousness Over Ritual

*"To do righteousness and justice is more acceptable to the LORD than sacrifice." (Proverbs 21:3)*

Humans are the crown jewel of God's creation because only humans have been made in the image of God. Though we are the pinnacle of God's creative work, that doesn't mean we are no longer accountable to the Lord. What does God really expect of us? The answer to that question will depend on who you ask, but judging from human activity throughout the ages, humans tend to think that God is impressed with buildings, pageantry, and rituals.

Just stop to consider the things humans have done in an attempt to make themselves "acceptable" to God. Humans have built some of the most beautiful and ornate buildings — we call them cathedrals or churches. Humans have given billions and billions of dollars to what they feel is the work of the Lord. And of course we have a great deal of rituals — ordinances, sacraments, confessions, etc. None of these things is inherently evil, but sometimes we lose sight of the most important things.

In this case, Solomon was very clear — "to do righteousness and justice is more acceptable to the Lord than sacrifice." In other words, we can go through all of our rituals — going to church, giving tithes and offerings, listening to Christian music, etc. But if all we have is ritual without righteousness, then our traditions mean nothing. "Behold, to obey is better than sacrifice" (1 Samuel 15:22). We thought God wanted our rituals, when He was really looking for our righteousness. Be a doer of the Word and not a hearer only (James 1:22).

## July 15 – Does Hell Know Your Name?

*"And the evil spirit answered and said, 'Jesus I know, and Paul I know; but who are you?'" (Acts 19:15)*

Have you ever seen the movie "The Exorcist"? If you did, there's a good chance it gave you some bad dreams. Why? It's the story of a young girl that was incredibly vexed by demons, and those who sought to help her were often tortured or murdered. Some of the movie's most iconic moments involve the 360-degree turn of the girl's head, some weird green stuff spewing from her mouth, and an uncanny levitation above her bed. That's enough to give anyone bad dreams!

That's Hollywood, but the fact is that demon possession is a real part of the human experience. Most people have never truly been demon-possessed, but all of us are demon-influenced at times. And yet Jesus exorcised scores of demons during His earthly ministry. In the days of Paul, there were some demon-possessed individuals in Ephesus where he was ministering. The Bible says some "itinerant Jewish exorcists" attempted to handle the problem by using the name of Jesus as an incantation.

On one occasion, an evil spirit answered the exorcists and said something that is best understood in the original Greek. He said, "Jesus I know (*ginosko*), and Paul I know (*epistomai*), but you — who are you?" *Ginosko* denotes intimate knowledge, while *epistomai* means general knowledge. In essence the demon was saying, "We know Jesus really well, and we're getting to know Paul, too, but who are you clowns?" I wonder — does hell know your name because you're living sold out to Jesus?

## July 16 – When Least Is Best

*"For a day in Your courts is better than a thousand. I would rather be a doorkeeper in the house of my God than dwell in the tents of wickedness." (Psalm 84:10)*

As humans, we all desire the best, including any places of privilege we can find. We like to be first in line, we like to have our order delivered first, etc. When we go to restaurants, we want to be seated in the nicest areas. When we go on vacations, we like to stay for long periods of time and do everything our wallets allow us to do. You could say we often like to treat ourselves to the nicest and best things, and we save and spend our money accordingly.

Today's verse reminds us there is something far greater than the nicest possessions, places, and positions. The sons of Korah said it well in Psalm 84 — "a day in Your courts is better than a thousand." You can spend a whole year at Disney World, but 365 days can't compare to one day spent in the presence of God. And yet, it's amazing how Americans save and spend thousands of dollars to make the all-important pilgrimage to Disney without regularly coming to the house of God for free.

The psalmists said it so well — "I would rather be a doorkeeper in the house of my God than dwell in the tents of wickedness." To use our modern vernacular, it's better to be a servant in God's kingdom than to serve at the "table" of the world. The lowest place in the kingdom of God is better than the highest position among men. There's nothing wrong with affluence or promotion, but we should never forget that the only One we truly need is Jesus. God's least is better than the world's best!

## July 17 – Corners Are Better Than Contentions

*"Better to dwell in a corner of a housetop, than in a house shared with a contentious woman." (Proverbs 21:9)*

What comes to mind when you think of your home's attic? I'm guessing your thoughts are not-so-good. Why? Because attics are usually tight spaces that we cram full of stuff we probably don't need. Who among us likes that tiny, narrow ladder that pulls down from the ceiling? And when you climb your way up to the attic, it's probably 100-plus degrees in the summer and below freezing in the winter. That said, most of us try to avoid very many trips to the attic.

And yet, Solomon was very clear — "better to dwell in a corner of a housetop, than in a house shared with a contentious woman." Wow! I wonder if Solomon ever tried to say this to one of his many wives. For the record, Scripture says that Solomon had 700 wives and 300 concubines! What was he thinking? Even though he was the king, there's no doubt he experienced his share of contention with spouses. And, of course, we know contention goes both ways — husbands can be just as contentious!

The point is simple — it's better to be alone and at peace than to be accompanied and agitated. All of us should take this to heart. Do our family members really enjoy living with us? Do our coworkers enjoy time spent with us, or do they try to avoid us? If your personality is to seek an argument and create strife, you need to ask God to help you become a peacemaker. As the old saying goes, "Be a lover, not a fighter." Be the sort of person who gives life to others rather than taking it from them.

## July 18 – The Whole Counsel of God

*"For I have not shunned to declare to you
the whole counsel of God." (Acts 20:27)*

Today's verse is taken from the lips of the Apostle Paul. On this occasion, he was leaving behind the Ephesian elders — the men who would be left to pastor the churches of Ephesus and the surrounding area. It was a bittersweet moment for Paul — sweet because he was leaving the church in the hands of capable men, but bitter because he would no longer see the men he had poured his heart and soul into. I'm sure he felt much like a parent dropping off his/her child at college.

Before he departed, he left the elders with some final words. He reminded the men of his own ministry and encouraged them to carry on in the same vein. When it came to preaching, Paul reminded them, "I have not shunned to declare to you the whole counsel of God." For that reason, Paul could leave Ephesus with a clear conscience, knowing he had faithfully delivered God's message as it is revealed in the Word of God. He encouraged all the Ephesian pastors to do the same.

This is such a timely word for us in the 21st century. It has become popular for pastors and churches to provide their people with "sermonettes" that often fail to capture the whole counsel of God. It is vitally important for pastors to share all of God's truth with all of God's people. Otherwise, we're like doctors who tell their patients only what they want to hear — tickling the ears on the outside while the body is diseased on the inside. As Paul commanded young Timothy — "Preach the Word!" (2 Timothy 4:2).

## July 19 – Keep Your Ears Open

*"Whoever shuts his ears to the cry of the poor will also cry himself and not be heard." (Proverbs 21:13)*

There are times when all of us just want to shut out the noise and relieve ourselves of the burden of listening to anyone or anything. Manufacturers know that, and they've even begun to use technology to help us block out the noise. The headphones I make regular use of have noise-canceling technology built in, and sometimes it's a pleasure just to put them on and have some peace and quiet. We would do well to remember that sometimes silence really is golden.

There are certainly times we need to close our ears and set aside the noise, but there are other times we must keep our ears open, like when we are driving, having a conversation, etc. If we close our ears when something important is happening, it could produce detrimental consequences. Today's verse reminds us that we should never shut our ears to the cry of the poor. Why? Because those who close their ears to the cries of the less fortunate may someday find themselves calling on deaf ears.

Sometimes we justify our unwillingness to help the less fortunate. We say things like, "I don't want to enable someone's laziness, addiction, etc." While it's true that we shouldn't consent to every request a person might make of us, that doesn't mean we should refuse to listen and help. Though we may not be able to provide everything a person wants, we can certainly be used of God to provide what the less fortunate might need. God help us all to open our ears, our hearts, and our hands.

## July 20 – I Will Call Upon the Lord

*"In the day of my trouble I will call upon You, for You will answer me." (Psalm 86:7)*

Who can you call on when you're really in trouble? When all the chips are down, who are the people in your life you can really depend on? I would hope that your spouse and children fall into that list. I'm sure your parents and siblings fall into that list as well. If you're fortunate enough to have a wonderful church family, then I'm sure you would throw your brothers and sisters in Christ in there as well. We thank the Lord for those people we can call on at any time for any reason.

The reverse of that is true as well — there are some people you would not call on if you were in distress. Why? Because there are some who are only along for the ride in your life. Some people may only maintain their relationship with you because of something you can do in exchange for them. But if you were in a predicament, you know you couldn't call on them because they wouldn't care. Thankfully, God is not like that. The psalmist said we can call on Him "in the day of my trouble."

Not only that, but the Scripture says God "will answer me." What an awesome truth. Of course, we know this promise belongs to the people of God — those whose sins have been covered by the blood of Jesus. We know He loves us and hears us when we pray. We shouldn't wait until we're in trouble to call on the name of the Lord, but we certainly shouldn't hesitate to call on Him when we're in distress. He knows where we are and what we need. He will answer us when we call on Him!

## July 21 – Forgiveness and Consequences

*"All the people shouted with a great shout, when they praised the Lord, because the foundation of the house of the Lord was laid. But many of the priests and Levites and heads of the fathers' houses, old men who had seen the first temple, wept with a loud voice when the foundation of this temple was laid before their eyes." (Ezra 3:11-12)*

God sent the children of Israel into captivity because of their refusal to believe His Word and order their lives accordingly. History tells us the northern kingdom of Israel was overthrown in 722 BC, and the southern kingdom of Judah was overtaken when the city of Jerusalem fell in 586 BC. At that time, nearly all the men were forced into slavery in Assyria and Babylon. Women and children were often treated as plunder by the new inhabitants of the land.

The Jews were in captivity to Babylon and the Persians throughout most of the 6th century BC. And yet, the Lord moved on the heart of the Persian king who decreed that the Jewish people were to be released so they could rebuild their homeland. The Book of Haggai tells us the Jews began by rebuilding their own homes. The Lord reminded them that the temple was lying in ruins while they slept and slumbered in their own homes (Haggai 1:4). In no time, temple reconstruction was under way.

Today's verses show us two sets of emotions. The younger generations were thrilled when the temple foundation was laid. I'm sure their joy was focused on the mercy and forgiveness of God. And yet, the elders were not quite so happy because they "had seen the first temple." They knew that the new temple was only a fraction of the original temple. These verses remind us that God's forgiveness doesn't always remove sin's consequence. Keep that in mind the next time you flirt with sin.

## July 22 – Saving Rather Than Squandering

*"There is desirable treasure, and oil in the dwelling of the wise, but a foolish man squanders it." (Proverbs 21:20)*

Are you a saver or a spender? Judging by the numbers, most Americans are better at spending than saving. Consider this: The typical American household now carries an average debt of $137,063. That includes things such as mortgages, car payments, student loans, etc. In fact, the average American household owes over $16,000 in credit card debt. On the other hand, 69 percent of Americans are saving 10 percent or less of their income. We're great spenders but sorry savers!

In today's verse, Solomon reminds us "there is desirable treasure, and oil in the dwelling of the wise." In other words, the wise see the value of saving and make adequate preparation for the future. Solomon mentions oil, and so did Jesus in His parable of the ten virgins (Matthew 25:1-13). The foolish virgins had no oil for their lamps when the bridegroom returned, but the wise virgins were ready for the coming of their lord because they had set aside adequate oil and trimmed their lamps.

Rather than setting aside adequate resources, "a foolish man squanders it." "Squander" is just a fancy word for waste. We need to admit we waste money on lots of things — food, clothes, toys, entertainment, etc. None of those things is inherently evil, but it is foolish for us to spend and spend without making any preparation for the future. A wise man once said, "You should give at least 10 percent of your income, save another 10 percent, and live off the remaining 80 percent." May God help us all to be so wise.

## July 23 — Priorities

*"A wise man scales the city of the mighty, and brings down the trusted stronghold." (Proverbs 21:22)*

Do you struggle with prioritizing the most important things? If so, you're not alone. Practically all of us allow ourselves to get sidetracked with things that aren't that important, while the most crucial things in our lives are neglected. For instance, there's the guy who puts so much time into his job that he has no energy left for his wife and children. There's the woman who spends so much of her income on non-essential items that she fails to faithfully give tithes and offerings to the Lord.

Solomon gives us some very good wisdom in today's verse — "A wise man scales the city of the mighty, and brings down the trusted stronghold." Think about it — if a man were really trying to secure a military victory, would he focus on small targets that have no real meaning? If an army were bombing an enemy nation, would they strike in insignificant places or would they shoot for the capital city? I'm guessing they would set their sights on the places where they could make the greatest impact.

What has God called you to be? Perhaps He's called you to be a spouse, parent, child, etc. If you've placed your faith in Jesus, then He's clearly called you to be a disciple maker. When you assess your life, are you prioritizing the things that help you be a faithful follower of Christ, or have you made majors out of minors? All of us should reassess our activities and recalibrate around those things that are most important. Sometimes saying "yes" to God means saying "no" to everything else.

## July 24 — Guard Your Mouth

*"Whoever guards his mouth and tongue keeps his soul from troubles." (Proverbs 21:23)*

Our world is much more concerned with security than it's probably ever been. Who can forget that terrible day — 9/11/01 — when terrorists flew jetliners into both of New York's iconic twin towers? Now we talk about the pre-9/11 world and the post-9/11 world. In pre-9/11 days, I can remember meeting someone as soon as they stepped off the plane and walked through the gate. These days, not even ticketed passengers are permitted to walk to the gates without passing through heavy security.

As much as we hate to admit it, we can all agree that the increased security measures of the last two decades were necessary. The need for additional security is further evidence of the wickedness of the world and our desperate need for Jesus. Wouldn't it be something if we were just as serious about guarding our mouths as we are airports, businesses, and homes? Sometimes things slip right through our mouths because we weren't standing guard. We wreak havoc because of our careless remarks.

Solomon reminds us that "whoever guards his mouth and tongue keeps his soul from troubles." How many times have we said something, only to regret it later and wish we could take our words back? All of us have caused trouble through the foolish things we've said. Each one of us needs to put a "Holy Spirit filter" over our mouths. Before you say something, ask yourself, "Is this going to build others up or tear them down?" Never forget, "death and life are in the power of the tongue" (Proverbs 18:21).

# July 25 – Teamwork

*"So they said, 'Let us rise up and build.' Then they set their hands to this good work."* (Nehemiah 2:18)

Nehemiah is a biblical character you might not know much about. Scripture tells us he was the cupbearer for the Persian king Artaxerxes. Nehemiah was a Jew who found favor in the eyes of Persian nobility when he and his countrymen were taken captive to Babylon. While he was serving the Persian king, distressing news came to Nehemiah. He was told that his beloved city of Jerusalem was lying in ruins and that even the walls of the city were fallen and in great disrepair.

While serving the king, Nehemiah was provided the opportunity to share his heartbreak over what had become of Jerusalem. In an act of God's providence, Nehemiah was permitted to leave the king's court in Persia so he could return home and rebuild the wall of Jerusalem. Upon returning to his city, Scripture says that Nehemiah spent three days at home before he finally went to survey the damage. Upon seeing the devastation, he recruited many others to join him in the restoration.

When he asked his countrymen to join him in rebuilding the wall, they said, "Let us rise up and build." They were determined to work together to see the wall rebuilt. In one accord, "they set their hands to this good work." And because the people had a mind to work, the Bible tells us it only took them fifty-two days to complete the project. They had their share of detractors and critics, but they were not deterred. It's amazing what God's people can do when we join hands and work together!

# July 26 — Are You Almost a Christian?

*"Then Agrippa said to Paul, 'You almost persuade me to become a Christian.'" (Acts 26:28)*

During one of his missionary journeys in Ephesus, Paul was taken into custody on account of his witness for Christ. Paul's incarceration led to a series of appeals he would make before a number of Roman magistrates. One of those officials was a man named Agrippa. Given the opportunity to share his story with the Roman authority, Paul proceeded to share his testimony. Acts 26 is a beautiful picture of Paul's life before and after Jesus. Such a powerful testimony!

After Agrippa listened to Paul's words, he was deeply moved. He said these sobering words — "You almost persuade me to become a Christian." Almost persuaded — so close to surrendering his life to Christ without actually doing so. I'm afraid there are many people in the world like that today. They're almost persuaded to place their faith in Jesus and be born again, but for some reason they never have. Many times, it's because they're afraid of what they might lose.

If Agrippa had genuinely given his life to Christ, he could've lost his position as king. Many others have faced the same dilemma. Remember the rich young ruler? The Bible says he walked away from Christ very dismayed because he was not willing to lose everything for Jesus. Dear friend, you might think you're saved, but could it be that you're "almost" a Christian? Almost will not be enough on the day of judgment. Make certain you've surrendered your life to Christ through faith in Jesus!

# July 27 – Peace in the Midst of the Storm

*"Therefore take heart, men, for I believe God that it will be just as it was told me." (Acts 27:25)*

After giving his life to Jesus on the road to Damascus, Paul lived quite an adventurous life. Not only was he apprehended and beaten many times on account of his faith in Jesus, but he was even forced to travel to places he didn't want to go. Today's verse is taken from an occasion where Paul was making his way toward Rome where he could potentially make an appeal to Caesar. He and his companions were traveling by boat, but Paul urged them not to make the trip.

Paul had been warned that their boat ride would not be smooth sailing. I'm sure Paul's words were much like nonsense to those who were responsible for his journey, so they sailed on. Not too far into the trip they realized that Paul was right. The winds became tempestuous and the waves beat against the ship. They threw anything out of the ship that was not essential, but no matter what they did, nothing seemed to work. Everyone was losing heart the further they sailed.

In the midst of the distress, Scripture says an angel of God came and stood next to Paul and assured him that he would make it all the way to Rome. Paul immediately believed the words of the angel, and placing his confidence in God, he moved to infuse hope in others. He said, "Take heart, men, for I believe God that it will be just as it was told to me." What an awesome reminder — when you trust in Christ and His Word, you can have peace in the midst of any storm that comes your way.

## July 28 – Strength for Every Day

*"Do not sorrow, for the joy of the Lord is your strength." (Nehemiah 8:10)*

Nehemiah led a major campaign to rebuild the wall of Jerusalem, and because the people had a mind to work the project was completed in fifty-two days. Because God blessed the people of Israel with His favor, a national revival was on. But the revival was not only built on architectural prowess — it was centered around the Word of God. Today's passage is taken from the occasion when all the nation was gathered together to celebrate the work of the Lord and to hear the Word of God.

The Bible tells us that Ezra brought out "the Book of the Law of Moses" — that is, the first five books of the Bible. The Jews call it the Torah (Law) and scholars call it the Pentateuch. Scripture tells us that a wooden platform was built for Ezra, and that he began to read the Law once he ascended into the pulpit. As Ezra read the Word of the Lord, "they bowed their heads and worshiped the Lord with their faces to the ground" (Nehemiah 8:6). The people were overjoyed when they heard the Law.

And yet there was also an air of sadness — "all the people wept, when they heard the words of the law" (Nehemiah 8:9). I'm sure it's because the reading of the Law reminded them just how far they had strayed from the will of God as a nation. And yet, God saw their brokenness and responded with hope — "the joy of the Lord is your strength." The people were to live empowered, knowing that God was smiling on their repentance. May God help each of us to live for the Lord and allow His joy to strengthen us daily!

## July 29 – Snake-Handling Preacher?

*"But when Paul had gathered a bundle of sticks and laid them on the fire, a viper came out because of the heat, and fastened on his hand. ... But he shook off the creature into the fire and suffered no harm." (Acts 28:3, 5)*

I count it a tremendous blessing to have been born and raised in East Tennessee. My life has been lived in the hills and hollers of the Smokies, and I'm no stranger to Appalachian culture. Some elements of our culture are truly wonderful — hospitality, kindness, and even our "hillbilly" dialect. And yet some things about our culture can leave you scratching your head. I'll never forget when I learned that there were churches in East Tennessee that utilized "snake-handling" as part of their worship.

When I was a student at UT, I watched a documentary on snake-handling churches in East Tennessee and the Appalachian area. Not only did the church members handle venomous snakes as part of their worship, but they also drank poison such as strychnine. I learned that snake-handling churches incorporate the practice as a result of Mark 16:18: "They will take up serpents; and if they drink anything deadly, it will by no means hurt them."

Is snake-handling a biblical practice based on that verse? Let's ask the Apostle Paul — while shipwrecked on the island of Malta, he was bitten by a venomous viper. Paul didn't see the viper as an instrument of worship — rather, he shook it off in the fire. The words of Jesus in Mark 16 were given to the disciples as they began to fulfill the Great Commission — a promise of His protection. God has not called His church to handle snakes, but He has promised to protect us as we continue to serve Him.

# July 30 – I Am Not Ashamed

*"For I am not ashamed of the gospel of Christ, for it is the power of God to salvation for everyone who believes, for the Jew first and also for the Greek." (Romans 1:16)*

During all his missionary journeys, the Apostle Paul desired to return to Rome, where he had seen many souls won to Christ and where he had also planted churches. Unfortunately, Paul was hindered from making the trip to Rome (Romans 1:13), but it was still his desire to encourage the Roman Christians. For that reason, he penned a letter to the church around the year AD 58. Paul's letter to the Roman believers is the most organized theological statement we have in all the Bible.

From the beginning of his letter, Paul wanted to make some things very clear. He gave us several "I am" statements. First, he said, "I am a debtor both to Greeks and to barbarians." In other words, Paul saw it as a divine obligation to share the Good News with people from every tribe, tongue, and nation. Furthermore, he said, "I am ready to preach the gospel to you." Just as he had preached the Gospel throughout the known world, Paul was now ready to share it with the Romans.

And then he gives us one last powerful statement — "I am not ashamed of the gospel of Christ." Why? Because "it is the power of God to salvation for everyone who believes." Through the Gospel, God has the power to save anyone who is willing to turn from his/her sins by trusting in Christ alone. And though the Gospel came to "the Jew first," it also has the power to save anyone in any age. That being the case, instead of being ashamed of the Gospel, we should open our mouths and share it! Never be ashamed of your Savior Jesus!

# July 31 — Train Up a Child

*"Train up a child in the way he should go, and when he is old he will not depart from it." (Proverbs 22:6)*

In the Bible, there are many promises that encourage us as we serve the Lord. In addition, there are also many principles in Scripture. And while principles are not promises, they provide godly wisdom that guides us as we seek to follow Jesus. One such principle is today's verse. Solomon encourages us to "train up a child in the way he should go." Paul said it like this in the New Testament — "bring them up in the training and admonition of the Lord" (Ephesians 6:4). We should raise our children to follow God.

How can we "train up" our children in the way of the Lord? It's impossible to list all the ways, so I'll attempt to summarize. First, there is what we teach our children. We need to teach our children that the Word of God is 100 percent true, and as such we believe that God is our Father, Christ is our Savior, and the Holy Spirit is our Helper. In addition, there is what we model for our children. We can teach them the truth all day, but if we live as hypocrites, our children will not be persuaded to follow God.

Some have raised an objection to this verse. They say, "I know parents that have raised their children to follow the Lord, and yet those children chose a different path when they grew older." We need to understand something: This verse is not a promise — it is an overarching principle that is generally true in life. Raising your children in the Lord is no guarantee they will always follow God, but one thing is certain — our kids will be much more likely to love the Lord if they see us loving Him first.

## August 1 — Justified by Faith

*"Therefore we conclude that a man is justified by faith apart from the deeds of the law." (Romans 3:28)*

As a first-year seminary student, I'm sure I thought there were a great many things I understood about the Christian faith. One or two semesters in seminary is about all it takes to show you that there's still a lot you don't know. It was in that first year that my pastor handed me a book comparing the doctrinal commitments of Protestants and Catholics. At that time, there were pastors and other Christian leaders stepping forward to say that both groups should be doing evangelism together.

As I read the book, I began to understand that there is one major difference between Protestants and Catholics — a difference so big that it sparked the Reformation. Catholics (and many others) believe that salvation is earned through a mixture of faith and good works. In other words, one's entrance into heaven is based on whether or not they did enough work to get there. The Reformation was born out of the conviction that salvation is gained ONLY through faith in Jesus.

Martin Luther was a former Catholic monk who spearheaded the Reformation. Today's verse was a monumental revelation to him. Though he had been taught all his life that the way to be justified before God was good works, he learned that "a man is justified by faith apart from the deeds of the law." Don't get me wrong — good works are a daily part of our Christian faith. But we don't do good works in order to be saved — we do good works because we ARE saved through faith alone in Jesus.

## August 2 – The Imputed Righteousness of Christ

*"But to him who does not work but believes on Him who justifies the ungodly, his faith is accounted for righteousness." (Romans 4:5)*

Has anyone ever gone to bat for you before, maybe even when you were undeserving? Think of someone who's been arrested. An innocent person comes to pay his/her bond so they can be released from captivity. When you bought your first car, perhaps someone co-signed for you. By adding their signature to your car loan, he/she promised to make good on the loan if you failed to make payments. Their good name (and good credit) was applied to you.

Salvation is much like that. Jesus Christ was born the perfect Son of God, and we know that He lived a perfectly sinless life. He never did one thing wrong, but that didn't keep the religious right from falsely accusing Him and sentencing Him to death. Jesus was turned over into the hands of sinful men who beat Him unmercifully and crucified Him at Calvary. It was on that cross that Jesus shed His blood for the sins of mankind. Only His blood is the perfect payment for the sins of every human being.

The good news is this — because Jesus has made atonement for your sins and mine, when we place our faith in Jesus, not only are our sins covered by the blood of Christ, but the spotless righteousness of Christ is "imputed" to us. When it comes to righteousness, we are all spiritually bankrupt because every one of us has sinned. But through faith in Jesus, the righteousness of Christ is lavished on us, and we stand before God totally justified — just as if we had never sinned! Through His righteousness, we have a right standing with God!

## August 3 – True Peace with God

> *"Therefore, having been justified by faith, we have peace with God through our Lord Jesus Christ." (Romans 5:1)*

I know our culture has radically shifted toward selfishness and wickedness, and we're led to believe most people don't think about God. In fact, even in my own community (where the Bible belt buckles) statisticians tell us that 8 out of 10 people are in no one's church anywhere on any given Sunday. And yet, I firmly believe that people know in the depths of their soul there is a God to whom they must give an account, and they really want to know they're at peace with Him.

The Apostle Paul was clear in this verse — there is only one way to have true peace with God. That is, "having been justified by faith." When you place your faith in Jesus, not only are your sins forgiven and covered by the blood of Jesus, but you also have a right standing with God. The Bible calls that justification — standing before God as though I'd never sinned based on the perfect righteousness of Jesus. Knowing that you have a right standing with God is the only thing that can give you lasting peace.

Don't get me wrong — Christians often anger the Lord. Any of us can walk the paths of sin and refuse to make the changes brought to our attention by the Holy Spirit. In those cases, the Lord will often rebuke us and sometimes even punish us, just like we would punish our children. But just because we punish our children doesn't mean we disown them. They still belong to us, and we belong to them. No matter how tough times get, take comfort in knowing that you've found eternal peace with God through faith alone in Jesus.

## August 4 – Life in the Secret Place

*"He who dwells in the secret place of the Most High shall abide under the shadow of the Almighty." (Psalm 91:1)*

Do you have a place you like to go just to get away from everything and everyone? It could be the hour you spend taking a walk around your neighborhood. It could be in the comfort of your own bed at night, just listening to relaxing music before you go to sleep. Maybe the place you like to go when you want to get away from it all is private and secluded. I'm thinking a nice hike along a beautiful mountainside, or maybe even a small chalet that your family rents from time to time.

Today's passage reminds us of the importance of finding the secret place, but not just any secret place. We've been called to dwell "in the secret place of the Most High." The psalmist doesn't tell us exactly where that is, but Jesus gave us a pretty good idea in the New Testament. Teaching on prayer, Jesus said, "When you pray, go into your room, and when you have shut your door, pray to your Father who is in the secret place" (Matthew 6:6). At the very least, the secret place is a place of prayer.

When your life is lived in the secret place yearning for God, you will "abide under the shadow of the Almighty." What does that mean? In the arid Middle Eastern climate, the shadow was a place of protection from the harmful and exhausting rays of the sun. So then, the psalmist wants us to know that God's protection belongs to those who spend their lives pursuing Him in the secret place. How is your current pursuit of God? How much time are you currently spending in the secret place?

## August 5 — Trusting God in Goodness and Adversity

*"But he said to her, 'You speak as one of the foolish women speaks. Shall we indeed accept good from God, and shall we not accept adversity?' In all this Job did not sin with his lips." (Job 2:10)*

There are a wide variety of opinions about God. Many say He is loving, some say He is holy, and others say He rewards those who serve Him. Among the myriad of opinions about God, nearly everyone would agree that God is good, meaning He is benevolent, kind, and giving. I think we would all agree God has been good to each one of us! Just think about all He's blessed you with — a home, food, clothes, family, friends, etc. He has blessed all of us immensely!

We love it when God blesses us, but we're not so thrilled when we go through the trials of life. When the doctor gives us a bad diagnosis, when we've been laid off from work, when a child is going through a terrible time — these are the moments we despise. And by the way — no one says you have to enjoy the trial that you're experiencing or even that you need to welcome adversity into your life, but Scripture makes it clear that we should accept every adversity knowing that God is sovereign.

Job is a wonderful example of this truth — after he lost everything he had (animals, barns, and even children), the Scripture says the only things he had left were a nagging wife and some painful boils from head to toe. His wife encouraged him to curse God and die, but Job refused to do so. The question he posed to his wife should resonate with each of us — how can we receive countless blessings from God without also accepting burdens as well? Dear friend, you can love God through the good, bad, and ugly when you know He's promised to work all things together for your good (Romans 8:28).

## August 6 – The Spirit of Adoption

*"For you did not receive the spirit of bondage again to fear, but you received the Spirit of adoption by whom we cry out, 'Abba, Father.'" (Romans 8:15)*

We live in a world that has legalized infanticide through the grizzly practice of abortion. Since 1973, over 60 million babies have been legally aborted in the US alone. That is a tragedy — not only because abortion is murder in the eyes of God, but because there are so many loving adults that are willing to adopt children. The children that are not murdered are often adopted into families where they are showered with love and given the opportunity to pursue their dreams.

Through adoption, a person enters into a new family. Maybe you didn't realize it, but when you placed your faith in Jesus you were adopted as well. The fact is that everyone of us was conceived in sin and born outside the family of God. Maybe you've heard it implied that every human being is a child of God, but that simply is not true. All of us were born outside of God's family, but through faith in Jesus we were adopted into the family of God. God's family includes every person that has trusted in Jesus.

Today's verse explains it all — through faith in Jesus a person receives a Spirit, but not just any spirit. We certainly didn't receive "the spirit of bondage" when we were born again, causing us to live in a state of perpetual fear. Through faith in Jesus we have received "the Spirit of adoption" — the Holy Spirit. By the Spirit's indwelling presence, all God's children can cry out "Abba (Aramaic for "Daddy"), Father." Through faith in Jesus, your Creator became your Father by the Spirit of adoption.

## August 7 — Nothing Can Separate Us

*"For I am persuaded that neither death nor life, nor angels nor principalities nor powers, nor things present nor things to come, nor height nor depth, nor any other created thing, shall be able to separate us from the love of God which is in Christ Jesus our Lord." (Romans 8:38-39)*

God has put some truly amazing people in our lives. Just think of all the folks who bless you on a daily basis — for you that might include your spouse, children, parents, friends, teachers, pastors, etc. When you really love and appreciate someone, there are times when you hate to be separated from their presence. Parents of adult children can understand this — for two decades you prepare them to live on their own, but when they finally leave the house it is a bittersweet moment of separation.

If you've ever lost someone you love, then you know how hard separation can be. We lose many things in this life, but God promised us there's one thing we can never be separated from — His amazing love. The fact is that God loves every person in the world, so much so that He willingly sent His only begotten Son to redeem the human race. Sadly, many of those whom God loves have refused His offer of salvation, but by the Spirit's power, many others have received His gift of grace.

Those who have placed their faith in Jesus have been born again by the regenerating power of the Holy Spirit, and they've also been added to the family of God. God has a special love for all those who belong to Him, and absolutely NOTHING can separate us from God's love. Death, demons, past, present, future, sin — none of it can separate us from God's love. If you belong to God, He will discipline you when you sin, but He will never stop loving you. His love is the greatest love of all!

## August 8 – What Are You Grieved About?

*"I tell the truth in Christ, I am not lying, my conscience also bearing me witness in the Holy Spirit, that I have great sorrow and continual grief in my heart." (Romans 9:1-2)*

Can you remember the last time you were really grieved about something? Let me guess — was it when they announced your favorite ice cream had been discontinued? Maybe it was the last time you went to the store and there were no parking spots close to the door? Maybe it was when your favorite team lost their last ball game? I hope none of those things made you "have great sorrow and continual grief," but you've got to admit that we get pretty torn up about lots of trivial things.

When Paul wrote his letter to the Roman Christians, he came to the point where he wanted to provide a fuller explanation of Israel's place in God's plan of salvation. He began by explaining his great sorrow over the fact that his Jewish countrymen were still under condemnation because they had not placed their faith in Jesus. Paul even went on to say he would allow himself to be cut off from Christ if it meant the rest of the nation of Israel would be saved.

Think about that — Paul actually said he would be willing to go to hell if it meant his countrymen would be saved. Of course, he knew he couldn't do that, and that's why he was so grieved — he was brokenhearted because he knew many of them would die lost apart from Christ. We need to examine ourselves — do we get more grieved by ice cream and parking spots than we do lost people dying and going to hell? Let's be grieved for those who need Jesus and do all we can to lead them to Christ.

## August 9 — Eternal Truth and Holiness

*"Your testimonies are very sure; holiness adorns Your house, O Lord, forever." (Psalm 93:5)*

We live in an age where things are not meant to last forever. Think about it — it doesn't matter if you're buying a microwave, a phone, or a computer — none of them are really designed to last very long. It used to be when something broke down, you took it to a repairman to fix it. These days, we spend our money, enjoy our product for just a little while, then when it's all used up we just throw it away and buy a new one. It's been said many times, "They don't make 'em like they used to."

In a throwaway world, it's hard to find very many things that last. The great thing about our God is that He is timeless — He literally exists outside the realm of space, time, and matter. Our God has no limitations — He has always been, and He will always be! Scripture also teaches us that God is immutable — He never changes. He is the same yesterday, today, and forever — and rightfully so, because why would you change perfection? He is the eternal God of heaven and earth.

Because God is eternally the same, that means He has always been eternally true and eternally holy. The psalmist said, "Your testimonies are very sure" — that's because they originate from the One who is the Truth! Every word of God is certain! Furthermore, "holiness adorns Your house, O Lord, forever." To say God is holy is to say He's never been stained with sin. He is the eternally perfect God. As followers of Jesus, it's so good to know we serve a God who is both true and holy forever!

## August 10 — Believe and Confess

*"If you confess with your mouth the Lord Jesus and believe in your heart that God has raised Him from the dead, you will be saved." (Romans 10:9)*

I remember teaching each of our six kids the ABCs. It's so vitally important that our kids learn the alphabet, because letters are the building blocks of words, and words are the vehicles of our language. No matter where a child goes, we know they will need their ABCs and 123s. And just as we taught our kids the ABCs of the English language, we also taught them the ABCs of salvation. Do you know what I'm talking about? Let me break it down for you — Admit, Believe, and Confess.

The Scripture is very clear that every human has sinned and fallen short of the glory of God (Romans 3:23). As such, every one of us stands condemned apart from Christ, but through Jesus there is hope of salvation. In order to receive God's greatest gift, we must ADMIT that we have violated God's plan of perfection. We must admit that we are sinners. Upon admitting our guilt to God, Paul said we must BELIEVE — "believe in your heart that God has raised Him from the dead."

The only way to receive God's grace is through faith in Jesus — believing that He truly is the Son of God and Savior of the world. When a person places his faith in Jesus, then he CONFESSES — "with your mouth the Lord Jesus." Paul said that "with the heart one believes unto righteousness, and with the mouth confession is made unto salvation" (Romans 10:10). It's really that simple — if you want to be born again, all you must do is place your faith in Jesus and confess Him alone as Lord of your life.

## August 11 – Grafted into the Covenant

*"And if some of the branches were broken off, and you, being a wild olive tree, were grafted in among them, and with them became a partaker of the root and fatness of the olive tree, do not boast against the branches." (Romans 11:17-18)*

The Apostle dedicated three chapters of his Roman epistle to explaining God's covenant of salvation with the nation of Israel. An honest reading of the New Testament reveals that God is not done with His people Israel and that the church has not replaced the nation of Israel. The church and Israel are two separate entities, and while it's true that some Israelites are part of the church, not all Jews are a part of the Body of Christ. And yet, there are some things we can be sure of.

Paul makes one thing clear — salvation came first to the nation of Israel. He said in Chapter 1 that the Gospel is the power of God to salvation for all who believe — "for the Jew first and also for the Greek." The Jews were the first to enter into a covenant of salvation with the Lord — a covenant that has always been based on faith in Jehovah (Romans 4:3). And while many Jews have rejected God's offer of salvation by rejecting Christ, it doesn't negate the fact that salvation came to us through the Jews.

So then, speaking to Gentiles (non-Jews), Paul said that "some of the branches were broken off" — that is, not every person born Jewish is saved. And likewise, "a wild olive tree" (Gentiles) was "grafted in among them." Though Gentiles were born outside the Jewish heritage, through faith in Jesus we have been grafted into the covenant of salvation. Now we have become partakers "of the root and fatness of the olive tree." That should not make us prideful — rather it should cause us to boast about Jesus!

## August 12 – God's Irrevocable Blessings

*"For the gifts and the calling of God are irrevocable." (Romans 11:29)*

When Christians think about the nation of Israel and Jews in particular, our hearts break because the majority of Jews have refused to receive Jesus as their Messiah. And yet, Paul said that God has used Israel's unbelief to extend God's salvation to the Gentiles. While many Jews have rejected God's grace by refusing to place their faith in Jesus, it doesn't mean God has discarded the nation of Israel. Paul helps us understand that our God remains faithful even when His people are unfaithful.

Today's verse is some of the best news in Scripture — "the gifts and the calling of God are irrevocable." When we think about the gifts of God, there are too many to mention. In this case, it seems Paul's focus is the gift of salvation. Earlier in Romans, Paul said, "the wages of sin is death, but the gift of God is eternal life in Christ Jesus our Lord" (6:23). Salvation is the greatest gift of all, and based on these words of Paul it is an irrevocable gift — you can't lose your salvation!

What does Paul mean by "the calling of God?" In this case, it seems clear Paul is talking about God's sovereign call of the Jews to be His chosen people. The gift of salvation is an irrevocable gift available to the nation of Israel, and Israel has an irrevocable call to be the people of God. Even Gentiles like us can find so much hope in this promise! If the Lord has called you to salvation and you've received the gift of His grace through faith in Jesus, your place in the family of God is eternally secure!

## August 13 — Living Sacrifices

> *"I beseech you therefore, brethren, by the mercies of God, that you present your bodies a living sacrifice, holy, acceptable to God, which is your reasonable service. And do not be conformed to this world but be transformed by the renewing of your mind, that you may prove what is that good and acceptable and perfect will of God." (Romans 12:1-2)*

After spending 11 chapters laying out God's plan of salvation for Jews and Gentiles alike, Paul turns the last five chapters of his epistle into a practical theology. Based on God's covenant mercies, it is our privilege to present our bodies to God as living sacrifices. Throughout history God has been opposed to human sacrifice, even punishing His own people for slaughtering their own children. Paul is talking about something different here — being crucified with Christ and yet still living for His glory!

What does it mean to sacrifice your life for the cause of Christ? It means living "holy, acceptable to God" — living our lives in submission to His perfect will. Living a life sacrificed to Christ is "your reasonable service." Think about it — if the Heavenly Father sacrificed His own Son for us, the very least we can do is sacrifice all of ourselves to Him. Living surrendered to God means we're no longer "conformed to this world" — in other words, we don't live how everyone else is living.

Instead, we should seek to be "transformed by the renewing of our minds." When you live your life submitted to God through prayer and the study of His Word, something amazing happens — your mind is renewed by the cleansing power of the Holy Spirit, causing you to be transformed into something beautiful for the glory of God. Being a living sacrifice comes with a tremendous blessing — "that you may prove what is that good and acceptable and perfect will of God."

## August 14 — My Redeemer Lives

*"For I know that my Redeemer lives, and He shall stand at last on the earth; and after my skin is destroyed, this I know, that in my flesh I shall see God, whom I shall see for myself, and my eyes shall behold, and not another. How my heart yearns within me!" (Job 19:25-27)*

It's probably safe to say the only man who suffered more than Job is our Savior Jesus. But outside of Christ, Job suffered some of the greatest internal and external torture a man can endure. I'm sure you recall his situation — in one moment he lost nearly everything he owned, even his children. The only thing left was a wife who encouraged him to curse God and die. Job rebuked his wife's foolish counsel, only to later be surrounded by three friends who accused him of wickedness.

Job tried to help his friends understand he was not responsible for all the calamity that had entered into his life, but they would not listen. So there he was — stripped of nearly all he had enjoyed and surrounded by friends who thought he was an unrepentant sinner. It's in that moment Job had to encourage himself. He took his eyes off the present and set his gaze on the future — "I know that my Redeemer lives, and He shall stand at last on the earth." Job looked forward to Jesus!

If that were not amazing enough, Job then detailed a remarkable truth — "after my skin is destroyed, this I know, that in my flesh I shall see God." The fact is that all of our bodies are going to die and decay following our passing. When Job prophesied he would see God in his own flesh, he was affirming the bodily resurrection of the saints. Here's the truth — if you have placed your faith in Jesus, your body will be gloriously resurrected at the end of time to spend eternity in the presence of God! Encourage yourself with that amazing truth!

# August 15 — Our Liberty in Christ

*"One person esteems one day above another; another esteems every day alike. Let each be fully convinced in his own mind." (Romans 14:5)*

As Paul began to set forth his practical theology at the end of Romans, he entered into an explanation of Christian liberty. Understand this — following the resurrection of Jesus, both Jews and Gentiles were being saved. Jews had grown up with a great deal of customs and observances that most Gentiles knew nothing about. When Jews placed their faith in Jesus, some desired to continue some of their Jewish observances, while others did not. That led to problems in the early church.

In this case, Paul said that well-meaning believers were arguing over dietary restrictions and holy days. The issues those first Christians were arguing about were not essential matters of faith and practice. Instead, they were secondary issues of Christian liberty — issues where believers are free to exercise different practices without disobeying the Word of God. We're reminded of the Jerusalem Council in Acts 15. There, a question arose — is it necessary for Gentiles to be circumcised upon coming to faith in Christ?

The apostles agreed that circumcision was not necessary for salvation or sanctification. But they said it was non-negotiable "that you abstain from thing offered to idols, from blood, from things strangled, and from sexual immorality" (Acts 15:29). Here's the point — some aspects of our faith are non-negotiable, while others are matters of Christian liberty. When it comes to the latter, "let each be fully convinced in his own mind" without shaming a brother or sister who sees things differently.

## August 16 – When Being Quiet Is Best

*"Do not speak in the hearing of a fool, for he will despise the wisdom of your words." (Proverbs 23:9)*

You've heard the serenity prayer — "God, grant me the serenity to accept the things I cannot change, the courage to change the things I can, and the wisdom to know the difference." That's a beautiful, powerful prayer, but maybe there's one more phrase that needs to be added — "and help me to know when to keep my mouth closed." It seems that all of us struggle with knowing when to shut our mouths, and consequently we end up saying things we wish we could take back.

Today's verse reminds us that it's entirely possible for you to be right about something and still need to be quiet. Solomon said, "Do not speak in the hearing of a fool." That is, don't enter into a conversation with someone who chooses to remain ignorant. Why? Because "he will despise the wisdom of your words." Rather than being persuaded by your wisdom, a fool will actually hate your wisdom and make a mockery of you. Not everyone wants to hear what you've got to say.

For that reason, it's best that we keep our convictions to ourselves when we're convinced they're going to fall on deaf ears. Jesus said something similar — "Do not give what is holy to the dogs; nor cast your pearls before swine, lest they trample them under their feet, and turn and tear you in pieces" (Matthew 7:6). It's absurd to place jewels in a pig pen, and sometimes it's just as absurd to share the truth with those who refuse to hear it. God help us all to know when to speak up and when to shut up.

## August 17 – The Mere Edges of His Ways

*"Indeed these are the mere edges of His ways, and how small a whisper we hear of Him! But the thunder of His power who can understand?" (Job 26:14)*

As Job reflected on all his sorrow, he didn't neglect to remember the amazing power of God. In Job 26, he recounted God's power in creation. Among other things he said, "He stretches out the north over empty space; He hangs the earth on nothing. He binds up the water in His thick clouds" (Job 26:7-8). The fact is that God created everything out of nothing, and even now the whole of creation is being held together by His power. Despite what evolutionists say, without God there is no creation!

How difficult is it for the Lord to be the Creator and Sustainer of all there is? Job said it was like nothing at all to God — "these are the mere edges of His ways." The entire created order is only a blip on the radar screen of God's power. Job further reflected: "How small a whisper we hear of Him!" As awesome as creation is, it is not even a hint of God's real power. He is able to do "exceedingly, abundantly above anything we ask or think" (Ephesians 3:20). We've only witnessed the whisper of His power!

Job asks a question we all need to consider — "the thunder of His power who can understand?" If the whisper of God's power is already overwhelming to us, how in the world could we comprehend "the thunder of His power"? Think of it like this — earth and the created order are God's whisper, while heaven and the hereafter are His thunder. It's for good reason God is going to resurrect us with a glorified body. As we are, there's no way any of us could survive the glorious thunder of His power in heaven. What an awesome God we serve!

## August 18 – Avoid the Doctrinally Divisive

*"Now I urge you, brethren, note those who cause divisions and offenses, contrary to the doctrine which you learned, and avoid them." (Romans 16:17)*

As Paul closed out his epistle to the Roman believers, he provided some final practical instructions designed to spur God's people toward holiness. In today's verse, Paul mentioned the approach believers should take in regard to those who spread divisive doctrines. First, Paul said we need to "note those who cause divisions and offenses." Just like taking notes of noteworthy items in class, we should make a mental note of those who refuse to be peacemakers in the Body of Christ.

Divisions and offenses could be any number of things. Sometimes people cause divisions simply because they have a combative, argumentative personality. In Proverbs, Solomon says those "who sow discord among brethren" are an abomination to the Lord (6:19). Christ has called us to make peace with one another by resolving our differences. He has not called us to keep things stirred up just because we didn't get our way. And clearly, He's not pleased with those who divide brothers with false doctrine.

So then, Paul says we need to note those who divide the flock, and especially those who raven the fold with heresy. Not only should we make note of them, but Paul says we are to "avoid them." Understand that avoiding someone is only a last resort, after all attempts at reconciliation have been exhausted. But if the divisive person will not listen to you or godly friends or the church, then it is your Christian duty to avoid them. Otherwise, they can begin to tear down your faith and cause you to sin.

## August 19 – God Chooses Fools Like Us

*"For you see your calling, brethren, that not many wise according to the flesh, not many mighty, not many noble, are called. But God has chosen the foolish things of the world to put to shame the wise, and God has chosen the weak things of the world to put to shame the things which are mighty."* (1 Corinthians 1:26-27)

When Paul wrote his first letter to the church at Corinth, he had his hands full. The church at Corinth was known for its spiritual immaturity and wickedness, and Paul spent the majority of his letter dealing with their shortcomings. And yet, he began the letter by reminding the church that God had called him to preach the Gospel (1:17). He helped them understand that while the Gospel is the power of God to salvation for all who believe, it is foolishness to a world that is perishing (1:18).

Of course, we know the Gospel is not really foolishness, but it appears to be lunacy to those who don't know Christ. It's for good reason that God would choose what appears to be a foolish message to reveal His saving power. God also chooses fools like us to accomplish His work! Paul helped his readers understand that they were not among the wise, mighty, or noble. That's not quite the power of positive thinking, self-help gospel approach we see in much of the world today.

And yet, Paul had a purpose — to help us understand that God doesn't often call the wise, mighty, or noble. Instead, he often chooses folks like us — simple, weak, and burdened. But why would God do that? Paul answers that question — "that no flesh should glory in His presence." God chooses to use fools like us so that when great things are accomplished through us, only He can get the glory. If you feel like you're "not enough," that's OK — you're just the sort of person God loves to use.

## August 20 – The Preaching We Need

*"And my speech and my preaching were not with persuasive words of human wisdom, but in demonstration of the Spirit and of power, that your faith should not be in the wisdom of men but in the power of God." (1 Corinthians 2:4-5)*

Paul had already identified himself as a preacher of the Gospel in Chapter 1, and in Chapter 2 he wanted his readers to understand his sermon methodology. Paul was a man of learning. From his youth, he was raised to be a Pharisee, sitting at the feet of prominent, learned men like Gamaliel. And when he made a missionary trip to Athens he was surrounded by pagan gods, but even there he demonstrated his knowledge of secular learning by quoting Greco-Roman poets (Acts 17:28).

Though he probably could've held his own on any debate stage, when he came to Corinth he did not elect to share some sort of doctoral dissertation. Instead, he said, "My speech and my preaching were not with persuasive words of human wisdom." There's not always something wrong with human reason — we know the human race has made many amazing discoveries! And yet there is a power much greater than anything carnal — it is the Spirit-born wisdom that comes from above.

Paul said his preaching was "in demonstration of the Spirit and of power." What is Spirit-filled preaching? Simply put, Spirit-filled preaching is biblical preaching. The same Spirit who authored the Bible also adds His power to the preaching of the Word. The goal of the preacher is not to deliver some new word — it is to reveal the time-tested truth of Scripture. The Spirit-filled, powerful preaching we desperately need in our churches encourages us to place our faith in the Lord rather than men.

## August 21 — God Is the Lord of the Harvest

*"Who then is Paul, and who is Apollos, but ministers through whom you believed, as the Lord gave to each one? I planted, Apollos watered, but God gave the increase." (1 Corinthians 3:5-6)*

The Corinthians were well acquainted with both Paul and Apollos. As with many churches, Paul helped plant the church at Corinth, and following his conversion to Christ, Apollos was sent to shepherd the new church. The Corinthians had clear admiration for the men who helped form their congregation, but in some cases admiration turned into division. Some who had been impacted by the ministry of Paul begin to swear allegiance to him, while others aligned themselves with Apollos.

Paul had to address the unholy division that splintered the church. He helped the Corinthians understand that both he and Apollos were only "ministers through whom you believed." He wanted to remind them that only God was responsible for their salvation. He used the beautiful analogy of sowing and reaping — "I planted, Apollos watered, but God gave the increase." His words remind us that while each minister does his own part, only God is the Lord of the harvest.

The salvation of the lost, the sanctification of the saved, and the planting of churches — all of it happens because our God is the Lord of the harvest. Even the ministers who facilitate salvation and discipleship would not be in their positions if it weren't for God. We need to keep this in mind — while all of us might have pastors or teachers we prefer to listen to, we need to understand that all of them are just flawed men tending the Lord's harvest. God alone deserves the glory and the praise!

## August 22 – The Power of the Kingdom

*"For the kingdom of God is not in word but in power." (1 Corinthians 4:20)*

Words are something we use every day. We speak words, read words, write words, type words, etc. Our thought patterns even consist of words! Some people are not very good at using words. My experience is that most people either excel in math and science or in English and logic. For those who aren't big fans of language arts, writing a book report or delivering a speech can be a terrifying proposition. Thankfully not everyone has to make a living primarily out of words.

And yet, there are many others who have their livelihood directly tied to words — the President, governors, professors, pastors, etc. All of them attempt to make great use of their language as they convey ideas and attitudes. In today's verse, Paul reminds us the kingdom of God is not primarily about words. That statement seems ironic, especially since our faith is anchored to the many words of Scripture. In this case, Paul is talking about an abundance of words that may or may not be biblical.

At Corinth, there were a good number of teachers troubling Paul and persuading the masses. Paul wanted us to understand that while the kingdom of God includes words, it is much more concerned with God's power. In the case of Paul, God's preaching had power because it was based on the Gospel. Only the power of God has the potency to see the lost saved and the saved sanctified. May God help us all to move beyond mere words of human reason by tapping into the power of the Holy Spirit.

## August 23 – Entering into God's Presence

*"Enter into His gates with thanksgiving, and into His courts with praise. Be thankful to Him, and bless His name. For the LORD is good; His mercy is everlasting, and His truth endures to all generations." (Psalm 100:4-5)*

I know we live in a day where people elect to remain more secluded, choosing virtual interaction through social media rather than face-to-face fellowship. And yet there are times when we invite others into our homes, and we also receive invitations as well. When you are invited to someone else's house, how do you enter their home? Do you come in loud and boisterous? Do you kick your shoes off and make yourself at home in the La-Z-Boy? I'm guessing you were probably raised better than that.

There is a better way to enter someone's home — saying hello, thanking your friends for the invite, and perhaps even bringing a gift. Have you ever thought about your entrance into the presence of God? The psalmist said we should "enter into His gates with thanksgiving, and into His courts with praise." Gratitude and glory are two sure ways into the presence of God. And likewise, if you have an ungrateful spirit that refuses to praise the Lord for all He's done, you won't experience His presence.

Why should we come into God's presence with thanksgiving and praise? There are too many reasons to mention, but the psalmist gives us three — "the LORD is good; His mercy is everlasting, and His truth endures to all generations." The goodness of God assures us of His character, the mercy of God assures us of His kindness, and the truth of God assures of His authority. If God's goodness, mercy, and truth are not enough to compel you to praise, then you need to make sure you truly know Him.

## August 24 — The Consequences of Alcohol Use

*"Who has woe? Who has sorrow? Who has contentions? Who has complaints? Who has wounds without cause? Who has redness of eyes? Those who linger long at the wine, those who go in search of mixed wine." (Proverbs 23:29-30)*

When I was a child, I can remember a pack of cigarettes selling for about a dollar. I can even remember seeing cigarette vending machines in fast-food restaurants. My, how times have changed! These days, a pack of cigarettes goes for about $5. Cartons of cigarettes are now more than $50! A mission team from our church went to New York City in late 2015. Upon walking into a convenience store, a member of the team read a sign that said, "It is unlawful to sell cigarettes in New York City for less than $10.15 a pack." Talk about sticker shock!

Why are cigarettes so expensive? In many places, it's because so many taxes have been attached to cigarettes. It's seems the powers-that-be are attempting to eliminate cigarette smoking altogether. There would certainly be many positive results if cigarettes went away — fewer people would get cancer, money used for cigarettes could be used for other things, etc. I hope the time comes when no one will want to smoke anymore.

While our culture has cracked down on tobacco, it seems that alcohol has received a free pass. That's very unfortunate, especially since alcohol kills just as many people as tobacco and heart disease. The words of Solomon here are very clear — if you want to waste your life, become an alcoholic. Many would agree that the Bible condemns alcoholism, but there's nothing wrong with a few drinks. Not only can alcohol use be a bad witness for a Christian, but it is also poor stewardship. As with tobacco, the price of alcohol is also astronomically high. Wouldn't we be better off sticking with water, coffee, tea, juice, etc.? I don't know about you, but "as for me and my house," we will abstain from alcohol.

# August 25 — Marriage, Divorce, and Remarriage

*"Now to the married I command, yet not I but the Lord: A wife is not to depart from her husband. But even if she does depart, let her remain unmarried or be reconciled to her husband. And a husband is not to divorce his wife." (1 Corinthians 7:10-11)*

The Bible is very clear that marriage was created by God Himself: "Therefore a man shall leave his father and mother and be joined to his wife, and they shall become one flesh" (Genesis 2:24). Jesus quoted these foundational words when He issued His own teaching on marriage. Jesus said, "So then, they (husband and wife) are no longer two but one flesh. Therefore what God has joined together, let not man separate" (Matthew 19:6). Many marriage vows include the phrase, "'til death do us part." When a man and a woman marry, it is God's will for them to remain together until one or both of them die.

That said, the Bible does grant two allowances for divorce. One is adultery (Matthew 5:32, 19:9) and the other is abandonment (1 Corinthians 7:15). A person is not forced to divorce for these reasons. In fact, the Bible says that God hates divorce (Malachi 2:16) and wants us to seek reconciliation when possible (1 Corinthians 7:15). Though God hates divorce, He does NOT hate divorced people. He died to save them just as He died to save everyone else.

While the Bible grants two allowances for divorce, even an "admissible" divorce doesn't guarantee remarriage. Today's verses show us there are two options once a divorce has taken place: remaining single or reconciling with the former spouse. An exception to this would be the death of the former spouse: "A wife is bound by law as long as her husband lives; but if her husband dies, she is at liberty to be married to whom she wishes, only in the Lord" (1 Corinthians 7:39).

## August 26 — What's New?

*"That which has been is what will be, that which is done is what will be done, and there is nothing new under the sun." (Ecclesiastes 1:9)*

We live in a culture where many folks strive for originality. I guess there's a thrill that comes with being the first person to do something or discover something. While there are some brand new things that come along, for the most part we are standing on the shoulders of those who've gone before us. Rather than being original, we should seek to be biblical — whether that involves something old or something new.

I've heard well-meaning Christians say, "I want a new word from God." Perhaps they mean that they want God to give them a new perspective on their current situation. If that's the case, I think we can all appreciate the request. But could it be that in our search for something new, we gloss over the old? We have a time-tested Word from God contained in the sixty-six books of the Holy Bible. Every line of Scripture is "God-breathed, and profitable for doctrine, reproof, correction, and instruction in righteousness, that the man of God may be complete, thoroughly equipped to every good work" (2 Timothy 3:16-17).

That being the case, we would be much better off digging into the time-tested Word of God rather than trying to search for some new truth somewhere else. "The grass withers and its flower falls away, but the Word of the Lord endures forever" (1 Peter 1:24-25). Anchor your life to the time-tested Word of God.

## August 27 — A Time for Everything

*"To everything there is a season, a time for every purpose under heaven." (Ecclesiastes 3:1)*

And you thought these words were part of a Byrds song released in 1965! To the contrary, these words go all the way back to the wisest man who ever lived — Solomon. In beautiful, picturesque language, he reminds us that there is a time for everything that happens. Of course, that includes all the good times — the birth of a child, being healed of a disease, laughing with friends. I don't know about you, but as I look back through life I have much to be thankful for. God has blessed me with some great family and friends who have transformed my life. He's provided my every need. I thank God for all the good things of life!

But as there is a time for all those mountaintop experiences, there is also time for the valley. There is a time to die, a time to weep, and a time to mourn. We welcome the mountains of life, but we dread the valleys. If this verse does anything, it should remind us that our human experience is going to be filled with all sorts of outcomes and emotions. We will experience the highest of highs and the lowest of lows. When the hard times come, we must remember the words of this passage.

God has sovereign control over everything that happens on this earth and He can see us through the good times and the bad. While we don't know what the future holds, if we know Jesus we know the One who holds the future. We do well to remember that "He has made everything beautiful in its time" (Ecclesiastes 3:11). No matter what, let's continue to hold on to the One who holds all things in His hands.

## August 28 – A Man of Few Words

*"Do not be rash with your mouth, and let not your heart utter anything hastily before God. For God is in heaven, and you on earth; therefore let your words be few." (Ecclesiastes 5:2)*

Studies have found that men say about 7,000 words a day. Sounds like a lot, doesn't it? Not really, when you consider that women average about 20,000 words a day! That's a lot of talking! But both sexes only average about 500-700 words a day of real value — words that are meant to communicate an item of importance to both parties. Clearly, many of us love to talk.

It has been well-said that God gave us two ears and one mouth so we can listen twice as much as we talk. Think about the words you say throughout the course of the average day. Who or what are most of your words about? I know some people that seem interested in talking only about themselves. I know others that want to tell you all about their families. Rarely do some of those people ever take an interest in you or your family. Perhaps our conversation is an indication that we've become too focused on ourselves.

Rather than spending all our time talking, we ought to stop and listen for the still, small voice of God (1 Kings 19:12). Listening for God's voice begins by spending time in prayer and the study of His Word. The way I see it, prayer is the time we spend talking to God. Bible study is the time He talks to us. Though He may not speak audibly, He communicates with His children by the indwelling presence of the Holy Spirit. So then, let's vow to speak less and listen more — especially to our Savior Jesus.

## August 29 – No One is Perfect

*"For there is not a just man on earth who does good and does not sin." (Ecclesiastes 7:20)*

If I asked you to think of the greatest people in the world, who would you think of? I'm sure many would think of Dr. Billy Graham who was one of the great preachers and evangelists of the 20th century. Through his Gospel ministry, thousands upon thousands of folks have come to faith in Jesus Christ. His service to God forced him to spend much time away from family and friends, but he willingly made the sacrifice.

Others might think of Mother Teresa. She was born in Macedonia, but lived the remaining years of her life in Ireland and India. She founded the "Missionaries of Charity" through which many people were cared and provided for — those with AIDS, leprosy, tuberculosis, etc. So amazing were her contributions that the Catholic Church recognized her as a saint in December 2015. Mother Teresa literally gave her life for the welfare of the poor.

Surely these were two of the finest people to ever grace the planet, but as good as they were, neither of them were perfect. In fact, the Bible says that no one is perfect — we all sin and fall short of the glory of God (Romans 3:23). Being the sinners we are, God knew we couldn't save ourselves. That's why He sent His only begotten Son, Jesus, to take on human flesh and die in our place. Christ is the only perfect person who ever lived — He "was in all points tempted as we are, yet without sin" (Hebrews 4:15). We may be sinners, but thank God we've got a sinless Savior!

## August 30 – The Result of Wisdom

*"If the ax is dull, and one does not sharpen the edge, then he must use more strength; but wisdom brings success." (Ecclesiastes 10:10)*

Have you ever attempted to cut down a tree or split wood? I've split my fair share of wood and there's one thing I can tell you for certain — I'd much rather use a sharp ax than a dull one. Will a dull ax split wood? I know firsthand that it will because I've used a dull ax on several occasions. But using a dull ax will cause a man to take many more swings to split the same piece of wood that could've been chopped easily with a sharp edge.

Wisdom is the sharp edge of our lives. It begins with a saving knowledge of Jesus Christ. Have you trusted in His death, burial, and resurrection as a complete payment for your sins? And of course, once we have trusted Christ, like newborn babies we must "desire the pure milk of the word, that you may grow thereby" (1 Peter 2:2). Daily time spent in God's Word will supply us with the wisdom we need to be successful in all life's pursuits.

Another great way to gain wisdom is through education. I've heard people discourage education before, implying that a man who trusts God doesn't really need "book learning" — he just needs to rely on the Holy Spirit. Obviously, we should lean on the Holy Spirit each moment of our lives, but we should also sharpen our minds through continuing our education. Whether it's in the classroom or at home, let's continue to "grow in the grace and knowledge of our Lord and Savior Jesus Christ" (2 Peter 3:18).

## August 31 — What It's All About

*"Let us hear the conclusion of the whole matter: Fear God and keep His commandments, for this is man's all. For God will bring every work into judgment, including every secret thing, whether good or evil." (Ecclesiastes 12:13-14)*

The Book of Ecclesiastes is a unique book. Written by Solomon, he chronicles the highs and lows of the human experience. His assessment of our situation is not too encouraging: "'Vanity of vanities,' says the preacher, 'All is vanity'" (Ecclesiastes 12:8). Solomon tells us that many of the things we place great emphasis on have very little eternal consequence. And even at times when we're trying to do the right things and live with integrity, life can still blow up in our face.

Knowing the volatile nature of our human experience, Solomon offered some much needed advice. He gives us two guiding principles — fear God and keep His commandments. What does it mean to fear God? Fearing God speaks of a holy reverence we have for our Maker, knowing that if we are disobedient to His commands, He can punish us as He pleases. Some suggest that we no longer need to fear the Lord. They say, "We are New Testament Christians." They need to understand that fearing God is for those under grace just as it was for those under the Law. The early church was found "walking in the fear of the Lord" (Acts 9:31) and so should we.

As we have a holy reverence for God, we will find ourselves obeying His commands. God knows we are sinners. We will never keep all His commands perfectly on this side of heaven, but that doesn't mean we shouldn't try. Remember, Paul said, "I can do all things through Christ who strengthens me" (Philippians 4:13). Our lives can be transformed by fearing God and obeying His Word!

## September 1 — The Lord's Supper

*"For as often as you eat this bread and drink this cup, you proclaim the Lord's death till He comes." (1 Corinthians 11:26)*

While observances vary according to denomination, there are two main elements to any Lord's Supper service — the bread and the cup. When Jesus instituted the Lord's Supper, He was actually celebrating the Passover with His disciples at what is called the Last Supper. Jesus picked up the bread, "broke it and said, 'Take, eat; this is My body which is broken for you; do this in remembrance of Me'" (1 Corinthians 11:23-24). The bread of the Lord's Supper represents the body of Jesus that was broken and battered as He suffered on the cross for our sins.

The cup of the Lord's Supper represents the blood of Jesus — "This cup is the new covenant in My blood. This do, as often as you drink it, in remembrance of Me" (1 Corinthians 11:25). The Old Covenant included a system of sacrifices and ceremonial laws that had to be obeyed. The blood of those animal sacrifices was never able to remove anyone's sins. That's why God sent His Son Jesus to be "the Lamb of God who takes away the sin of the world" (John 1:29). Only through the blood of Jesus can anyone receive salvation and the forgiveness of sins (Hebrews 9:22).

What's the importance of the Lord's Supper? It is a time of memorial where we look back and reconsider the precious body and blood of Jesus Christ that was offered up as a payment for our sins. Clearly, we thank God for the resurrection of our Savior, but in celebrating the Lord's Supper we proclaim "the Lord's death 'til He comes" (1 Corinthians 11:26). As the old song says, "I will cling to the old rugged cross, and exchange it someday for a crown."

## September 2 — Spiritual Gifts

*"There are diversities of gifts, but the same Spirit. There are differences of ministries, but the same Lord. And there are diversities of activities, but it is the same God who works all in all. But the manifestation of the Spirit is given to each one for the profit of all." (1 Corinthians 12:4-7)*

When a person places his faith in Jesus Christ, he confesses that Jesus is Lord and receives the Holy Spirit. The Holy Spirit serves a variety of functions — conviction, leadership, intercession, illumination, etc. When the Holy Spirit indwells a believer, He gives the new Christian a spiritual gift. There are a variety of spiritual gifts mentioned in the New Testament. In fact, there are five separate lists of spiritual gifts (Romans 12:6-8, 1 Corinthians 12:8-10, 28-30, Ephesians 4:11, 1 Peter 4:9-11).

Every Christian possesses at least one gift that is to be used "for the profit of all" (1 Corinthians 12:7). Clearly we don't all possess the same gifts, and that's the way God intended for it to be. In this chapter, Paul says the church is the "body of Christ." If each member of the body does its part, then you've got a healthy body. If several members fail to do their job, then you've got a weak, handicapped body.

It's time for all of us to discern our spiritual gifts and put them to use. If you're unsure of your gift, talk to your pastor. He will probably ask you to complete a spiritual gifts inventory and pray with you about your gift. If each of us will do our part, we can have a strong body of Christ! The world has yet to see what can be done through a church in which all members are using their spiritual gifts for the glory of God!

## September 3 — The Supremacy of Love

*"And now abide faith, hope, love, these three;
but the greatest of these is love." (1 Corinthians 13:13)*

Faith is one of the most important elements of our Christian faith. By faith, great men and women of God have "subdued kingdoms, worked righteousness, obtained promises, stopped the mouths of lions, quenched the violence of fire, escaped the edge of the sword" and a multitude of other amazing things (Hebrews 11:33-34). As the old hymn says, "Faith is the victory that overcomes the world" (cf. 1 John 5:4).

The Word of God also commends the importance of hope. The Bible says God allows us to go through tribulations so we can develop perseverance, character, and finally hope (Romans 5:3-4). Hope is a faithful expectation that God is going to do exactly what He said He would, including coming back to take all those who have placed their trust in Him. As believers, we keep hope on our horizon as we walk through all the trials of life.

As great as faith and hope are, love stands far above both of them. Paul goes to great lengths to explain that it doesn't matter how talented or gifted someone is. It's doesn't even matter how much a person is able to accomplish. If someone labors apart from love, then their work is done in vain. Love is not envious, haughty, proud, rude, self-seeking, easily provoked, evil-minded, or happy about sin. Love IS patient, kind, glad about truth, and it bears, believes, hopes, and endures all things. Let the love of God lead you today and every day.

## September 4 — Speaking in Tongues

*"I thank my God I speak with tongues more than you all; yet in the church I would rather speak five words with my understanding, that I may teach others also, than ten thousand words in a tongue." (1 Corinthians 14:18-19)*

In his letter to the Corinthians, Paul clearly identifies speaking in tongues as a spiritual gift. The Bible indicates that tongues-speaking is like all the other gifts — it has been given for the edification of the church. But tongues are also "a sign, not to those who believe but to unbelievers" (1 Corinthians 14:22). We see this use of tongues many times in the Book of Acts. On the day of Pentecost, God allowed men to speak in tongues so those of different languages could hear the Gospel in their own tongue (Acts 2).

But there are times God might allow a believer to speak in an unknown tongue so the church can be built up. On those occasions, the Bible says there are to be "two or at the most three" (1 Corinthians 14:27). When those two or three begin to speak, there is to be someone available to interpret the utterance. "If there is no interpreter, let him keep silent in church, and let him speak to himself and to God" (1 Corinthians 14:28). Based on these standards, it's not hard to see that there are some unbiblical things taking place.

On the other hand, there are some who teach that speaking in tongues is no longer a gift of the Holy Spirit. Nowhere does the Bible say that tongues have ceased — only that they will cease when Jesus comes back because they will no longer be needed (1 Corinthians 13:8-10). So when it comes to the gift of tongues, the Bible says we shouldn't seek it, but neither should we forbid it when practiced biblically.

## September 5 — The Power of Forgiveness

*"'Come now, and let us reason together,' says the LORD, 'though your sins are like scarlet, they shall be as white as snow; though they are red like crimson, they shall be as wool.'" (Isaiah 1:18)*

Today's passage captures the words of Isaiah as He shares the Word of God with the inhabitants of Jerusalem and Judea. Through the leadership of several ungodly kings, God's people had done a great deal to incite the wrath of God by disobeying His commands. Isaiah told his fellow Jews that God was going to bring judgment, but that even in the midst of judgment there would be an opportunity for forgiveness.

The Lord invited His people to "reason" with Him. The word could also be translated "judge." In essence, God is inviting His people to join Him in judging between the fate of a faithful, repentant believer, and an ungodly, rebellious sinner. The fate of those who are willing and obedient will be forgiveness. Even though his/her sins are red as scarlet or crimson — much like a dirty stain on a garment — they shall be washed white as snow or wool. God cleanses us of our sins when we turn to Him!

Yet, the opposite can be said for those who refuse to repent. God says, "If you refuse and rebel, you shall be devoured by the sword" (Isaiah 1:20). God promised that His people would be judged and removed from their land, and so they were by the Babylonians. If God didn't allow His rebellious people to go unpunished back then, what would lead us to believe He would allow us to go unchecked now? Why not receive the cleansing touch of God that comes through faith in Christ? Once we've trusted Him, let's be sure to keep a close account by seeking His cleansing on a daily basis.

# September 6 — The Heart of the Gospel

*"For I delivered to you first of all that which I also received: that Christ died for our sins according to the Scriptures, and that He was buried, and that He rose again the third day according to the Scriptures, and that He was seen by Cephas, then by the twelve." (1 Corinthians 15:3-5)*

The word "Gospel" comes from an old English word — *godspel*. It means "good news," and has its roots in the Greek *euangelion* (meaning "good message"). When Christians speak of the Gospel, we are talking about the good news of Jesus Christ. The good news is that Jesus was born of a virgin, lived a perfect sinless life, was met with the hatred of the religious establishment, was arrested, tried, and condemned to death. The heart of the Gospel lies in the fact that "Christ died for our sins according to the Scriptures."

The death of our Savior may not seem like good news. Think about it — are we glad when someone very dear to us passes away? Of course not, but the death of Jesus was like no other death. Without His suffering and death, there would be no payment for the sins of mankind. "Without shedding of blood there is no remission (of sin)" (Hebrews 9:22). Jesus died to pay the price, "was buried, and … rose again the third day according to the Scriptures." Without the cross, there would be no need for a resurrection — but without a resurrection, the cross would be useless. Because Jesus rose again, we can also receive the promise of everlasting life (John 3:16).

When Jesus rose from the dead, Paul says He was seen first by Peter (Cephas) and then the twelve — a reference to the remaining disciples. After that, He was seen by hundreds of others before He ascended back to heaven. And the best news is, He's coming back to save all those who belong to Him! "Even so, come, Lord Jesus" (Revelation 22:20).

## September 7 – A Good Model for Worship

*"And one cried to another and said, 'Holy, holy, holy is the L*ORD *of hosts; the whole earth is full of His glory!'" (Isaiah 6:3)*

Isaiah was an amazing prophet of God. He records his call to ministry in Isaiah 6. I think the circumstances surrounding his call would serve as a great model for Christian worship. Notice first that Isaiah was forced to look *upward*. He beheld the awesome glory of God when he "saw the Lord sitting on a throne, high and lifted up, and the train of His robe filled the temple" (v. 1). Isaiah witnessed some amazing fiery angelic creatures flying around God's throne, declaring His holiness. By looking up toward the presence of God, Isaiah learned why the Lord is worthy of worship.

The glory of God caused Isaiah to be afraid as he looked *inward*. He said, "Woe is me, for I am undone! Because I am a man of unclean lips, and I dwell in the midst of a people of unclean lips" (v. 5). Isaiah thought his death was certain because he realized he was a sinful man standing in the presence of a holy God. I think Isaiah's response was entirely appropriate. When we consider the perfection of God, we should consider the imperfection of man. Only then can we understand our need for forgiveness, which Isaiah also received: "Your iniquity is taken away, and your sin purged" (v. 7).

Having looked upward and inward, Isaiah was then called to look *outward*: "Whom shall I send, and who will go for us?" (v. 8) Without hesitation, Isaiah responded, "Here am I! Send me" (v. 8). He was eager to take God's message to a lost and dying world. How awesome would it be if we followed Isaiah's example each week in worship? Each time we come to God's house, we should look upward to consider His holiness, look inward to consider our sinfulness, and look outward to consider those whom He loves and sent His Son to save.

## September 8 – The Source of All Wisdom

*"And when they say to you, 'Seek those who are mediums and wizards, who whisper and mutter,' should not a people seek their God? Should they seek the dead on behalf of the living? To the law and to the testimony! If they do not speak according to this word, it is because there is no light in them." (Isaiah 8:19-20)*

People seek wisdom in a number of places. Often we seek the counsel of friends or coworkers. Some folks turn to books or even to the magazines that line the supermarket shelves. Still others turn to TV, radio, internet, and a number of other media outlets. I even know some people who look to horoscopes seeking wisdom for the day. Back in Isaiah's day, some of his countrymen were in the habit of visiting mediums and spiritists to gather wisdom from the dead!

Isaiah profoundly reminds Israel of her source of wisdom: "Should not a people seek their God?" Why are we so inclined to seek wisdom from other humans when the supernatural Creator of the universe has given us all the guidance we need? His wisdom is contained the Word of God — "to the law and to the testimony!" Rather than running to gather conventional wisdom, we should run to take our Bible off the shelf and seek the insight that rests with our Maker.

Just in case anyone were unclear, Isaiah offered his people one more condition — "If they do not speak according to this word, it is because there is no light in them." In other words, if what someone is telling us does not line up with the Bible, it needs to be discarded. All of us should seek to be like the Bereans of Acts 17 — we should be in the habit of searching the Scriptures to confirm the things we have seen and heard. The psalmist said it best, "Thy Word is a lamp unto my feet, and a light unto my path (Psalm 119:105).

## September 9 — The Names of Jesus

*"For unto us a Child is born, unto us a Son is given; and the government will be upon His shoulder. And His name will be called Wonderful, Counselor, Mighty God, Everlasting Father, Prince of Peace." (Isaiah 9:6)*

In the midst of pronounced judgment, God provided His people with hope — a Son who would come from God. Of course, we know Jesus was and is the Son of God. Prophesied hundreds of years before His coming, the Word of God tells us that Jesus would be called "Wonderful." The Hebrew word translated "wonderful" means marvelous, extraordinary, and hard to understand. Jesus Christ is so amazing that we could not even understand Him apart from the illuminating power of the Holy Spirit!

Isaiah also prophesied that Jesus would be called "Counselor." On the night before He died, Jesus promised He would not leave His followers as orphans, but He would send the Holy Spirit who would guide them into all truth (John 16:13). When we need counsel, we should always begin with our Savior and His inerrant Word. Jesus is also identified as "Mighty God." This stands as proof that Jesus was and is completely and fully God. "In the beginning was the Word, and the Word was with God, and the Word was God" (John 1:1).

The Son of God is also called "Everlasting Father." This is not to say Jesus is the Heavenly Father, but that He acts fatherly toward all those who surrender to Him. Just as a father loves and sacrifices for His child, so Christ loves and sacrifices for those who belong to His Father. And of course we can't miss the "Prince of Peace." Remember that Jesus was able to stop the winds and waves by saying "Peace, be still" (Mark 4:39). Just as He brought peace to the waters, He can bring peace to your life.

## September 10 — The Kingdom of Christ

*"The wolf also shall dwell with the lamb, the leopard shall lie down with the young goat, the calf and the young lion and the fatling together; and a little child shall lead them. ... They shall not hurt nor destroy in all My holy mountain, for the earth shall be full of the knowledge of the LORD as the waters cover the sea." (Isaiah 11:6, 9)*

We live in a world filled with violence. Terrorism has become a word used all too often. We read stories of men and women strapping bombs to themselves, walking in public places, and blowing themselves up in an attempt to kill many others. We read stories of one nation invading another nation and countries joining in coalition to attack someone else. Will the violence ever end?

When you think about it, violence is as old as the earth. Adam and Eve had two sons — Cain and Abel. You may recall that both men brought sacrifices to God. The Lord respected Abel's offering, but He rejected Cain's because he refused to offer his best. Overtaken with jealousy and anger, Cain "rose up against Abel his brother and killed him" (Genesis 4:8). Since that time, brother has fought against brother, sister against sister, and neighbor against neighbor.

The good news is that the violence won't last forever. Jesus Christ is the Prince of Peace, and the Bible says He is coming to establish His kingdom following His victory at the battle of Armageddon (Revelation 16:16). Christ's eternal kingdom will be filled with peace, pictured in the beautiful words of our passage — a wolf with a lamb, leopard with the goat, etc. All the violence will be done away, and we will spend our eternity enjoying everlasting rest and endless peace. If you have placed your faith in Jesus, your future is bright indeed!

## September 11 — Liberty in the Spirit

*"Now the Lord is the Spirit; and where the Spirit of the Lord is, there is liberty." (2 Corinthians 3:17)*

Maybe you've heard that praise song that says, "My chains are gone, I've been set free; my God, my Savior has ransomed me." The good news is that, in Christ, sinners are set free! No longer are we bound by chains of death and wickedness. Of course, we'll never be perfect on this side of heaven — we still battle with sin in our daily lives. But the eternal effects of sin have been removed from our lives when we receive the unconditional love and forgiveness that comes through faith in Jesus. Praise God, we've been set free!

As awesome a reality as that is, some have interpreted their liberty to be a license to sin. I've heard some professing believers say things like, "I'm at liberty to live how I want since Jesus has saved me." Nothing could be further from the truth. While the grace of God freed us from the ceremonial obligations of the Law (animal sacrifices, ceremonial washing, etc.), we have not been released from God's moral demands, nor would we want to be. God's moral code is summarized in the Ten Commandments, and they are still binding on Christians today.

For that reason, we should not use our liberty in Christ as a license to sin. Be honest — when faced with a decision about something, have you ever said, "Well, I know God doesn't want me to do this, but it's OK because He'll forgive me later"? If we ever take this sort of attitude, we need to check our hearts to see if Jesus is really the Lord of our lives. Those who have genuinely been born again will seek to live according to the precepts of God's Word. Think of it like this — through Christ we are FREE to please the Lord and fulfill our God-given purpose. That's the only life worth living!

## September 12 — Down But Not Out

*"We are hard-pressed on every side, yet not crushed; we are perplexed, but not in despair; persecuted, but not forsaken; struck down, but not destroyed — always carrying about in the body the dying of the Lord Jesus, that the life of Jesus also may be manifested in our body." (2 Corinthians 4:8-10)*

Think about some of the hard times you've been through — the death of a spouse or a child, the diagnosis of cancer, the loss of a job, etc. When you were in the midst of the valley, were you tempted to throw in the towel? Be honest — when life was the hardest, did you consider taking your own life? If we're not careful, everyone can reach the point of despair — that point when you think there is no hope left and life is not worth living.

Paul suffered immensely for the cause of Christ: "In labors more abundant, in stripes above measure, in prisons more frequently, in deaths often. From the Jews five times I received forty stripes minus one. Three times I was beaten with rods; once I was stoned; three times I was shipwrecked; a night and a day I have been in the deep; in journeys often, in perils of waters, in perils of robbers, in perils of my own countrymen, in perils of the Gentiles, in perils in the city, in perils in the wilderness, in perils in the sea, in perils among false brethren; in weariness and toil, in sleeplessness often, in hunger and thirst, in fastings often, in cold and nakedness — besides the other things, what comes upon me daily: my deep concern for all the churches" (2 Corinthians 11:23-28). And we thought we had it rough!

Yet, amid all the suffering, Paul and his companions didn't lose heart. He explains in verse 16: "Even though our outward man is perishing, yet the inward man is being renewed day by day." When Satan harasses you about your present, remind him of his future! You may be down, but you're not out! Through Christ, you are more than a conqueror (Romans 8:37).

## September 13 – The Judgment Seat of Christ

*"For we must all appear before the judgment seat of Christ, that each one may receive the things done in the body, according to what he has done, whether good or bad." (2 Corinthians 5:10)*

Have you ever stood before a judge? I'm not trying to dig up unpleasant memories, but look back and remember how you felt. As you awaited his judgment, were you nervous? Excited? Uncertain? Many men and women have stood nervously before a judge as they awaited his judgment. You might say, "I've never stood before a judge and I don't intend to." Hopefully you will never stand before a judge on this earth, but God's Word assures all of us that we will stand before the Judge of heaven and earth.

Paul said that "we must all appear before the judgment seat of Christ." Paul was talking to believers in this passage, but that doesn't mean it will only be Christians who will stand in judgment before Jesus. Hebrews 9:27 tells us that "it is appointed to man once to die and after that the judgment." No one will be exempt from standing before Christ. Some have called the judgment of unbelievers "the Great White Throne Judgment." The title is taken from Revelation — "Then I saw a great white throne and Him who sat on it … anyone not found written in the Book of Life was cast into the lake of fire" (20:11, 15).

For those who have trusted Christ, they won't have to be afraid of being cast into hell. Yet, that doesn't mean believers will escape judgment. The amount of our heavenly reward will be determined by the work we have done for Christ on this earth. Let me be clear — we gain heaven ONLY through faith in Jesus, but the amount of our eternal reward will be determined by our works. For that reason, we are wise to lay up treasure in heaven "where moth and rust do not destroy and thieves do not break in and steal" (Matthew 6:20).

## September 14 — Unequally Yoked

*"Do not be unequally yoked together with unbelievers. For what fellowship has righteousness with lawlessness? And what communion has light with darkness? ... Therefore, 'Come out from among them and be separate,' says the Lord. 'Do not touch what is unclean and I will receive you.'"* (2 Corinthians 6:14, 17)

What does it mean to be "unequally yoked"? A yoke is a wooden crosspiece fastened over the necks of two animals and attached to the plow or cart that they are to pull. It keeps the two animals in close proximity so they can work together to accomplish a task. So then, Paul was saying that believers should not enter into a close relationship with unbelievers. In particular, Christians should not date or marry unbelievers, nor should they develop close friendships with unbelievers.

Why would God command such a thing? Is it because Christians are better than unbelievers? Of course not! The Bible says all of us have sinned and fallen short of the glory of God (Romans 3:23). God did not give His people this command so they could exalt themselves above those who reject Jesus. Rather, the purpose of this command is to keep us in close relationship with our brothers and sisters in Christ. Drawing close to unbelievers can draw, and has drawn, many believers away from God.

While Christ-followers should not develop close relationships with unbelievers, believers should not stop associating themselves with the lost altogether. Remember that Jesus was criticized as "a friend of tax collectors and sinners" (Matthew 11:19). That's because He was willing to go to those whom society cast aside. He loved them and pointed them to His Heavenly Father. We should do the same thing, but we must beware that our association doesn't turn into a relationship that would distract us from serving God.

## September 15 – It's Time to Say So

*"Oh, give thanks to the LORD, for He is good! For His mercy endures forever. Let the redeemed of the LORD say so, whom He has redeemed from the hand of the enemy." (Psalm 107:1-2)*

The phrase "His mercy endures forever" appears forty-one times in the Bible and in all twenty-six verses of Psalm 136. Mercy is compassion or forgiveness shown toward someone whom it is within one's power to punish or harm. When we speak of the mercy of God, we're saying God would have been justified in annihilating our forebears, Adam and Eve, when they sinned in the Garden of Eden. But instead of destruction, He chose mercy — the kind of mercy that would send His only begotten Son to this world to suffer and die in our place.

Because of God's limitless mercy, every member of the human race has an opportunity to experience redemption. "Redeem" means to gain or regain possession of something (or someone) in exchange for payment. When Adam and Eve chose sin, they made us all adversaries of God. The only way humans could be reconciled was for sin's price to be paid. Through His death, burial, and resurrection, Jesus came and paid the price we could not pay. In other words, His shed blood was the only payment that could salvage us from hell.

If we have placed our faith in Jesus alone for salvation, the good news is that we are redeemed. If we've been redeemed, we need to open our mouths wide and "say so." We need to worship God every day through a personal walk with Him. We need to join God's people in praising the name of Jesus. We need to go to a lost and dying world and share with them how they can be redeemed as well. You've been bought with a price — let the world know! It's time to say so!

## September 16 – You Can Be Rich

*"For you know the grace of our Lord Jesus Christ, that though He was rich, yet for your sakes He became poor, that you through His poverty might become rich." (2 Corinthians 8:9)*

Our culture is obsessed with wealth. Everywhere you turn, it seems that someone's got a "get rich quick" scheme they're trying to market. While some have achieved amazing wealth, the reality is that most of us will struggle to make ends meet. And for those who are able to pay the bills, it can still be a challenge to save resources for the future. Bottom line — very few of us will become wealthy in this life.

But just because we may not achieve great wealth doesn't mean we can't be rich. Spiritual wealth has been made available to us through the Son of God, Jesus Christ. Our verse says that Christ "was rich." Does that mean He was a successful businessman and multi-millionaire? Of course not. In fact, Jesus once said, "Foxes have holes, and birds of the air have nests, but the Son of Man has nowhere to lay His head" (Luke 9:58). He may not have had great earthly wealth, but being God Himself, He possessed great heavenly glory!

Yet, "He became poor." In other words, He took on our human flesh, lived a life of poverty, suffered at the hands of evil men, and endured the cruel mockery of death by crucifixion. Why would the God of the Universe leave such wealth to accept such poverty? Jesus said it is because we are loved by God (John 3:16). The good news of the Gospel is that "you through His poverty might become rich." Through faith in Jesus, you can become the richest person in the world! Someone once said, "The Christian life doesn't pay much, but the benefits are out of this world."

## September 17 – A Cheerful Giver

*"So let each one give as he purposes in his heart, not grudgingly or of necessity; for God loves a cheerful giver. ... Thanks be to God for His indescribable gift!" (2 Corinthians 9:7, 15)*

Everyone loves to receive gifts. Just think about all the occasions we get gifts — birthdays, Christmas, wedding showers, graduation, Mother's/Father's Day, etc. Most of us love to receive, but we're not always quite as excited about giving. Yet, Jesus once said, "It is better to give than to receive" (Acts 20:35). So then, it usually lights our fire to receive, but it also ought to make us just as happy to give to God and to others.

In today's verse, Paul instructed the Corinthians about a collection that was to be received for him and his missionary companions so the work of the Lord could continue. Paul could have told them to give just because it was the right thing to do, but instead he appealed to their attitude. He instructed his readers to give, not just because they had to, but because they saw it as an opportunity to join God in His work. The word translated "cheerful" in this verse is the Greek *hilaros*, from which we get our English word "hilarious." God loves a hilarious, joy-filled giver!

If we ever run into trouble giving to the work of the Lord and to others who might be in need, we should stop to remember what God has given us. Paul provided the reminder — "Thanks be to God for His indescribable gift." What was he talking about? The earth? Our houses? Our clothes? Our food? While all those are great gifts, the greatest Gift of all is Jesus Christ, freely given so you and I might be saved. God willfully sacrificed for us, now it's our turn to joyfully give back to Him!

## September 18 — Our Weapons of Warfare

*"For the weapons of our warfare are not carnal but mighty in God for pulling down strongholds, casting down arguments and every high thing that exalts itself against the knowledge of God, bringing every thought into captivity to the obedience of Christ, and being ready to punish all disobedience when your obedience is fulfilled." (2 Corinthians 10:4-6)*

Have you ever stopped to think about all the weaponry that is available to the men and women of our armed forces? There are planes — fighter planes, bombers, etc. There are sea-faring vessels — battleships, submarines, etc. And of course, there are a multitude of guns — handguns, rifles, semi-automatics, Gatling guns, etc. Our brave men and women have some amazing weapons, but none of them are as powerful as the weapons available to God's children.

Paul said, "The weapons of our warfare are not carnal." In other words, God has not called us to take up arms and be crusaders against infidels. Rather, our weapons are spiritual — prayer, Bible study, fellowship, evangelism, etc. These spiritual weapons are powerful enough to "pull down arguments … and every high thing that exalts itself against God." The lies and deceits of Satan are no match for the truth of God. By sharing His truth with others, we can bring our thoughts and theirs "into captivity to the obedience of Christ." Are you captivated by God?

These spiritual weapons are not only effective for confronting the lies of the world, but they are also necessary to deal with sin and deceit in the church. There were some in Corinth who were trying to discredit the ministry of Paul. Rather than taking up swords and clubs to come against those who were reviling him, he armed himself with truth that would lead to church discipline. Considering this, let's put on the whole armor (Ephesians 6:10ff) and use our spiritual weaponry for the glory of God.

## September 19 – An Angel of Light?

*"For such are false apostles, deceitful workers, transforming themselves into apostles of Christ. And no wonder! For Satan himself transforms himself into an angel of light." (2 Corinthians 11:13-14)*

It might surprise you to know that Satan can and does transform himself into an angel of light. In this verse, light is clearly a reference to that which is good, as opposed to darkness (evil). We know Satan is evil, but would masses of people really be attracted to him if he presented himself in all his darkness? Maybe some would, but it is doubtful God's people would be attracted to his darkness. For that reason, he often presents himself as something good to those in the church, in hopes that he might deceive them.

In the Garden of Eden, Satan called into question the Word of God and acted as though he had Eve's best interest in mind. Unfortunately, she and her husband bought in to Satan's lie, and all of us now pay for the sins they committed. Satan is so good at presenting himself as God's messenger because he is a master of taking God's perfect truth and counterfeiting it into something it is not. In other words, his deceptions sound good, but they are often laced with just enough error to make them wrong. He has many false teachers in this world who perpetuate his lies.

Because our adversary is very crafty, we need to prepare ourselves to discern his tricks. The only way we will know whether or not we're dealing with something godly or something satanic is to know the Word of God. The psalmist said, "Thy Word is a lamp unto my feet and a light unto my path" (Psalm 119:105). God's Word will cast light onto Satan's lies and help us stay on the right path. All the more reason for us to read and meditate on God's Word every day (Psalm 1:1-2).

## September 20 – The Source of My Trust

*"Woe to those who go down to Egypt for help, and rely on horses, who trust in chariots because they are many, and in horsemen because they are very strong, but who do not look to the Holy One of Israel, nor seek the Lord." (Isaiah 31:1)*

Where do you place your trust? When you think about it, there are a variety of options. Some place their trust in our economy. They think that through stocks, bonds, and various other investments they will find the security they're searching for. Some place their trust in education. Through academic pursuits, they hope to find the answers to all of life's questions. Some have placed their trust in hard work. They're convinced that if they can just land the right job and work long and hard enough, all of life's details will fall in place.

While financial security, education, and hard work are all commendable, we misplace our trust if we put it in any of these. We're not the first ones to place our trust in the wrong things. Years after Israel was released from their bondage in Egypt, they had a new threat surrounding them. The Assyrians threatened to attack and displace Israel from their land. Rather than turning to "the Holy One of Israel" to protect them, they actually turned to Egypt — the nation that had enslaved them for over 400 years!

Unfortunately, Israel failed to remember how God had delivered them through many amazing signs, wonders, and miracles. Is it possible that we also forget to trust in God? Why is it that we turn to everything and everyone besides our Creator when we are in need of help? The truth is that if we would keep our trust in God, we probably wouldn't find ourselves in a mess to begin with. Let's make the declaration of the psalmist our own — "Some trust in chariots, and some in horses; but we will remember the name of the Lord our God" (Psalm 20:7).

## September 21 — Who Is the Lord?

*"For the LORD is our Judge, the LORD is our Lawgiver, the LORD is our King; He will save us." (Isaiah 33:22)*

Over 6,000 times, the Old Testament makes reference to "the Lord." In the original Hebrew, the word is *Yahweh* and it means "the existing One." When Moses had his encounter with the burning bush (Exodus 3), he discovered that it was actually the Lord in the midst of the flame. When Moses asked the Lord about His name, He responded, *"Ehyeh asher ehyeh"* — "I AM WHO I AM." In other words, the Lord was saying, "I'm not dependent on anyone or anything for My existence. To the contrary, everything depends on Me."

Through the prophet Isaiah, Yahweh says He is our Judge. The Bible says, "It is appointed to man once to die, and after that the judgment" (Hebrews 9:27). Every member of the human race will have to stand before Yahweh in judgment. The only thing that will save us from eternal torment is faith in Jesus Christ. And even before our death, the Lord judges our daily activity and shows us how we can live more acceptable to Him.

The Lord is also our Lawgiver. Through His Word (the Bible), He has shown us how we can please Him. That's all the more reason for us to be students of the Word, that we may be "complete, thoroughly equipped for every good work" (2 Timothy 3:17). Yahweh is also our King. This world has many presidents, prime ministers, dictators, etc., but there is One that stands far above them all — the "King of kings and Lord of lords" (Revelation 19:16). And thankfully, the Lord is our Savior. When we were all bound for hell because of our sin, Yahweh came to spare us from everlasting punishment. Who is the Lord? He is the One who deserves ALL our praise!

## September 22 — Examine Yourself

*"Examine yourselves as to whether you are in the faith. Test yourselves. Do you not know yourselves, that Jesus Christ is in you? Unless indeed you are disqualified." (2 Corinthians 13:5)*

Paul wrote these words to the church at Corinth. Isn't it interesting that he asked members of the church to "examine themselves"? That is, he was asking them to search their hearts to make sure they were really Christians. Paul's instruction makes one thing clear — it is entirely possible for lost people to talk like Christians, dress like Christians, and even attend church like Christians, while being unsaved and unreconciled to God.

Every one of us should search our hearts as well. Are we certain that Jesus Christ is the Lord of our lives, or could it be that we are just playing church? One of the best indicators of being born again is assurance of salvation. If we have been born again by the grace of God, then there should be no doubt in our minds that we belong to Jesus. The Apostle John said, "These things I have written to you who believe in the name of the Son of God, *that you may know that you have eternal life*, and that you may continue to believe in the name of the Son of God" (1 John 5:13).

Another indicator of one's salvation is the fruit of their life. Jesus once said, "You will know them by their fruits." In other words, a believer will act like a believer. That being the case, what are your actions saying about your soul? If you have examined yourself and you have no doubt that Jesus is the Lord of your life, then let the world know! "Let your light so shine before men, that they may see your good works and glorify your Father in heaven" (Matthew 5:16).

## September 23 — A Different Gospel

> *"I marvel that you are turning away so soon from Him who called you in the grace of Christ, to a different gospel, which is not another; but there are some who trouble you and want to pervert the gospel of Christ. But even if we, or an angel from heaven, preach any other gospel to you than what we have preached to you, let him be accursed."* (Galatians 1:6-8)

Paul wrote his letter to the Galatians to contend against some who had come and perverted the true Gospel. The false teachers were called Judaizers, and they taught that unless people kept the Law of Moses, they could not be saved. This question was actually taken up by the early church in Jerusalem. Speaking of Old Testament believers, Peter said, "We believe that through the grace of our Lord Jesus Christ we shall be saved in the same manner as they" (Acts 15:11). In other words, the true Gospel is that humans — past, present, and future — can only be saved by faith in God.

Paul did not mince words. He said that a person — even an angel — should be condemned if he preached another gospel. Why was he so passionate about the false teachers? Because they were teaching a false gospel that would mislead people and prevent them from turning to Jesus in faith alone.

There are still many false teachers promoting a different gospel today. There are some who preach a prosperity gospel — that through faith in Jesus a person can be rich and receive all their heart desires. Others teach a social gospel — that the Christian life is not really about faith in Jesus, but helping to eliminate human suffering. And yes, there are still some who teach a works gospel — that we must do good works to earn our salvation. Don't be deceived! There is only one Gospel — through faith alone in Jesus' death, burial, and resurrection we can become children of God. All other "gospels" are to be rejected and refuted with the Good News of the Bible.

## September 24 – Wait on the Lord

*"He gives power to the weak, and to those who have no might He increases strength. Even the youths shall faint and be weary, and the young men shall utterly fall, but those who wait on the Lord shall renew their strength; they shall mount up with wings like eagles, they shall run and not be weary, they shall walk and not faint." (Isaiah 40:29-31)*

I don't know about you, but I'm not a very patient person. I consider myself to be pretty driven and determined — I don't like to wait for things to get done. If you're like me, I think it's fair to say that we're not the only ones responsible for our impatience. Our culture has conditioned us to despise waiting. A fast-food chain released a jingle several years ago that said, "Your way, right away." To this day, some pizza delivery companies will give you the pizza if it's not there in thirty minutes or less!

Waiting on pizza is one thing, but have you ever had to wait on God? If you've been following Jesus for any amount of time, I bet you've had times when you asked God to do something. You read the words of Jesus to "ask, seek, and knock" (Matthew 7:7), so you didn't give up — you persevered in your praying. But no matter how frequently or fervently you prayed, it just seemed like God didn't hear you because nothing was happening.

Trust me — it's happened before and it will happen again. In those times when you're eager for God to answer, learn to wait on Him. God has taught me some of my greatest lessons while I was waiting on Him. He has matured me more as a child of God while waiting on Him than at any other time. I promise you this — if you prayerfully and patiently wait on God, soon you will find yourself soaring with eagles, running with the energized, and walking with the faithful. Let me tweak Momma's advice — "The best things in life come to those who wait ON THE LORD."

## September 25 — One in Christ Jesus

*"There is neither Jew nor Greek, there is neither slave nor free, there is neither male nor female; for you are all one in Christ Jesus." (Galatians 3:28)*

This is one of the most awesome and most misinterpreted verses in all the Word of God. It's awesome for obvious reasons — through faith alone in Jesus Christ we are born into the family of God. It doesn't matter about a person's race, gender, socioeconomic status, etc. — anyone can become a child of God through faith in Jesus Christ. It's sad to say that we still live in a world filled with discrimination, but it's good to know that all forms of self-centered discrimination don't exist with God! It's been well-said that "the ground is level at the foot of the cross."

This amazing verse is often misused by those who try to make the Bible say something different than what it actually says. Some people have used this verse to say that wives are no longer obligated to provide faithful submission to their husbands. Others have used this verse to argue that women should be allowed to serve as pastors and deacons in our local churches. Many others have twisted this verse to say a variety of things.

Could they be correct in their interpretations? Let's ask ourselves — when a Jewish person receives Jesus, does he cease to be Jewish? When a woman asks Christ to save her, does she stop being a woman? Of course not! This verse does not mean there are no longer races, genders, etc., when God saves us. What it means is that He saves us and unites us in spite of our differences. Through Jesus, we are all one great big family of God! So then, let's glory in that which unites us — not those things that divide us.

## September 26 — Right on Time

*"But when the fullness of the time had come, God sent forth His Son, born of a woman, born under the law, to redeem those who were under the law, that we might receive the adoption as sons." (Galatians 4:4-5)*

I'll have to admit that I'm not a patient person. I don't like waiting for anything very long at all, but waiting is an essential part of life. For instance, I love a good hamburger, but let's say I took the raw beef out of the fridge, formed it into a bloody patty, and slapped it on a bun. Would I be wise to eat an uncooked hamburger? Of course not, unless I'm a fan of E. coli. I'd be much wiser to fire up the grill and cook the meat thoroughly. Burgers are great at the right time.

Paul tells us it was in the fullness of time that God sent His Son into the world. Basically, that means God sent His Son to earth at just the right time. According to God's salvation plan, there were some things that needed to happen before Jesus came — mankind falling into sin, God giving us His Law, His people consistently disobeying the Law, etc. At the perfect time, God sent His only begotten Son to be born of the virgin Mary in the little town of Bethlehem.

Paul tells us that Jesus was "born under the law." That is, just like us, He was required to keep every precept of the Law. The Bible tells us that Jesus was the only man to ever keep the Law perfectly — "(Jesus) was in all points tempted as we are, yet without sin" (Hebrews 4:15). Because He kept the Law perfectly, He was the only one fit "to redeem those who were under the law." That is, He was the only One capable of paying the price for our sins. Because He paid the price, through faith in Him we can be adopted as sons and daughters of God forevermore, never to be orphaned again!

## September 27 — Fruit of the Spirit

*"The fruit of the Spirit is love, joy, peace, longsuffering, kindness, goodness, faithfulness, gentleness, self-control. Against such there is no law." (Galatians 5:22-23)*

I love all kinds of fruit. I love apples, oranges, strawberries, peaches, kiwi — have I made you hungry yet? My favorite fruit of all is banana. It makes a quick breakfast, or it can provide a nice little energy pick-me-up in the middle of a busy day. I'm no fruit expert, but I do know that bananas grow on banana trees. I've never witnessed a banana tree producing apples, oranges, or anything else but bananas. As Jesus said, "Every tree is known by its own fruit" (Luke 6:44).

In Galatians 5, Paul lists the fruit of an unbeliever's life and that of a Christian as well. If a person's life matches the fruit of an unbeliever, then it's proof they have not placed faith in Jesus. On the other hand, if a person demonstrates Christian fruit, then it serves as proof of salvation. Of course, that's not to say that someone could not fake being a Christian. It's entirely possible for someone to fool you and me, but there is no one that can fool God. He knows everything — even the secret things of our lives (Romans 2:16).

If we have truly surrendered ourselves to God through faith in Jesus, our lives will be filled with selfless love, abounding joy, constant peace, patience toward others, kindness that is noticeable, goodness that is expressible, faithfulness that is durable, gentleness that is touchable, and self-control that is radical. Who would create a law against such things? Instead of outlawing these things, the world wants to experience them for themselves. Through our lives, let's encourage them to "taste and see that the Lord is good" (Psalm 34:8).

## September 28 — Keep on Going

*"And let us not grow weary while doing good, for in due season we shall reap if we do not lose heart." (Galatians 6:9)*

Have you ever thrown in the towel? Did you ever feel like you were working as hard as you could without seeing any results? I think this has happened to a lot of people trying to get in better shape. I'll use the example of a runner. When he begins his exercise regimen, he's only able to run a quarter mile, but then it turns into half a mile in just a week. Before long he's running a full mile and feels like he could begin to go the second mile. He's losing weight, his clothes are falling off, and everyone talks about how good he looks.

Then it happens — he hits the wall. He's running just as much as he ever did, but the pounds are no longer melting away. No one has commented about his weight loss in weeks. Let's face it — this guy is dangerously close to throwing his hands up and going back to his Little Debbie cakes. He says to himself, "What's the use? Nothing I do seems to work anymore."

Satan is elated when we give up! When we're tempted to throw in the towel, we've got to remind ourselves that if God has called us to it, He'll see us through it. What has God called you to do? What adversity has landed in your path? You may not see the results you want right now, but whatever you do, *do not give up!* When you stop persevering, you play right into the devil's hands. Claim this awesome promise of God — you will reap a harvest at just the right time if you don't give up!

## September 29 — Sealed by the Holy Spirit

*"In Him you also trusted, after you heard the word of truth, the gospel of your salvation; in whom also, having believed, you were sealed with the Holy Spirit of promise, who is the guarantee of our inheritance until the redemption of the purchased possession, to the praise of His glory." (Ephesians 1:13-14)*

Allow me to unpack the great theology of these verses. Paul says the Christians at Ephesus trusted the Lord Jesus as their Savior after they heard the word of truth. This should tell us how pivotal the Bible is to our salvation. In another place Paul said it like this: "Faith comes by hearing, and hearing by the word of God" (Romans 10:17). The only way a person can be saved is to place their faith in Jesus after hearing the good news.

Once a person places his faith in Jesus, he is "sealed with the Holy Spirit of promise." The word "promise" is applied to the Holy Spirit here because Jesus promised His Heavenly Father would send a "helper" to those left on earth following His resurrection. At the moment we accept Jesus as our Savior, the Holy Spirit actually takes residence in our hearts and guides us into all truth (John 16:13). The Holy Spirit's presence in our lives is a guarantee of future glory, namely heaven. A Christian is eternally secure because he can never be lost again after the Holy Spirit enters his life.

Paul speaks of a "purchased possession," but what is he talking about? The Bible answers that question too: "Do you not know that your body is the temple of the Holy Spirit who is in you, whom you have from God, and you are not your own? For you were bought at a price" (1 Corinthians 6:19-20). So, when Paul speaks of the purchased possession, he's talking about us — every person that has trusted in Jesus. Jesus bought us out of sin and death through His own blood. What an awesome Savior He is!

## September 30 — Saved by Grace

*"For by grace you have been saved through faith, and that not of yourselves; it is the gift of God, not of works, lest anyone should boast. For we are His workmanship, created in Christ Jesus for good works, which God prepared beforehand that we should walk in them." (Ephesians 2:8-10)*

These verses tell us how and why God saves lost people. Paul could not have been any clearer: "By grace you have been saved." What is grace? Someone once gave me this definition — God's Riches At Christ's Expense. Basically, grace is God's gift of salvation to us, but it cost Him the life of His only begotten Son. We receive the grace of God "through faith." The only way anyone can be saved is through faith in Christ's death, burial, and resurrection. That's it!

Some say that faith alone sounds too easy. They say if we do enough good works, we will be saved. In fact, it was this issue that caused the Protestant Reformation. The Catholic Church taught (and still teaches) that a person has to work in conjunction with God's grace to experience salvation, while the Protestants (Martin Luther, Huldrych Zwingli, John Calvin, etc.) taught that no one can do enough work to be saved. That's why grace is a gift — it cannot be earned. In this case, I think it's clear to see that the Protestants were on the right side of the Bible.

We know how God saved us, but why? Paul tells us God has had a plan from all of eternity and that we were included in His plan. "We are His workmanship." In other words, He has created us for the purpose of walking in good works. This might seem contradictory to what we've already discussed, but rest assured it is not. We don't do good works because we want to be saved — we do good works because we *are* saved and want to please our Father in all we do. How will you please Him today?

## October 1 — Healed by His Stripes

*"But He was wounded for our transgressions, He was bruised for our iniquities; the chastisement for our peace was upon Him, and by His stripes we are healed. All we like sheep have gone astray; we have turned, every one, to his own way; and the Lord has laid on Him the iniquity of us all." (Isaiah 53:5-6)*

The most detailed Old Testament account of the Messiah is found in Isaiah 53. Some 700 years before Jesus was born, Isaiah prophesied in great detail about the life and death of Jesus Christ. Verse 5 tells us that God's Messiah, Jesus, would be wounded, bruised, chastised, and whipped. When we read the Gospels, we see that Jesus was slapped in the face, His beard was pulled out, He was spit on, and of course He was beaten over and over again with a vicious whip called a "cat of nine tails" that had bits of metal, bone and rock on the ends of the straps.

But Isaiah is clear that Jesus was not brutalized for His own sins — He was punished in our place! He never did anything wrong! The Bible tells us Jesus "was in all points tempted as we are, yet without sin" (Hebrews 4:15). We were the ones who deserved to be tortured, because the Bible also says that each of us "have sinned and fall short of the glory of God" (Romans 3:23). Yet, when we could not pay for our own sins, Jesus stepped into our place and paid the price.

As Jesus hung on the cross, just think about what took place. The Heavenly Father laid all our sins on Jesus — He became the perfect sacrifice. Because He was willing to take our punishment, these verses tell us that we can experience peace and healing. Through faith in Jesus we are healed, not of our physical infirmities, but of our sin-sickness. When God forgives our sins, we have peace in our relationship with Him forever.

## October 2 — The Danger of Anger

*"'Be angry and do not sin': do not let the sun go down on your wrath, nor give place to the devil." (Ephesians 4:26-27)*

Someone once explained to me the subtle difference between anger and danger — only the letter "d" separates the two. When a person is angry, danger is probably not too far away. Anger leads to all sorts of danger. One can be physical danger. We've all heard stories where someone got so enraged that he started beating someone else. Sadly, many women and children have felt the effects of anger and physical abuse.

Anger also produces emotional danger. I know the old saying says, "Sticks and stones may break my bones, but words will never hurt me." Unfortunately, that saying is very wrong. For many people, their emotional scars run deeper than anything they've ever suffered physically. Many people struggle with saying some very nasty things when they are angered. Even though the person may not have meant what they said, the damage was done when the words were spoken.

And of course, the greatest damage anger does is spiritual. Anger adversely affects our relationship with God. So what's the solution? The Bible says, "Be angry and do not sin." That tells me that anger, in and of itself, is not sin — but left unchecked, it can lead to sin. Remember, our Savior angrily turned over the money-changer tables in the temple, but in His case He was angry for a righteous cause. But self-serving anger needs to be snuffed out as soon as we feel it rising within us. Otherwise, we will "give place to the devil" to have a field day in our lives. Ask God to remove your anger and replace it with His love and forgiveness.

## October 3 — Expose the Works of Darkness

*"And have no fellowship with the unfruitful works of darkness, but rather expose them. For it is shameful even to speak of those things which are done by them in secret." (Ephesians 5:11-12)*

Probably the most misquoted verse in all the Bible is "Judge not, that you be not judged" (Matthew 7:1). Jesus commanded that we should not make premature judgment of any person or situation, but that's not to say we should fail to use spiritual discernment as we assess the facts. Remember, Jesus also said, "You will know them by their fruits" (Matthew 7:16, 20). The Apostle John also instructed us to "test the spirits" (1 John 4:1). In other words, God has called us to use spiritual criteria to determine if something is good or evil.

That brings us to today's verses. God has commanded us to "be holy, even as I am holy" (1 Peter 1:16). That means we are to separate ourselves from "the unfruitful works of darkness." Lying, stealing, adultery, pornography, etc. — all these and many more are the works of a lost person. Since God has saved us through faith in Jesus, He has called us to depart from these evil acts. Peter said it well — "We have spent enough of our past lifetime in doing the will of the Gentiles" (1 Peter 4:3).

Rather than doing evil deeds, God has called us to expose them. This is where it's easy for a Christian to get in trouble. We live in a culture that commands us to mind our own business. That's impossible for us as followers of Jesus. Christ has called us to be salt and light. Sharing the Gospel is the best way to illumine someone else's life. These verses not only instruct us to emphasize the good, but to expose the evil. Why? So God's people will be kept from the paths of sin. Make it your aim today to lovingly light the world by exposing the darkness.

## October 4 – Filled with the Spirit

*"And do not be drunk with wine, in which is dissipation; but be filled with the Spirit." (Ephesians 5:18)*

Alcohol is a major industry in our country. Every year, about $211 billion in alcoholic beverages are sold in America. I don't know about you, but I really don't have any use for alcohol for several reasons. First, it can be a bad witness. What if someone were to see me drinking alcohol? Would they be inclined to do the same? Also, it is poor stewardship because alcohol is expensive. Couldn't our money be used on something else? With all the other beverage alternatives, alcohol just seems to be unnecessary.

Of course, that's not to mention all the lives that have been ruined by alcohol. Just think of all the fights it has caused. Think of all the mothers who have lost their children because they were driving under the influence of alcohol. As a pastor, I routinely minister to people whose lives have been hijacked by booze. People have lost their jobs, homes, cars, and families all as a result of consistently filling themselves with intoxicating beverages.

There's got to be a much better way. Paul provides the alternative — "be filled with the Spirit." Filling oneself with alcohol leads to dissipation (wastefulness), but being filled with the Holy Spirit leads to a life beyond our wildest dreams. Understand that there's a difference in being "indwelt" by the Spirit and being "filled." The Holy Spirit came to indwell you when you placed your faith in Jesus, but being filled with the Spirit is something that occurs every day as you pursue a closer walk with God through prayer, Bible study, etc. Put away the spirits, and be filled with the Spirit!

# October 5 — The Whole Armor of God

*"Finally my brethren, be strong in the Lord and in the power of His might. Put on the whole armor of God, that you may be able to stand against the wiles of the devil." (Ephesians 6:10-11)*

Did you know there is someone plotting your destruction? There is someone who hates you so much that he is devising a plan to ruin your life and send you to hell. His name is Satan, and he is a powerful adversary. The Bible says he "walks about like a roaring lion seeking whom he may devour" (1 Peter 5:8). There's no way you or I could overcome a lion by ourselves, but sadly, there are people who try to overcome Satan every day in their own strength. He often chews them up and spits them out.

The truth is we are engaged in a daily battle. Yet, our battle is not against "flesh and blood" (Ephesians 6:12). In other words, we're not really warring against one another. Rather, our battle is against Satan and all his demonic minions. It is a battle we will not win by ourselves. The only way we can be victorious is to "put on the whole armor of God." Paul doesn't leave us to wonder what that armor includes.

First, we must put on the helmet of salvation which comes through faith in Christ. Then we must put on the breastplate of righteousness — that is, seeking to do the will of God at all times. Next, we must gird ourselves with the belt of truth. We've got to separate ourselves from all the lies of the devil, the father of lies (John 8:44). We must have our feet outfitted with the gospel of peace. We must share the good news with those who still need to hear. Finally, we take up the shield of faith for protection, and the sword of the Spirit (the Word of God) so we can resist our enemy. Only in arming ourselves this way will we cause the devil to flee from us (James 4:7).

## October 6 – To Live Is Christ

*"For to me, to live is Christ, and to die is gain."* *(Philippians 1:21)*

Have you ever been in a win-win situation? Perhaps something like this: Let's say it's your birthday. Your spouse and mother haven't talked about the details of your party, so both of them decide to make you a cake. Your spouse makes a nice big chocolate cake. Your mom makes a coconut cake. The good news is you love both, so no matter what you pick you come out a winner either way. Eat up and enjoy your birthday!

As followers of Jesus Christ, we are in the greatest win-win situation of all time. Paul said, "To live is Christ." In other words, Paul is going to live each day for the glory of God as long as God gives him life. Think about what life with Christ means. Jesus said, "I have come that they may have life, and that they may have it more abundantly" (John 10:10). As long as Jesus is the Lord of our lives, we have the promise of an abounding life on this earth.

But what happens when this life is over? Paul says, "To die is gain." Wait a minute — it sounds like he's calling death a good thing. Could that possibly be right? Absolutely — for a Christ-follower, death is the doorway into the greatest life we'll ever know. When a believer dies, there is no more suffering, pain, tears, sickness, sin, or anything else that causes harm. We'll be in the presence of Jesus forever and nothing could be greater than that! Let's agree with the Apostle Paul — each day with Jesus is a great day, but eternity with Him is even better! "Even so, come, Lord Jesus!" (Revelation 22:20).

## October 7 — The Name Above Every Name

*"Therefore God also has highly exalted Him and given Him the name which is above every name, that at the name of Jesus every knee should bow, of those in heaven, and of those on earth, and of those under the earth, and that every tongue should confess that Jesus Christ is Lord, to the glory of God the Father." (Philippians 2:9-11)*

These verses are part of what theologians call the Christ Hymn — a song used in worship by the early church. There are two main stanzas of the song. The first pertains to the humiliation of Jesus in verses 6-8. Paul tells us that Jesus was willing to leave the glory of heaven to come to earth and take on human flesh. Not only that, but He was willingly subjected to torture, "even the death of the cross." He humbly experienced the most awful torture anyone has ever endured.

But thank God the song has a second stanza! The first stanza details the humiliation of Jesus, but the second emphasizes His exaltation. By virtue of His death, burial, and resurrection, Jesus defeated death once for all. Therefore, God granted Him a name above every name — Jesus. The name Jesus is a transliteration of the Hebrew name *Yeshua*, meaning "Yahweh (God) is salvation" — a fitting name for the Son of God and the only Way of salvation (John 14:6).

Notice that the worship of Jesus doesn't stop at the front steps of the church. The Bible tells us that every person from every age is going to bow down at the feet of Jesus and acknowledge Him as King. Every person in heaven and earth is going to worship Him! Even those who have been cast into hell will acknowledge that Jesus is the Savior they refused to acknowledge while they were alive. Truly, there is no one like Him! Bless that wonderful name of Jesus!

## October 8 — Pressing On

*"Brethren, I do not count myself to have apprehended; but one thing I do, forgetting those things which are behind and reaching forward to those things which are ahead, I press toward the goal for the prize of the upward call of God in Christ Jesus." (Philippians 3:13-14)*

Unfortunately, I know many people are bound in shackles and chains. No, you won't find them in the local jail or state penitentiary. Their chains are not physical, rather they are mental and emotional. Too many people are imprisoned by the events of their past. Some people were victims of unspeakable abuse. Some people have experienced a life-altering tragedy. Others are imprisoned by the sins of their past. I've known more than one person who believes that God can no longer use them.

If anyone had a past, it was the Apostle Paul. In his letter to the Philippians, he tells us all about his strict Jewish upbringing. In fact, he was known as a "Hebrew of Hebrews" — a zealous Pharisee who had climbed to the top of his national ladder. In his zeal, he would go from town to town persecuting Christians. We know he was present when Stephen was stoned to death because the Bible says "the witnesses laid down their clothes at the feet of a young man named Saul (Paul)" (Acts 7:58).

After Jesus saved him on the road to Damascus (Acts 9), Paul's life was radically changed. He was transformed from a murderer to a missionary. Yet, Paul could have allowed his past to dictate his future. Instead, he chose to "forget those things which are behind" while "reaching forward to those things which are ahead." As a result, he became the greatest missionary the world has ever known. *Don't sacrifice your future on the altar of the past!* What do you need to leave behind today?

## October 9 — No Reason to Worry

*"Be anxious for nothing, but in everything by prayer and supplication, with thanksgiving, let your requests be made known to God; and the peace of God, which surpasses all understanding, will guard your hearts and minds through Christ Jesus." (Philippians 4:6-7)*

It's been said that death was walking toward a city one morning. A man noticed death on the scene and asked, "What are you going to do?" Death replied, "I'm going to take 100 people." The man was visibly shaken as a result of the bad news and hurried to warn everyone about death's plan. As evening fell, the man ran into death once more. "You told me you were going to take 100 people, so why did 1,000 die?" Death replied, "I kept my word. I only took 100 people — worry killed the rest."

That fictitious story has a very real meaning. Unfortunately we tend to worry about everything — health, bills, kids, school, work, terrorism, war, violence, etc. The list goes on and on. What's especially troubling is that Christians are not immune to worry — at times it seems that we worry more than many others. Has God really called us to live in fear and doubt? Of course not!

God has invited us to enjoy a worry-free life. He's even told us how to do it. Rather than worrying, we ought to come to God in prayer, thanking Him for the things He's already blessed us with. God invites us to go into detail about the things we're tempted to worry about. He invites us to cast all our anxieties on Him because He cares for us as a father cares for his child (1 Peter 5:7). When we leave our prayers with God, He takes the worry from us and replaces it with perfect peace. How good it is to know that worry-free living is only a prayer away through our Savior Jesus.

## October 10 — Creator and Sustainer

*"For by Him all things were created that are in heaven and that are on earth, visible and invisible, whether thrones or dominions or principalities or powers. All things were created through Him and for Him. And He is before all things, and in Him all things consist." (Colossians 1:16-17)*

Life is filled with some foundational questions such as, "How did we get here?" The secular humanist will probably tell you that there was a big bang about 14 billion years ago that set everything in motion. From there, evolution has been working non-stop to eliminate the weak and establish the strong. When I speak to someone of this opinion, I always ask, "If space, time, and matter didn't exist, how was a big bang even possible?" None of them have ever successfully answered that question.

Thankfully, we don't have to wonder how everything came into existence. The Bible is very clear: "In the beginning, God created the heavens and the earth" (Genesis 1:1). In today's verses, Paul goes a step further to tell us which member of the Trinity did the creative work. While God the Father and God the Holy Spirit were all involved in the creative work, Paul tells us that it was primarily God the Son (Jesus) through whom "all things were created."

Paul provides even further detail to clear up any ambiguity. It doesn't matter if something is visible or invisible, mighty or weak, permanent or passing — from the outhouse to the penthouse, Jesus is the Creator of ALL things. Just as amazing, He also sustains everything He created — "in Him all things consist." If Jesus were to stop caring for the created order, it would vanish in a millisecond. How awesome it is to know that the Creator and Sustainer of everything wants to be our Savior too!

## October 11 – The Balm of Gilead

*"Is there no balm in Gilead, is there no physician there? Why then is there no recovery for the health of the daughter of my people?" (Jeremiah 8:22)*

Including today's reference, the balm of Gilead is mentioned three times in the Bible. A balm is an aromatic, medicinal substance derived from plants. Gilead was an area east of the Jordan River, well known for its spices and ointments. Thus, the balm of Gilead was a high-quality ointment with healing properties. The Bible uses the balm of Gilead metaphorically as an example of something with healing or soothing powers.

Jeremiah was one of God's many prophets who tried to call the southern kingdom of Judah to repentance. Already they had seen their countrymen, Israel, carried away by the Assyrians. Now the Babylonians were breathing down their necks. All Judah had to do was turn back to God, but time and again they chose to "steal, murder, commit adultery, swear falsely, burn incense to Baal, and walk after other gods" (Jeremiah 7:9).

By speaking of Gilead, God wanted His people to know that healing was available. Just as there are balms and doctors in Gilead, so the Great Physician dwells in the heavens. The forgiveness and salvation He provides is much better than any medicine produced by a pharmaceutical company. And yet Judah was not healed because she wouldn't turn to the Healer. How about you? Is there a sin-sickness in your life? The Great Physician is on duty, but will you set aside time for an appointment? Let Him apply His healing balm to your suffering soul.

## October 12 – Something to Brag About

> *"Let not the wise man glory in his wisdom, let not the mighty man glory in his might, nor let the rich man glory in his riches; but let him who glories glory in this, that he understands and knows Me." (Jeremiah 9:23-24)*

Our moms always told us not to brag, but sometimes we just can't help ourselves. My goodness — sometimes we brag about nearly everything. We've been known to brag about the car we drive, the house we live in, the clothes we wear, the people we've met, the place we work, etc. Part of our fallen, sinful nature includes a desire to draw attention to ourselves rather than placing the focus on Jesus where it rightfully belongs.

We can take solace in knowing that we're not the first ones to suffer with a pride problem. God had to remind His people that they shouldn't brag about the things they held in high esteem. For instance, while wisdom is a fine thing, we shouldn't gush just because we know more than someone else. Physical strength is commendable, but we shouldn't gloat just because we can outlift or outrun our friends. Nor should we promote ourselves just because we have earned or inherited lots of money.

If any of us wants to brag on something or someone, let's brag on the Almighty God who created us. We ought to make much, not of ourselves, but of the Lord who loved us enough to send Jesus to pay the price for our sins through His death, burial, and resurrection. We should spend our time rejoicing that we can understand and know God because He initiated a relationship with us. It's OK to brag — just make sure you're bragging on Jesus!

## October 13 — Seasoned Speech

*"Let your speech always be with grace, seasoned with salt, that you may know how you ought to answer each one." (Colossians 4:6)*

Do you ever stick your foot in your mouth? We've all said things we wish we'd never said, but once the words are out of our mouths there's no way to reel them back in. Thankfully, God has not left us to wonder about the words we should speak. In today's verses, He tells us our speech should always be "with grace." Our words should be spiritual, wholesome, fitting, kind, sensitive, purposeful, complimentary, encouraging, truthful, loving, and thoughtful.

Paul also tells us that our conversation should be "seasoned with salt." I'm a salt lover. Some people are crazy about sweets, but I'm much more a salt and starch guy. I add salt to potatoes, eggs, mixed veggies, etc. To me, salt makes good foods taste even better. In our verses, I don't think Paul is talking about pouring salt on our tongues before we speak. The salt he's speaking of is the Gospel of Jesus Christ. Remember, Jesus told us we are "the salt of the earth" (Matthew 5:13).

While I personally enjoy the taste of salt, good flavor is not its primary purpose. Salt is a preservative. It has been used throughout countless generations to keep food from decay. When we act as the salt of the earth by sharing the good news of Jesus and the commands of His Word, we are turning back the decay that comes from secular worldviews and wicked lives. Today, make it your aim to season our culture with the Gospel of our Savior. It's the only way to prevent "truth decay."

## October 14 – Disciplined but Not Dead

*"I shall not die, but live, and declare the works of the Lord. The Lord has chastened me severely, but He has not given me over to death." (Psalm 118:17-18)*

I grew up in a great family with wonderful parents. I'm thankful I had parents who loved me enough to correct me when I was wrong. I didn't enjoy the correction at the time — several times I remember getting a pretty good whipping, though I'm sure I deserved more than I actually received. My parents corrected me pretty sternly, but they never beat me, and certainly not to the point of death. It wasn't their goal to kill me, but to correct my mistakes by showing me a different path.

There are times when the Lord has to "take us behind the woodshed." We have a merciful, compassionate Heavenly Father who is "slow to anger and abounding in mercy" (Psalm 103:8). When we disobey Him, He'll go to great lengths to redirect us, but sometimes we simply don't listen. On those occasions, God often does a great deal to get our attention. There are even times when He will send tragedy into our lives in order to correct us.

Some say God shouldn't do that. "If He really loved us, He'd allow us to be ourselves." Let me ask you — do you always allow your children to be themselves? If I see my son walking into the middle of oncoming traffic, I'm going to push him out of the way and correct him afterwards. Through correction, he will learn never to walk out into oncoming traffic. Thankfully, though God may often correct us, it's proof that we belong to Him and that we will "live and declare the works of the Lord."

## October 15 – The Day the Lord Has Made

*"This is the day the LORD has made; we will rejoice and be glad in it." (Psalm 118:24)*

If you've been in church any amount of time, you've probably heard someone quote these words. Perhaps even you have said these words yourself. Maybe you were walking into church and the greeter said, "Boy, it's a great day, isn't it?" And you responded, "Sure is — it's the day the Lord has made!" While any believer can appreciate that kind of enthusiasm in giving glory to God, this verse is not really talking about today.

Psalm 118 is a messianic psalm. That means it is a prophetic psalm that looks forward to the coming of God's promised Messiah, Jesus. The psalm says that Jesus is "the stone the builders rejected," but by God's power "He became the chief cornerstone" (Psalm 118:22). Verses 25-28 also make reference to the words that were shouted when Jesus entered Jerusalem during His triumphant entry: "Blessed is He who comes in the name of the Lord."

So, "the day" our verse is speaking of is not today, but it was looking forward to the day when Jesus would ride into Jerusalem to the cries of "Hosanna." We now know that Jesus made that ride into Jerusalem about 2,000 years ago just before His death, burial, and resurrection. We rejoice that Jesus was willing to pay such a price. Of course, every day is a gift from God and we should thank Him for every moment. But the greatest day was when Jesus willingly paid the price for our sins. "We will rejoice and be glad in it!"

# October 16 – God Blesses Trust and Hope

*"Blessed is the man who trusts in the* Lord, *and whose hope is the* Lord. *For he shall be like a tree planted by the waters, which spreads out its roots by the river, and will not fear when heat comes; but its leaf will be green, and will not be anxious in the year of drought, nor will cease from yielding fruit." (Jeremiah 17:7-8)*

Did you know that "In God We Trust" is the official motto of the United States? It was adopted in 1956 as an alternative or replacement to the unofficial motto of *E pluribus unum*, which was adopted when the Great Seal of the United States was created and adopted in 1782. "In God We Trust" first appeared on US coins in 1864. A law passed in a Joint Resolution by the 84th Congress declared IN GOD WE TRUST must appear on all currency. This phrase was first used on paper money in 1957 when it appeared on the one-dollar silver certificate. The first paper currency bearing the phrase entered circulation on October 1, 1957.

Some have argued that the motto should be removed from our currency, saying that it is an establishment of religion and thus it violates the First Amendment. Nothing could be further from the truth. Not only is it perfectly legal for our lawmakers to add the motto to whatever they wish, but it would be wise to place even more trust and hope in God.

We're all going to go through adversity, but today's verses remind us that God will always sustain those who have placed their trust in Him — even through the worst droughts and storms of our lives. Like a tree that flourishes in the midst of severe famine, God will cause His children to prosper in the midst of this dark and dry world. Of course, that doesn't mean we'll never experience any poverty, but it does mean God will sustain us through it all. So then, "taste and see that the Lord is good, blessed is the man who trusts in Him" (Psalm 34:8).

## October 17 – Life After Death

*"For if we believe that Jesus died and rose again, even so God will bring with Him those who sleep in Jesus." (1 Thessalonians 4:14)*

Each year since 1994, the Roper Center for Public Opinion Research has asked American adults what they believe about life after death. In 2014, 73 percent of American adults said they believe there is life after death. When you ask those same Americans to get more specific about heaven, hell, and the other details of the afterlife, responses vary tremendously. Simply stated, there is no consensus among Americans what they think about life to come.

Paul told his Thessalonian readers, "I do not want you to be ignorant, brethren" (v. 13). In other words, he didn't want his brothers and sisters in Christ to be uninformed about what happens to a Christian when he/she passes away. At the moment of their death, all Christians will be in Paradise with Jesus (Luke 23:43). In another passage, the Apostle Paul said, "We are confident, yes, well pleased rather to be absent from the body and to be present with the Lord" (2 Corinthians 5:8).

In today's passage, Paul is talking about the order of events when Jesus comes back. One day, there is going to be a shout from heaven, accompanied by the voice of an archangel and the trumpet of God (v. 16). When that occurs, those who have died in Christ will be resurrected. Their souls were already in Paradise with God, but now their souls will be reunited with their perfect bodies. Those believers who are alive when Jesus comes back will be "caught up together with them in the clouds to meet the Lord in the air" (v. 17). Praise God, "we shall always be with the Lord" (v. 17).

## October 18 — The Will of God

*"Rejoice always, pray without ceasing, in everything give thanks; for this is the will of God in Christ Jesus for you." (1 Thessalonians 5:16-18)*

In Christian circles, very few subjects have received more attention than the will of God. Books have been written on how to discern it. Sermons have been preached encouraging us to discover it. Prayers have been prayed asking God to reveal it. It is true that parts of God's will are different for each of us because we're all unique. I've found that God often reveals His specific plans for my life when I focus on doing the parts of His will that He's already revealed.

That brings us to today's verses. If you want to know the revealed will of God for your life, here it is. First, be a person of joy at all times. Living a joy-filled life is a decision we must make every day, because life is not always filled with joyful moments. Someone once told me that joy is not the same as happiness, because happiness depends on what "happens." Joy is a decision to bless the Lord and walk in victory regardless of what happens.

Second, God expects us to "pray without ceasing." That doesn't mean that we're to walk around with our heads bowed and eyes closed all day long. It does mean that we have a lifestyle of prayer — praying in the morning, noon, afternoon, evening, and night. Prayer is our lifeline! Finally, God instructs us to "give thanks in everything." Those last two words make this one hard. It's easy to give thanks when all is well, but thanking God in the adversity is a different matter. Let's covenant to live each day rejoicing, praying, and thanking God — after all, it is His will for your life!

## October 19 – Open Our Eyes, Lord

*"Open my eyes, that I may see wondrous things from Your law." (Psalm 119:18)*

Growing up in church, I sang so many great songs — "Amazing Grace," "To God Be the Glory," "In Christ Alone." When I read this verse, I recall one of those old songs: "Open our eyes, Lord, we want to see Jesus, to reach out and touch Him, and say that we love Him. Open our ears, Lord, and help us to listen, open our eyes, Lord, we want to see Jesus." By singing these words, we asked God to help us understand the glory of His Son and the truth of His Word.

Calling on God for illumination is a wonderful thing to do. James said, "If any of you lacks wisdom, let him ask of God who gives to all liberally and without reproach, and it will be given to him" (James 1:5). Jesus promised He would provide us with a Helper who would show us His truth: "When He, the Spirit of truth, has come, He will guide you into all truth." The Helper Jesus spoke of is the Holy Spirit. He indwells every person who has placed his faith in Jesus.

So we know God has the power to open our eyes to the truth, but I wonder if we desire to hear from Him. Do we really want to know more about God and His Word? Do we want to pursue a deeper walk with God? When I learned to swim, I spent a lot of time in the shallow end. Yet, when I mastered swimming, I moved to the deep end. Frankly, too many Christians are in the shallow end of God's Word when they should've moved deeper years ago. Will you go deeper with God? Just as the psalmist did, I hope you'll ask Him to take you further than you've ever been.

## October 20 – The Value of a Friend

*"As iron sharpens iron, so a man sharpens the countenance of his friend." (Proverbs 27:17)*

God made us humans to be relational creatures. Just look back to the Garden of Eden — "It is not good that man should be alone; I will make him a helper comparable to him" (Genesis 2:18). From Eve's creation all the way until now, we've never had to worry about being in this world by ourselves. Yet, while there are about 8 billion people in this world, it is entirely possible for someone to feel all alone.

God does not intend for us to live the Christian life by ourselves. Someone once said, "There are no Lone Ranger Christians." God has given us one another as a gift, and He intends for us to use our relationships to strengthen one another and glorify Him. Today's verse tells us that just as iron sharpens iron, so a good friend will sharpen the countenance of his companion. In other words, we can blow wind into the sails of a friend's life through our love and encouragement.

Another great thing about friendships is the possibility for accountability. Some people use the term "accountability partner" to speak of a friend that challenges us to grow in our walk with Christ by encouraging us to steer clear of the sins of this world. Do you have someone in your life that can ask you the hard questions? If not, I encourage you to find such a person. Do all you can to strengthen his life and allow him to do the same for you.

## October 21 — Refusing to Work

*"For even when we were with you, we commanded you this: If anyone will not work, neither shall he eat." (2 Thessalonians 3:10)*

There are a variety of opinions when it comes to work. Some people love to work — they can't wait for the alarm clock to go off so they can punch in and get cracking. Others despise work — it wouldn't hurt their feelings if they never had to report for duty. I think many people are somewhere in between — they really don't look forward to work. Rather, it's something they have to do to pay the bills. It certainly helps if a person enjoys what he does.

It might surprise you to learn that work is as old as the Garden of Eden. From the very beginning, the Bible says that "the LORD God took the man (Adam) and put him in the garden of Eden to tend and keep it" (Genesis 2:15). In other words, God designed us to work. Some would have us believe that work was a result of man's fall into sin, but nothing could be further from the truth. That feeling of satisfaction you get when you do a good job is exactly what God intended.

In today's verse, Paul addressed so-called church members who didn't want to work. He couldn't be more clear — if they don't want to work, they don't get to eat. In other words, God designed us to pull our own weight by earning a living. Of course, some people are disabled or handicapped so they can't work. It is the church's responsibility to provide for such people. But if we are able to work, then that's exactly what God expects us to do. So then, "whatever your hand finds to do, do it with all your might" (Ecclesiastes 9:10).

## October 22 – Why Did Jesus Come?

*"This is a faithful saying and worthy of all acceptance, that Christ Jesus came into the world to save sinners, of whom I am chief." (1 Timothy 1:15)*

In the New Testament, the Apostle Paul gave us five "faithful sayings" (the others can be found in 1 Timothy 3:1, 4:8, 2 Timothy 2:11-12, and Titus 3:8). Today's verse is one of the most foundational statements in the whole Bible. If you've ever wondered why Jesus Christ came into the world, you don't have to wonder any longer: "Christ Jesus came into the world to save sinners." Apart from Jesus, there would be no way for men to be reconciled to God.

Some people think that "sinners" is too strong a word to describe mankind. Nothing could be further from the truth. The Bible is very clear that there is no one righteous — "no, not one" (Romans 3:10). That's because every single human being has sinned and "fallen short of the glory of God" (Romans 3:23). Our sin is a terrible problem that must be addressed because "the wages of sin is death" (Romans 6:23). The effects of sin are temporary and eternal. That is, sin causes us to die a natural death, and it will cause us to suffer eternal torment.

The greatest news mankind has ever heard is that no one has to suffer in hell forever. When we were hopelessly lost in our sins, the Bible says God "made Him who knew no sin to be sin for us, that we might become the righteousness of God in Him" (2 Corinthians 5:21). Though we are all guilty sinners deserving of hell, through faith in Jesus Christ we gain a righteous standing before God and the forgiveness of sins. Though each of us is a "chief of sinners," Jesus came to save sinners just like us. Hallelujah, what a Savior!

## October 23 – Savior and Mediator

*"For this is good and acceptable in the sight of God our Savior, who desires all men to be saved and to come to the knowledge of the truth. For there is one God and one Mediator between God and men, the Man Christ Jesus." (1 Timothy 2:3-5)*

These power-packed verses tell us a great deal about the God who loves and saves us. Paul says that God is our Savior — He is the One who saves us from a hopeless life on earth and eternal torment in hell. Through faith in Jesus, we can be totally set free! Notice that God is no respecter of persons — He "desires all men to be saved." There are some who teach that God only desires to save an elect few. This verse proves that God wants to save every man, woman, and child in this world.

Paul then explains that there is only one God. Statements like this don't make unbelievers very happy. Some religions teach that there are millions of gods. Some would call us narrow-minded for believing there is only one God. People believe what they will, but the Bible is clear that there is only one God (Deuteronomy 6:4) who exists eternally as Father, Son, and Holy Spirit (Matthew 28:19). Any other concept of God originates with Satan who wants to take as many people to hell as possible.

Not only is there one God, but there is only one Mediator between God and men. A mediator is someone who intervenes between two disagreeing parties to try and find a solution. The fact is that our sin made us enemies of God from birth. Sadly, we can't do anything to reconcile our relationship with God. When Jesus saw that we were hopeless and helpless, He stepped in to bridge the gap between us and God through His death, burial, and resurrection. For that reason, He alone is the Savior and Mediator for sinners like you and me. Through Him only we can now have peace with God.

# October 24 – The Mystery of Godliness

*"And without controversy great is the mystery of godliness: God was manifested in the flesh, justified in the Spirit, seen by angels, preached among the Gentiles, believed on in the world, received up in glory." (1 Timothy 3:16)*

In today's verse, Paul refers to the Gospel as the mystery of godliness. That's not to say that we can't know the Gospel — he's simply saying that no man would know the Gospel had God not revealed it to us. This mystery has everything to do with the earthly ministry of Jesus. First, he mentions the incarnation — "God was manifested in the flesh." Jesus, who is completely and fully God, took on human flesh when He was born of the virgin Mary. "The Word became flesh" (John 1:14).

Paul then makes reference to the baptism of our Lord — "justified in the Spirit." When Jesus was baptized, the Bible says that they "saw the Spirit of God descending like a dove and alighting upon Him" (Matthew 3:16). This was the Heavenly Father letting the world know that Jesus is His Son. Next, Paul points us toward Christ's resurrection — "seen by angels." When Jesus rose from the dead, it was an angel who rolled the stone away and spoke comfort to Christ's followers (Matthew 28:2ff).

Paul then points us to the preaching and receiving of the Gospel — "preached among the Gentiles, believed on in the world." Jesus said that "this Gospel of the kingdom will be preached in all the world as a witness to all the nations" (Matthew 24:14). It was men like Peter, Paul, Luke, Timothy, and many others who shared the Gospel everywhere and witnessed many professions of faith. And of course Paul concludes with the ascension — "received up in glory." The two angels who witnessed Jesus' ascension left us with great hope — "this same Jesus, who was taken up from you into heaven, will so come in like manner as you saw Him go into heaven" (Acts 1:11). Even so, come, Lord Jesus!

## October 25 – What God Thinks of Exercise

*"Reject profane and old wives' fables, and exercise yourself toward godliness. For bodily exercise profits a little, but godliness is profitable for all things, having promise of the life that now is and of that which is to come." (1 Timothy 4:7-8)*

It's just my opinion, but I think our culture is more health-conscious than it's ever been. Health club memberships are at an all-time high. The food industry has been revolutionized with the demand for organic foods. Even schools are beginning early, trying to educate children against the dangers of obesity. Twenty billion dollars is spent annually on the US weight-loss industry, including diet books, diet drugs and weight-loss surgeries. An estimated 108 million Americans are currently on a diet. Wow!

The emphasis on health and wellness is a good thing. The Apostle Paul reminds us that "bodily exercise profits a little." Regular exercise is a great way to prevent so many maladies — heart disease, diabetes, obesity, etc. Exercise is also proven to be a great stress reliever. I try to exercise regularly — I can't say I enjoy it, but I love the way it makes me feel. Through exercise, it's my hope that I'll be here for my wife and kids for a long time.

Our fascination with fitness also indicates a problem — it appears that we're more passionate about our physical health than our spiritual health. Paul tells us that physical exercise is good, but spiritual health is much better because it will profit us in this life and the life to come. After all, Jesus is not going to ask how many miles you ran and how much you bench pressed when you stand before Him in judgment. He'll want to know how much you loved Him, how much you prayed, and how many disciples you made. God help us to be both physically AND spiritually fit!

## October 26 – The Use of Alcohol

*"No longer drink only water, but use a little wine for your stomach's sake and your frequent infirmities." (1 Timothy 5:23)*

The alcohol industry does big business in the United States of America. Each year the liquor industry spends almost $2 billion on advertising and encouraging the consumption of alcoholic beverages. Apparently the advertising works, because Americans spend over $90 billion on alcohol each year. Unfortunately, over 15 million Americans are dependent on alcohol, and 500,000 are between the ages of nine and twelve. To put it bluntly, our nation has a serious alcohol problem.

Some people have pointed to today's verse as evidence that God has no problem with the use of alcohol. In fact, some would say God actually encourages consumption. To make sense of this verse, we need to know the context Paul was writing in. In the ancient world, water was often polluted and carried many diseases. Thus, Paul urged Timothy not to risk illness — not even for the sake of abstaining from alcohol. Drinking small amounts of wine would keep Timothy from continuing to get sick.

We need to ask ourselves, "Do we have the same problem with disease-laden drinking water in our culture?" Unsafe drinking water is a tremendous problem for many people all over the world. Many relief organizations dig wells for the underprivileged in an attempt to alleviate the problem. But in our modern culture of sewers and clean drinking water, we don't have those troubles. So then, if we don't need to drink alcohol to avoid sickness, why do we need to drink it at all? It's clear that Timothy wanted to abstain from alcohol — I think we'd be wise to do the same.

## October 27 — Contentment

*"Now godliness with contentment is great gain. For we brought nothing into this world, and it is certain we can carry nothing out. And having food and clothing, with these we shall be content." (1 Timothy 6:6-8)*

Our culture has conditioned us to make as much money as we possibly can. Through money, we can buy big houses, drive nice cars, and take fancy vacations. We're all familiar with the "American dream." It tells us to work hard, advance in our careers, and make lots of money. The "dream" is to have a comfortable life with a nice family and lots of cool toys. Pursuing the dream has presented quite a challenge to many people who are now overworked and in serious debt just to manage their expenses.

Should Christians aspire to be rich? There's nothing inherently evil about having a lot of money or possessions. Some of the most godly men in the Bible were also very wealthy — Abraham, Job, etc. So while there's nothing evil about being prosperous, seeking wealth should not be our primary pursuit. Rather, God has called us to be content with the things He has blessed us with — food, clothing, shelter, transportation, education, employment, etc. Too often, we take these wonderful blessings for granted.

Paul reminds us that we brought nothing into the world with us when we were born, and it's certain that we won't carry anything out when we die. The old saying is true — "You don't see any U-Hauls attached to hearses." Everything we accumulate will be left to someone else when we pass away. There's nothing wrong with leaving an inheritance to our loved ones. In fact, the Bible encourages us to do so. But the greatest legacy we can leave is spiritual — a life of Christ-honoring contentment that points others to Jesus.

## October 28 – A Spirit of Fear

*"God has not given us a spirit of fear, but of power and of love and of a sound mind." (2 Timothy 1:7)*

In his inaugural address in 1933, President Franklin Delano Roosevelt said these famous words: "The only thing we have to fear is fear itself." Keep in mind that America was in the midst of the Depression. The threat of war was still very real following World War I. Roosevelt was trying to tell his fellow Americans that fear would keep them from being what they could be. Some things never change — fear still has millions of people bound in shackles all over the world.

We're afraid for so many reasons. Sometimes we're afraid that we might get sick and not recover. In the turbulent world we now live in, many people are afraid of terrorism and the threat of nuclear war. Investors are always concerned that the stock market is going to crash and they're going to lose everything they have. Most people are afraid of everyday issues — paying the bills, the safety of their children, losing a job, etc. Sadly, many people are even afraid to die.

There's good news — if Jesus Christ is your Savior, you don't have to be afraid of anything. In fact, the only thing God has commanded us to fear is Himself: "The fear of the Lord is the beginning of wisdom" (Proverbs 9:10). If we have a holy reverence and respect for the Lord, we don't need to be afraid of anything else. As a follower of Christ, I know that God is my Provider and Protector. For that reason, I can live each day with power, love, and soundness of mind! "The Lord is my light and my salvation; whom shall I fear? The Lord is the strength of my life; of whom shall I be afraid?" (Psalm 27:1).

## October 29 — The Solid Foundation

*"Nevertheless the solid foundation of God stands, having this seal: 'The Lord knows those who are His,' and, 'Let everyone who names the name of Christ depart from iniquity.'" (2 Timothy 2:19)*

In His famous Sermon on the Mount, Jesus said that every person is building on one of two foundations — the rock or the sand. Jesus said a wise man builds his house on the rock because it can withstand all the storms of life. In today's verse, the Apostle Paul tells us a little more about the solid foundation that is found only in Jesus Christ. If we want our lives to withstand all the trials and temptations Satan sends our way, we need to learn more about the bedrock of our faith.

First, Paul tells us that "the Lord knows who are His." That's because every person who has placed their faith in Christ is now a child of God. I'm sure you've heard someone use the phrase "all of God's children" as a substitute for the word "everyone." That's an incorrect substitute because not everyone is a child of God. We're all His creation, but only those who have trusted Christ are His children. He has sealed His children with the Holy Spirit who guides them into all truth (John 16:13).

Second, Paul challenges us: "Let everyone who names the name of Christ depart from iniquity." I'm very concerned that some people treat salvation like it's a license to sin. They think to themselves, "I prayed a prayer, walked an aisle, had Christian parents, etc." Because they did something religious or emotional, they think they have a relationship with God and can now live however they want. Nothing could be further from the truth. "Shall we continue in sin that grace may abound? Certainly not! How shall we who died to sin live any longer in it?" (Romans 6:1-2). If we know Him, let's live for Him!

## October 30 – God-Breathed Scripture

*"All Scripture is given by inspiration of God, and is profitable for doctrine, for reproof, for correction, for instruction in righteousness, that the man of God may be complete, thoroughly equipped for every good work." (2 Timothy 3:16-17)*

Guinness World Records says there is little doubt the Bible is the world's best-selling and most widely distributed book. A survey by the Bible Society concluded that around 2.5 billion copies were printed between 1815 and 1975, but more recent estimates put the number at more than 5 billion. Those are amazing numbers, but what makes the Bible so special? Why do so many people desire to get a copy in their hands? Why do millions of people give the Bible to others?

The answer is very simple. The Bible is not just another book — it is the very word of God. Paul said that all Scripture is God-breathed. That means every paragraph, every line, and every word. Jesus said that even the smallest "jot or tittle" of Scripture would not pass away until everything it prophesies is fulfilled. Because the Bible comes to us from God Himself, it is useful for doctrine (what to believe), reproof and correction (when we fall short), and instruction in righteousness (for serving God).

Verse 16 tells us where Scripture comes from and what it can do, but verse 17 tells us the purpose of Scripture — "that the man of God may be complete, thoroughly equipped for every good work." Think of it like this. We are soldiers in God's army. No soldier goes into battle unprepared. A soldier secures the right clothes, weapons, supplies, etc. Soldiers of war are outfitted by their country, but soldiers of the cross are equipped by God through His Word. And praise the Lord, His Word is adequate to help us complete every good work He's called us to do.

## October 31 – Finish Well

*"I have fought the good fight, I have finished the race, I have kept the faith." (2 Timothy 4:7)*

When I was a senior in high school, I can remember a boxer named George Foreman trying to make a comeback. These days, he is known more for grills, but in his prime George Foreman was scary good. But at the age of forty-five, no one expected him to make any real noise on the heavyweight scene. All that changed when he fought Michael Moorer for the heavyweight title in November 1994. After taking a beating for nine rounds, in round number 10 George Foreman knocked out Michael Moorer to become the oldest heavyweight champion in the history of the United States.

I also recall watching a race in the 1992 Barcelona Olympics. A British runner, Derek Redmond, was competing in the 400-meter dash. About halfway through the race, Redmond checked up very quickly and it was obvious he had torn his hamstring. Overcome with pain, Redmond did not give up. In a moment for the ages, Redmond hopped down the track toward the finish line. About 100 meters from the end, a man came and put his arm around Redmond and helped him to the finish line. It was his father. Together, father and son finished the race.

The human tendency is to give up when life gets difficult. As a follower of Christ, no one experienced more adversity than the Apostle Paul (read 2 Corinthians 11:23-28). Yet, he was determined to be faithful to Christ until the very end of his life. In his last recorded letter of the New Testament, Paul was happy to announce he had not given up. Rather, he kept the faith. What about you? Are you on the verge of quitting? The Christian life is not a sprint, it is a marathon. When you think you can't take another step, your Heavenly Father will be there to see you safely home. Keep on fighting and running so that you can finish well!

## November 1 — The Value of Integrity

*"Better is the poor who walks in his integrity than one perverse in his ways, though he be rich." (Proverbs 28:6)*

We've all heard of the "American Dream." We've been told it's all about hard work and dedication, and that if you work hard enough you will be prosperous. Prosperity is something that drives the majority of Americans. Let's face it — we want to make a lot of money so we can buy big houses and drive nice cars. We want to take nice vacations and play with big toys. We want to put back lots of money in our retirement accounts and 401(k).

Sadly, many have allowed their lust for money to compromise their convictions. Think about it — how many people have ever lied to get a promotion or earn more money for the company? How many people have stepped on the back of a coworker as they climbed the corporate ladder? I've even heard stories of employees who began a sexual relationship with a boss just so that boss would look favorably on them and promote them before others.

Today's verse reminds us that integrity is much more important than wealth. Jesus said it like this: "For what profit is it to a man if he gains the whole world, and loses his own soul? Or what will a man give in exchange for his soul?" (Matthew 16:26). We can have everything the world affords, but if we don't have Jesus we have nothing. Even as children of God, we can get swept up in the rat race. Let's make a vow that we will not compromise our integrity on the altar of wealth and the American dream.

## November 2 — The Grace of God

*"For the grace of God that brings salvation has appeared to all men." (Titus 2:11)*

We've all heard the phrase "grace of God," but what does it mean? The Bible tells us that grace is a gift of God that brings salvation. Paul said it like this: "For by grace you have been saved through faith, and that not of yourselves; it is the gift of God, not of works, lest anyone should boast" (Ephesians 2:8-9). Someone defined grace using an acronym: God's Riches At Christ's Expense. Through the death, burial, and resurrection of His Son, God offers us an eternal relationship with Himself.

The Bible is clear how someone receives the grace of God. Paul said, "It's by grace you have been saved *through faith*." We might say that faith is the key that unlocks the door of salvation. No one explained it better than Jesus: "For God so loved the world that He gave His only begotten Son that *whoever believes in Him* should not perish but have everlasting life" (John 3:16). Faith is an absolute trust in Jesus Christ that results in a life surrendered to Him.

Today's verse tells us that "the grace of God that brings salvation has appeared to all men." Does that mean everyone knows and has heard the Gospel? Clearly that's not the case. Even the Bible tells us there are many who have not heard — that's why God has called you and me to share the Good News (Romans 10:14). Our verse means that the offer of salvation has been extended to every person on earth — all colors, genders, and classes of people are invited to receive the greatest gift of all. Have you received God's grace? If so, are you sharing it with others?

## November 3 — The Value of Good Works

*"This is a faithful saying, and these things I want you to affirm constantly, that those who have believed in God should be careful to maintain good works. These things are good and profitable to men." (Titus 3:8)*

Sometimes we treat salvation as a license. We might not say it, but we think to ourselves, "I've been saved. God will understand if I commit this sin. He knows I'm only human." Salvation is not a license to sin — it's the doorway to a new life in Jesus Christ. Thus, instead of looking for opportunities to sin, we should look for ways to glorify God. As Paul said, "Shall we continue in sin that grace may abound? Certainly not! How shall we who died to sin live any longer in it?" (Romans 6:1-2).

We'll never get this right until we understand our reason for living. Every human being was created for the same purpose — to glorify God. "Whether you eat or drink, or whatever you do, do all to the glory of God" (1 Corinthians 10:31). Of course, that's not to suggest that God's plan for each of our lives will be identical. God has a variety of plans for His people — pastors, doctors, teachers, policemen, etc. God's plan will be unique for each of us, but our purpose is the same.

By maintaining good works through obedience to God's Word, we bring glory to our Creator. But not only do our good works magnify the Lord, they are a blessing to us too. I mean, who couldn't benefit from a kind smile from a child of God? Who wouldn't like to have some of their bills provided for by some generous believer? It's an amazing truth — obedience to God's Word would usher in the awakening that our world desperately needs. Press on in your service to God and others!

## November 4 – The Faithfulness of God

*"Through the* Lord's *mercies we are not consumed, because His compassions fail not. They are new every morning; great is Your faithfulness." (Lamentations 3:22-23)*

One of the great hymns of the Christian faith is "Great Is Thy Faithfulness." I bet you've sung the beautiful words before:

*Great is Thy faithfulness, O God My Father*
*There is no shadow of turning with Thee,*
*Thou changest not, Thy compassions they fail not*
*As Thou has been Thou forever wilt be.*
*Great is Thy faithfulness! Great is Thy faithfulness!*

While you may be familiar with the song, I wonder if you know its origin. The prophet Jeremiah ministered to the southern kingdom of Judah when they were overthrown by the Babylonians in 586 BC. The overthrow of Judah was a punishment for the many sins they had committed — worshiping idols, sacrificing to false gods, refusing to listen to God's prophet, etc. Jeremiah had to watch his city be overtaken by pagan people who burned it to the ground while forcing its inhabitants into slavery.

Knowing that context, we have a greater appreciation for Jeremiah's words. Get this — He praised the faithfulness of God while his homeland was being burned to the ground! Wow! Most Christians will give glory to God when things are going well, but when things turn south it takes a true child of God to praise the Lord in the midst of the storm. Understand this — no matter what is happening in your life, God is faithful, and He will see you through everything that comes your way!

## November 5 — It's All True!

*"The entirety of Your Word is truth, and every one of Your righteous judgments endures forever." (Psalm 119:160)*

Unfortunately, many people do not believe that the Bible is true. In a Lifeway Research study released in 2016, only 58 percent of Americans said that God is the author of Scripture, 51 percent said the Bible can be interpreted however someone chooses, and only 50 percent said the Bible has the authority to tell us what to do. Less than half (47 percent) said the Bible is 100 percent accurate and 44 percent said that while the Bible is helpful, it is not literally true. Clearly, many Americans do not have a high view of Scripture.

We've seen what the general public thinks of the Bible, but what does God say about the Bible? God tells us plainly that the Bible is His Word — "all Scripture is God-breathed" (2 Timothy 3:16, NIV). When we hear the words of the Bible, we are listening to the very words of God! Because the Bible is the Word of God, and because God is perfect, it is impossible for Scripture to contain errors. That's why the psalmist said, "The entirety of Your word is truth."

The Bible is so true that every judgment pronounced by God in the Bible either has or will come to pass. Just think of all the prophecies concerning Jesus — the Bible prophesied His birth, life, death, burial, and resurrection. Every one of those things came to pass EXACTLY how the Bible said they would. What would lead us to believe that all the remaining prophecies and judgments will go unfulfilled? Clearly, the Bible is the 100 percent accurate Word of God. We've just got to decide if we believe it.

## November 6 – Every Christian Is a Watchman

*"Son of man, I have made you a watchman." (Ezekiel 3:17)*

We've all studied enough history to know what a watchman is. Ancient civilizations built walls around their cities to keep enemies out. The city's leadership appointed men to act as watchmen. They placed them at watch posts on various parts of the wall. If the watchman saw that everything was calm on the horizon, he didn't have to say anything. If he saw the enemy charging toward the city, it was his job to sound the alarm and warn the inhabitants about coming danger.

God made Ezekiel a watchman to his countrymen, Israel. God sent judgment to His people because they rebelled against Him. God called Ezekiel to warn His people about the coming judgment. If God told Ezekiel to say something and Ezekiel sounded the alarm, the people would die and their blood would be required at their own hands. But if God said "speak" and Ezekiel did nothing, the people would still die in their own sins, but their blood would be required at the hands of Ezekiel.

When you think about it, that's a huge responsibility God put on Ezekiel. But did you know that He has put the same responsibility on us? God has entrusted us with the Gospel — the Good News about the death, burial, and resurrection of Jesus Christ. If we share the message of salvation, many people will not receive it, but we will not be responsible for their eternal punishment. If we refuse to share the Good News, we will have to answer for our silence when we stand before God. I'm praying God will help us all do the work of faithful watchmen by sharing the Good News of Jesus Christ.

## November 7 – The Danger of Unbelief

*"So we see that they could not enter in because of unbelief." (Hebrews 3:19)*

The Book of Hebrews is truly amazing. We don't know who the author is, but speculations abound. Though we may not know the author's identity, we know he was a Jewish Christian who was an expert on all things Jewish. In today's passage, the author tells us that the ancient Israelites who were freed from their Egyptian captivity were not able to enter the Promised Land for one main reason — unbelief. Their lack of faith in God kept them from inheriting God's best for forty years.

The lesson is clear for us — there is grave danger in unbelief! Unbelief has temporary ramifications. Consider Israel once more — not only did they have to roam the wilderness instead of the Promised Land for forty years, but every man had to die before Israel could inherit God's promise. If you refuse to believe God and take Him at His Word, it will keep you from experiencing God's best. We need to be very careful not to exchange the truth of God for the lies of the devil.

The worst effects of unbelief are eternal. In fact, Jesus said there is only one sin that is unforgivable — "blasphemy against the Spirit" (Matthew 12:31). Essentially, blasphemy is refusing to believe God. It can take many forms — attributing the work of God to someone else, doubting the truth of Scripture, failing to surrender one's life to Christ, etc. The ultimate danger of unbelief is that it will send someone to hell forever. There's only one solution — we must place our faith in God and His Word every day!

## November 8 — The Man Who Never Sinned

*"We do not have a High Priest who cannot sympathize with our weaknesses, but was in all points tempted as we are, yet without sin." (Hebrews 4:15)*

I bet you've probably said to yourself, "No one knows what I'm going through." You may be right — no other human being may know the details of everything you're experiencing. Yet, even if no one else knows all you're enduring, Jesus knows EVERYTHING you are going through. He is able to sympathize with all your grief for one main reason — He experienced every temptation you experience. The details might be a little different, but still He knows where you are and what you're going through.

The author of Hebrews explains that Jesus "was in all points tempted as we are." Just look at how the devil tempted the Lord three times in Matthew 4. First, after forty days without food, Satan tempted Jesus — "If you are the Son of God, command that these stones become bread." Second, Satan tempted Jesus to test the Lord — "If you are the Son of God, throw Yourself down." With this temptation, Satan even quoted God's Word. Satan and his demons know the Word just as much or more than we do!

Finally, Satan tempted Jesus with power — "All these things I will give You if You will fall down and worship me." Each time Satan tempted the Savior, Jesus responded with the Word of God. Through all the temptation, Jesus came out spotless. He never committed one sin! He is perfect! That's why He is the only One who could die for our sins. Only a spotless Lamb could pay the price for the sins of mankind! You can entrust your life to the One who never did anything wrong!

## November 9 — The Source of My Help

*"I will lift up my eyes to the hills — from whence comes my help? My help comes from the LORD, who made heaven and earth." (Psalm 121:1-2)*

It doesn't matter who we are, we all need some help from time to time! Or as the old song says, "We all need somebody to lean on." If we are followers of Christ, we can always lean on the everlasting arms of our Heavenly Father. Today's verse tells us He is our constant source of help, but in what ways does He help? There are too many ways to count, but Psalm 121 gives us several ways God helps those that belong to Him.

First, God is our Sustainer. The psalmist says, "He will not allow your foot to be moved." That's because "He who keeps you will not slumber." God is never taken by surprise. He is always awake and attentive to the welfare of His children. When you don't think you can take another step, He will hold you up and give you the strength to persevere. These verses also tell us that God is our Protector. He is so close that "the sun shall not strike you by day, nor the moon by night." Truly, He is "a friend who sticks closer than a brother" (Proverbs 18:24).

Finally, we're told that God is our Provider — "the LORD shall preserve you from all evil." If we're battling with sin, God will provide a way of escape (1 Corinthians 10:13). The Lord will provide the means for you to grow in your relationship with Him. The Lord will provide everything you need to live. And the best news of all — God will provide abundantly for us on this earth, and He'll provide eternal life for us when we leave this world. If you need help, lift your eyes up to the Lord!

## November 10 – Going to God's House

*"I was glad when they said to me, 'Let us go into the house of the LORD.'" (Psalm 122:1)*

Psalm 122 is called a song of ascents. It is one of many psalms used by the Jews as they ascended the temple mount for worship. If you ever get the chance to go to Jerusalem, you will see something amazing on the southern steps of the temple mount. The steps are unusual — for every two short steps, there is one long step. That's so the Jews could pause at every third step and meditate on the Scripture as they prepared their heart for worship.

I've often wondered what would happen if Christians prepared their hearts for worship like that. When we think about gathering together with God's people, do we get excited? David was overjoyed with the thought of worshiping God at the temple! We should be just as excited to gather with God's people at God's house! For starters, it is our chance to approach God and offer Him "the sacrifice of praise" (Hebrews 13:15). The Jews brought animal sacrifices to God — we bring the praise of our lips!

Encouragement is another reason we should be excited to gather with God's people. The Bible commands us — Do not forsake "the assembling of ourselves together, as is the manner of some, but exhorting one another, and so much the more as you see the Day approaching" (Hebrews 10:25). When we gather with brothers and sisters in Christ, we are rubbing shoulders with people who are fighting the same battles we fight. So the next time someone tells you it's time for worship, glorify God and go!

## November 11 — Our God is Mighty to Save

*"Therefore He is also able to save to the uttermost those who come to God through Him, since He always lives to make intercession for them."* (Hebrews 7:25)

Perhaps you've heard the song that says, "Savior, He can move the mountains, my God is mighty to save, He is mighty to save." I love that song because it's so true. Today's verse tells us that Christ is able to save to the uttermost those who come to God through Him. A preacher once said, "Jesus takes us from the guttermost to the uttermost!" He is able to take us from being hopelessly lost to radically saved in just a matter of moments.

But how does someone "come to God through Him"? The Bible tells us there is only one way to approach God, and that is Jesus Christ. Jesus said it so clearly — "I am the way, the truth, and the life. No one comes to the Father except through Me" (John 14:6). Jesus is the only Way of salvation, but how do we access the salvation only He can provide? Paul answers that "If you confess with your mouth the Lord Jesus and believe in your heart that God has raised Him from the dead, you will be saved" (Romans 10:9). Faith is the key that unlocks the door of salvation.

The author of Hebrews says that Jesus "always lives to make intercession for them." We have to understand something about the Old Testament priesthood to make sense of that statement. The OT priests had to come offering sacrifices over and over again, but none of them could offer sacrifices forever because they passed away. Jesus offered His own body as an eternal sacrifice for sins, and He lives forever to ensure our standing before God! Surely He is mighty to save!

## November 12 – Faithfulness Better Than Riches

*"A faithful man will abound with blessings, but he who hastens to be rich will not go unpunished."* (Proverbs 28:20)

If you were to ask people about their life's goal, you would get a variety of answers. Many people pursue an education in hopes of securing a degree and a job. But what's so important about landing a nice job? Whether we'll admit it or not, a job is simply a means to an end for most people. A nice job is the path to lots of money. Isn't that what the "American dream" is built around? Marry a spouse, have kids, find a nice job, make lots of money, and retire happy.

Sadly, the pursuit of the American dream doesn't end up quite like many had hoped. Longing to get ahead of the competition, people are tempted to lie and steal. Relationships that once meant a great deal to us aren't quite as important when the opportunity for a promotion and more money is at stake. The sad truth is that many people have climbed their way to the top of the ladder only to find out that their money brings them no comfort when their life is falling apart.

In today's verse, Solomon reminds us there is something much more important than money — faithfulness. But here's the catch — if you live a life of faithfulness to God, you may not always get that promotion. Your salary might not be as much as your neighbor's. Faithfulness to God does not always produce temporary benefits, but it ALWAYS guarantees an eternal reward. So remember this — your earthly riches will all pass away, but your faithfulness to God will last forever.

## November 13 – How God Judges Us

*"The soul who sins shall die. The son shall not bear the guilt of the father, nor the father bear the guilt of the son. The righteousness of the righteous shall be upon himself, and the wickedness of the wicked shall be upon himself." (Ezekiel 18:20)*

I'm sure we've all heard the expressions, "He's his father's son" or "She's her mother's daughter." Others have said, "The apple doesn't fall far from the tree." Sometimes you get the impression that a person is prone to follow in his/her parents' footsteps. If the parents were lazy, the child will be lazy. If the parents were generous, the child will be generous. No one can argue that a person's environment and upbringing play a large factor in his/her life.

Some even have us to believe that the sins of the father are automatically passed down to the children. If the father was a drunk, the son will atone for the sins of the father. If the mother was a prostitute, the daughter will be punished for the sins of the mother. Today's passage makes it clear that God doesn't see things that way. "The soul that sins shall die." That means God will judge me for my own sins, not the sins of someone else.

The Bible is clear that every person will stand before the judgment seat of Christ at the end of time (2 Corinthians 5:10). When you stand before Jesus, someone else's faith will be no help to you. Your dad may have been a great pastor. Your mother may have been a compassionate soulwinner. Their faith will not grant you entrance into heaven. I will have to give an account for my own sins, and specifically whether or not I surrendered my life to Christ. Give your life to Jesus, and live each day knowing you will stand before God to give account for your own actions.

## November 14 — Jesus Paid It All

*"And every priest stands ministering daily and offering repeatedly the same sacrifices, which can never take away sins. But this Man, after He had offered one sacrifice for sins forever, sat down at the right hand of God, from that time waiting till His enemies are made His footstool." (Hebrews 10:11-13)*

Just about everyone has had the experience of paying off a debt. For instance, many people have a home loan. Most home loans are stretched out for fifteen to thirty years. When you're in the midst of paying the loan, sometimes you wonder if it's ever going to be paid off. You have to make payment after payment after payment, and still the debt is not paid. No matter how much we hate it, we have to keep paying until the debt is retired.

Human beings have a problem — we owe an unpayable debt to God. When our forefathers (Adam and Eve) sinned in the Garden of Eden, they passed to all the rest of us the curse of sin. Every human being is born a sinner (Romans 3:23). Because all of us are sinners, we are now objects of God's wrath. Throughout the ages, humans have offered a variety of sacrifices to God in their attempts to cover or remove their sins, but the blood of bulls and goats never worked.

That's where Jesus stepped in. When He saw we could do nothing to pay our sin debt, He took on human flesh, went to the cross, and paid our debt with His own blood. Following His death on the cross, the Bible says Jesus presented His own blood to the Heavenly Father as a perfect payment for the sins of mankind. Because His blood was a satisfactory atonement, Jesus did something the OT priests could never do — He *sat down* at the right hand of God. He sat down because the work was done. I don't know about you, but I'm so glad Jesus paid it all!

## November 15 – Everyone Belongs in Church

*"And let us consider one another in order to stir up love and good works, not forsaking the assembling of ourselves together, as is the manner of some, but exhorting one another, and so much the more as you see the Day approaching." (Hebrews 10:24-25)*

All of us were born into a family. I was born into the Stinnett family, and I'm very grateful for that. My parents, Larry and Ginny Stinnett, were the best parents any child could ask for. I also have one brother, Brad. Growing up, I found my identity as part of the Stinnett family. I've been told hundreds of times, "You look just like your dad." But I'm even happier when someone tells me, "You remind me so much of your dad." I take that as a high compliment. I love my family.

If you are a follower of Jesus Christ, you are also part of another family. That family is called the church. Jesus said to Peter, "On this rock I will build My church, and the gates of Hades shall not prevail against it" (Matthew 16:18). In his letter to the church at Corinth, Paul calls the church the Body of Christ. He said, "Now you are the body of Christ, and members individually" (1 Corinthians 12:27). Just as our bodies have many different parts (hands, feet, etc.), those parts make up one body.

In today's verse, the author of Hebrews reminds us that we should continue to meet together as the church. I've had many people tell me, "I don't have to go to church to be a Christian." I usually respond, "You're right, but if you are a Christian, you will want to be in church." Why? Because the church is my family of faith. There I find the love and encouragement I need to continue following Christ. If you aren't a member of a local church, find one that loves God and preaches the Bible. You will never regret taking your place in God's family.

## November 16 – The Definition of Faith

*"Now faith is the substance of things hoped for, the evidence of things not seen. For by it the elders obtained a good testimony." (Hebrews 11:1-2)*

Faith is something mentioned in every culture every day. Even people who may not necessarily believe in God will underscore the importance of faith. The world's definition of faith is much different than God's definition of faith. The NIV records our verse like this: "Now faith is being sure of what we hope for and certain of what we do not see." In other words, faith believes that which cannot always be seen or explained.

The author of Hebrews says we must have faith in at least two things. First, we must simply "believe that He is" (Hebrews 11:6). Faith begins when I confess that there is a God to whom I must give an account. Of course, this flies in the face of a secular culture that leads us to believe there is no God and that all human life evolved from apes. They tell us everything began with a big bang almost 14 billion years ago. Faith says God Himself is the Creator and Sustainer of all things.

Furthermore, the author of Hebrews says we must believe that "He is a rewarder of those who diligently seek Him" (Hebrews 11:6). We must believe God will reward every person that surrenders to Him, and the rewards will be both temporary and eternal. Temporarily, I am rewarded with love, joy, peace, and many other blessings. Eternally, I am rewarded with an indescribable heavenly home in the presence of Jesus. So, if you want a good testimony, place all your faith in Jesus Christ!

## November 17 – God Provided Something Better

*"And all these, having obtained a good testimony through faith, did not receive the promise, God having provided something better for us, that they should not be made perfect apart from us." (Hebrews 11:39-40)*

These two verses conclude one of the greatest chapters in the Word of God. After the author of Hebrews goes into great detail about the faithful men and women who've gone before us, he reminds us that each of them "obtained a good testimony through faith." What is a testimony? In this case, a testimony is a person's story. If the story is good, the person has a good reputation. If the story is wicked, the person has a wicked reputation.

Each of the faithful men and women in Hebrews 11 will always be associated with a good testimony because they were willing to believe God, even when it didn't make sense. For instance, Moses continued to defy Pharaoh by serving God because he was "seeing Him who is invisible" (Hebrews 11:27). And yet, with all their dynamic faith, none of the Old Testament saints mentioned in Hebrews 11 were able to "receive the promise."

What promise is that? The promise was an eternal atonement for sins provided through the blood of Jesus Christ. The OT saints looked forward to the penalty for their sins being paid once for all, but until Jesus came many years later they were not able to realize that promise. So the author of Hebrews says "they should not be made perfect apart from us." In other words, it's only through Jesus Christ that men and women from every age can have their sins atoned and forgiven. By virtue of their faith in God, the OT saints were able to receive the free pardon of sin that came through Jesus.

## November 18 — Running the Race

*"Therefore we also, since we are surrounded by so great a cloud of witnesses, let us lay aside every weight, and the sin which so easily ensnares us, and let us run with endurance the race that is set before us." (Hebrews 12:1)*

I'm not fast, and I've never really been fast, but I love to watch a good race. It's always exciting when the Olympics roll around every four years. You see men and women compete in a number of races — 100 meter, 200 meter, 400 meter, etc. I've watched a good number of races, and one thing I've noticed is that the runners want to get as light as possible prior to running. They wear skin-tight outfits and they lay aside their warmup clothes. They have one single focus — the finish line.

In today's two power-packed verses, the author of Hebrews likens the Christian life to a race. He says we are surrounded "by so great a cloud of witnesses." Much like Olympic athletes are surrounded by a stadium full of admiring onlookers, as followers of Christ we are reminded of all the saints who have gone before us. Their example inspires us to run the race, but we can only run if we "lay aside every weight and sin." Anything that prevents us from pursuing Christ to the best of our ability should be removed from our life.

The author of Hebrews says we must "run with endurance." There are times we all want to give up, but we've got to keep running for the finish line by "looking unto Jesus." Our ultimate example is Christ who "endured the cross, despising the shame." Because He was willing to do the will of His Father until the very end, He gained victory over sin and death and "sat down at the right hand of the throne of God." So, my Christian friend, keep looking to Jesus and running the race. Christ will see you safely home.

## November 19 — Content with Christ

*"Let your conduct be without covetousness; be content with such things as you have. For He Himself has said, 'I will never leave you nor forsake you.' So we may boldly say: 'The LORD is my helper; I will not fear. What can man do to me?'" (Hebrews 13:5-6)*

It seems that envy has overtaken the world. It starts young, doesn't it? When we're kids, we want our friend's toy. When we hit the teenage years, we want our friend's car. When we reach adulthood, we are envious our neighbors can take such glorious vacations. For years, it's been called "keeping up with the Joneses." In today's verses, the author of Hebrews tells us to set aside envy and to be content with all God has blessed us with.

But why should we be content? The answer is clear — "He Himself has said, 'I will never leave you nor forsake you.'" We may not have everything we want, but if we've got Jesus we've got everything we need. One of the sweetest promises in all the Word of God is that Jesus will never leave those He has saved. It doesn't matter where we go. Whether we're walking on one of life's mountaintops or through one of life's valleys, Jesus has promised to be with us each step of the way.

The presence of Jesus gives us great boldness to say, "The LORD is my Helper; I will not fear." That psalmist said, "Even though I walk through the valley of the shadow of death, You are with me. Your rod and Your staff, they comfort me" (Psalm 23:4). Because Jesus walks with us, we never have to be afraid of anything — no sickness, no heartbreak, no loneliness. In everything, we are more than conquerors through the One who has loved us (Romans 8:37). Decide every day to live in contentment and boldness, because after all, "what can man do to me?"

## November 20 – The Joy of Trials

*"My brethren, count it all joy when you fall into various trials, knowing that the testing of your faith produces patience. But let patience have its perfect work, that you may be perfect and complete, lacking nothing." (James 1:2-4)*

Everybody loves to experience hardship and trials, right? Of course not — it is not human nature to embrace any kind of pain. In fact, we try to avoid it at all costs. That's why today's verses are so different than anything the world can teach us. God actually commands us to "count it all joy" when we experience the hardships of life. Lost your job? Count it all joy! Your child is making some poor decisions? Count it all joy! You've been diagnosed with an illness? Count it all joy!

To be clear, Scripture is not saying we need to be excited about losing a job, hurting for a child, or dealing with an illness. But the Scripture says that even in the midst of our suffering there is cause for joy. Why? Because "the testing of your faith produces patience." I've often heard people say, "I prayed for patience once and I'll never do that again." What they mean is they don't want the adversity that comes with developing patience, but without trials there can be no perseverance.

James says we need to "let patience have its perfect work, that you may be perfect and complete, lacking nothing." James isn't saying that it's possible for human beings to be perfect on this side of heaven. There was only one perfect human being, and His name is Jesus Christ. What James means is that we can be mature. Trials equip us with perseverance that covers the "gaps" of our lives. So then, we don't go looking for trials, but when they come we rejoice because we know God is at work.

## November 21 — Love with Heart and Lips

*"So they come to you as people do, they sit before you as My people, and they hear your words, but they do not do them; for with their mouth they show much love, but their hearts pursue their own gain." (Ezekiel 33:31)*

There is so much good news contained in the Word of God, but there's also a good deal of bad news. The bad news usually comes to the people of God through the prophets of God. When God's people sinned, it was up to the prophets to expose the sins of the people and call them to repentance. In today's verse, God talks to one of His great prophets — Ezekiel. God wants Ezekiel to know that even though the people come to hear from him, they really aren't listening.

God says, "They come to you ... they sit before you ... they hear your words, but they do not do them." This reminds us of a key truth. God did not give us His Word for the purpose of *information*. God has given us His Word for the purpose of *transformation*. Ezekiel was faithfully preaching the Word of God to the people; they even heard what he had to say, but they never bothered to apply what they heard. Sadly, many people today still hear the Word of God but simply choose to disregard it.

God shares one final indictment — "with their mouth they show much love, but their hearts pursue their own gain." These words describe the person who puts a Christian bumper sticker on his/her car but then drives with road rage. Or, perhaps the person who wears a Christian T-shirt but is ruthless to fellow employees. *We can say we love God with our lips, but our lives will show it.* So then, we need to ask ourselves: Do I only love God with my mouth, or do I love Him with my whole heart?

## November 22 – A Stricter Judgment

*"My brethren, let not many of you become teachers, knowing that we shall receive a stricter judgment." (James 3:1)*

I was first introduced to this verse while pursuing my master's degree at Southeastern Baptist Theological Seminary. My professor, Dr. Greg Lawson, shared this verse with our class as something of a warning. Until I read the verse, I never knew that preachers and teachers of the Word would be held to a higher standard. But once I read the verse, it made perfect sense. If we're going to be teaching the Word, we should have a greater understanding of what it says.

The Bible says a great deal about the judgment reserved for all mankind at the end of time. Hebrews 9:27 says, "It is appointed to man once to die, and after that the judgment." In 2 Corinthians 5:10, the Apostle Paul says, "We must all stand before the judgment seat of Christ." Every person will stand before Jesus Christ in judgment at the end of this life. Some people have asked me, "Even Christians have to stand in judgment?" The answer is yes — every person will stand before Jesus.

When we stand before Christ, there's one thing that will matter more than anything else — did we receive the free pardon of sin that comes through faith in Jesus Christ? Has His precious blood covered our sins? If the answer is no, we will be eternally separated from God's grace and mercy. If the answer is yes, He will usher us into heaven. But for all the teachers among us, we will also give an account for how we led God's people. So then, teachers, let us be sure to "rightly divide the Word of truth" (2 Timothy 2:15) and do what it says!

## November 23 – Sins of Omission

*"Therefore, to him who knows to do good and does not do it, to him it is sin."* (James 4:17)

The Bible is very clear that all of us are sinners. Paul said, "All have sinned and fall short of the glory of God" (Romans 3:23). Humans commit sins every day — we say something we shouldn't have said, we look at something we shouldn't have looked at, we go somewhere we shouldn't have gone, etc. Thankfully, the blood of Jesus is enough to cover all our sins! But did you know our greatest sins are not sins of commission? They're often sins of omission.

Here's what I mean — unfortunately, we often do things that are displeasing to God. But there are many times we simply fail to do what God wants us to do. In those cases, it's not that we *committed* a sin, it's that we sinned by *omitting* the plan of God from our lives. For example, who among us has not sensed the leadership of the Holy Spirit to stop and pray, but we said to ourselves, "I'm too busy"? Or, the Spirit directed us to witness to someone, but we said, "There's no way I can do that"?

When I spend time confessing my sins to God, it seems I always bear more sin based on what I didn't do rather than what I did do. The point James makes in today's verse is clear — if we know the will of God and don't do it, we are just as guilty as if we had broken one of His commands. So, now would probably be a good time to do a spiritual inventory. Has God been leading you to do something for His glory? Have you done it? If not, what do you intend to do about it?

## November 24 – The Power of Prayer

*"Confess your trespasses to one another, and pray for one another, that you may be healed. The effective, fervent prayer of a righteous man avails much."* (James 5:16)

As James closes out his letter to the church, he leaves us with some wonderful practical instructions. Today's verse tells us first about the importance of confessing our sins to one another. Many conflicts and divisions would be healed immediately if one or both parties would simply say, "I'm sorry. I sinned. Would you please forgive me?" There is a great deal of love and healing that comes with humbling ourselves before someone else. Even our physical bodies can be made well!

James then commands that we pray for one another. In this context, he instructs us to pray specifically for someone's healing, as verse 14 says, "Is anyone among you sick? Let him call for the elders of the church, and let them pray over him, anointing him with oil in the name of the Lord." The ancients would use oil for a variety of medicinal purposes, but the healing was really found in faith. Verse 15 says, "The prayer of faith will save the sick."

But how can we know our prayers have power? James answers that question — "The effective, fervent prayer of a righteous man avails much." That being the case, there are two requirements. First, our prayers need to be fervent. That is, they need to be genuine and consistent. Furthermore, our prayers need to come from someone who lives a holy life. If we're not honoring God with our lives, what makes us think He would answer our prayers? So if we want prayer that prevails, we need to live holy and pray fervently.

## November 25 – The Goodness of Unity

*"Behold, how good and how pleasant it is for brethren to dwell together in unity!" (Psalm 133:1)*

Have you noticed how much division there is in the world today? All over the globe, nations war with one another. Evil dictators threaten to launch nuclear missiles toward rival countries. Even in our country, the division is strong. Races have divided against races in ways we haven't witnessed since the civil rights movement. The division has even reached professional sports. Football players have decided not to stand when their own country's national anthem is played.

The words of the psalmist desperately need to be heard today and every day. Notice first that his words are directed at "the brethren." In our New Testament context, I take this as a reference to the church. As followers of the Lord Jesus, there is much more that unites us than divides us. The Apostle Paul said, "There is one body and one Spirit, just as you were called in one hope of your calling; one Lord, one faith, one baptism; one God and Father of all, who is above all, and through all, and in you all" (Ephesians 4:4-6).

The world will never find peace until there is unity in the church. Stop to consider "how good and how pleasant" it is when the church works together without fussing and fighting. When the children of Israel returned to their homeland, they found it decimated. They joined hands, rolled up their sleeves, and got busy rebuilding the wall. Because the people had a mind to work, the wall was completed in only fifty-two days! So, brothers and sisters, let us set us aside our differences and pursue the glory of God TOGETHER! We're much better together than we are apart.

## November 26 – Rules for Many Relationships

*"Honor all people. Love the brotherhood. Fear God. Honor the king." (1 Peter 2:17)*

Today's verse is so simple, yet so profound. In one verse, we have clear direction about what our relationship should be with four groups of people — mankind, the church, the Lord, and governing officials. Peter begins by commanding us to "honor all people." In other words, every human being of every race, gender, socioeconomic status, etc., is worthy of dignity and respect. Why? Because every human being has been made in the image of God (Genesis 1:26). We must honor and love every person.

Peter then instructs us to "love the brotherhood." Clearly, this is a reference to the church — brothers and sisters in Christ. Every human being has a birth family, but if you've been born again by the power of God, you also have a spiritual family. Christ commanded us to love the church! He said, "By this all will know that you are My disciples, if you have love for one another" (John 13:35). Love your family of faith by taking your place in the Body of Christ.

Peter then reminds us to "fear God." Solomon said, "The fear of the LORD is the beginning of wisdom" (Proverbs 9:10). At all times, we are to remember that our God is holy and sinless — always worthy of our reverence and devotion. Finally, Peter instructs us to "honor the king." This is not always easy. Our governing authorities don't always act worthy of honor, but we are to submit regardless. The only exception is if the authorities ask us to do something ungodly. On those occasions, our response should always be, "We ought to obey God rather than men" (Acts 5:29).

## November 27 — When Suffering Is Better

*"For it is better, if it is the will of God, to suffer for doing good than for doing evil." (1 Peter 3:17)*

As human beings, we try to avoid suffering at all costs. We take medications, go to the doctor, and take many other preventative measures. But sometimes, no matter how hard we try, suffering becomes a part of life. We're diagnosed with an illness, a friend turns their back on us, a child goes down the wrong path, etc. Some of our suffering is self-inflicted, but much of our suffering is beyond our control. It's just part of living in a fallen world.

Though none of us would ever prefer suffering, Peter reminds us it's actually better to suffer sometimes than not to suffer at all. He says, "It is better ... to suffer for doing good than for doing evil." For example, you find yourself in a situation where people start using drugs and alcohol. The users begin to pressure you to join them in their substance abuse. If you say yes, you sin against God. If you say no, you will probably be mocked as a party-pooper. What do you do?

Peter is clear — it's much better to be mocked by the world and be honored by God. He and his fellow apostles knew something about suffering. Did you know that every apostle, except John, died a martyr's death? Some of them were hanged. Some were sawn in two. Some were beheaded. And Peter suffered the worst death. According to church history, Peter was sentenced to crucifixion, but he made one request of his executioners. He asked to be crucified upside down, as he didn't feel worthy to die in the same way as His Savior. So, suffering is difficult, but obedience to God is worth it all!

## November 28 – Love Above All Else

*"And above all things have fervent love for one another, for 'love will cover a multitude of sins.'"* (1 Peter 4:8)

As he approaches the end of his letter to the early church, Peter provides some practical commands focused on everyday Christian living. He reminds believers to be serious and watchful about praying, being hospitable to one another, and being good stewards of what God has provided. Yet above all the other commands, Peter says the church needs to have "fervent love for one another." The word translated "fervent" literally means "stretched out."

Consequently, Peter commands believers to have a passionate love for one another that will extend throughout the course of time. And why is loving one another so important? Peter says it's because "love will cover a multitude of sins." Here, Peter quotes Proverbs 10:12 — "Hatred stirs up strife, but love covers all sins." In other words, a contentious person loves drama and despises reconciliation. A loving person is willing to extend forgiveness and mercy for the sake of peace.

These words of Peter remind us of the words of Jesus — "By this all will know that you are My disciples, if you have love for one another" (John 13:35). In other words, the world will not know that we are followers of Christ just because we worship in a beautiful building. The world won't know we're followers of Christ just because we wear a Christian T-shirt. The world will know we belong to Jesus because we love God and we love one another. So then, set aside the hate and spread the love.

## November 29 — A Word for Pastors

*"Shepherd the flock of God which is among you, serving as overseers, not by compulsion but willingly, not for dishonest gain but eagerly; nor as being lords over those entrusted to you, but being examples to the flock." (1 Peter 5:2-3)*

Pastors do a lot of preaching, but sometimes they need to be preached to as well. Today's verses focus on the work of a faithful pastor. In verse 1, Peter addressed the pastors as "elders." The Greek word is *presbuteros*. It can be used to denote an older person, but it can also be used of the office of pastor. Basically, it implies that a pastor is a man worthy of respect because he lives a life above reproach.

Peter commands the pastors to "shepherd the flock of God." Of course, Peter is not talking about sheep — he's talking about the followers of the Lord Jesus Christ, the church. A pastor's job is to shepherd the church — to lead them in paths of righteousness for the glory of God. Further, the pastor is to act as "overseer." The Greek word is *episkopos*, and it is a derivative of words like telescope, stethoscope, etc. It means the pastor is to be the overseer of the church's ministries.

Peter says the pastor's service should be rendered willingly and not by compulsion. In other words, the pastor serves the Lord and the church because it is the passion of his life. Also, the pastor doesn't do his work for "dishonest gain." That is, he doesn't pastor to manipulate others and get rich. He serves because he has to serve — his love for God won't allow him to do otherwise. Peter also says the pastor is not to lord his authority over the church, but rather he's to be a servant leader. Every true pastor looks forward to the second coming of "the Chief Shepherd" — Jesus Christ. When Christ appears, He will reward every faithful pastor with "the crown of glory that does not fade away."

## November 30 – The Origin of Scripture

*"No prophecy of Scripture is of any private interpretation, for prophecy never came by the will of man, but holy men of God spoke as they were moved by the Holy Spirit." (2 Peter 1:20-21)*

While it's difficult to get exact numbers, experts agree the Bible is the best-selling and most widely distributed book of all time. A survey by the Bible Society concluded that around 2.5 billion copies were printed between 1815 and 1975, but more recent estimates put the number at more than 5 billion. The whole Bible has been translated into 349 languages, with 2,123 languages having at least one book of the Bible in that language.

As amazing as that is, the composition of Scripture is just as fascinating. The sixty-six books of the Bible were composed by forty different writers over a period of roughly 1,500 years. That's fifteen centuries! And yet, when someone reads the Bible, they're amazed to find it has one consistent message — there is a holy God who longs to redeem mankind through the blood of His Son Jesus. But how can Scripture be so consistent when so many people were involved in its composition?

It's very simple — though the Bible is the product of forty different writers, there is only One Author. Peter says the Author of Scripture is the Holy Spirit. Evangelicals believe in what theologians call the "verbal plenary inspiration" of Scripture. That is, the Holy Spirit moved the forty writers as they penned the words of the Bible. God worked through each of their unique personalities to give us His inerrant Word. Because God is the Author of Scripture, you can trust every word of the Bible!

## December 1 — God Delivers His Children

> *"Now the king was exceedingly glad for him, and commanded that they should take Daniel up out of the den. So Daniel was taken up out of the den, and no injury whatever was found on him, because he believed in his God." (Daniel 6:23)*

The Word of God is amazing. One of the most amazing stories in Scripture is found in Daniel 6. You might remember that Daniel and his three friends were carried away into Babylon following the fall of Israel in 586 BC. Though they were far from their homeland, Daniel and his friends remained faithful to God. His friends were so faithful that they were condemned to the fiery furnace, but God delivered them from the midst of the fire. Not even the smell of smoke was on their clothes.

Daniel found favor in the eyes of the pagan kings he was forced to serve. One of the kings was Darius. After being tricked into signing a foolish law, Darius was forced to throw his beloved Daniel into a hungry den of lions. The Bible says Daniel was placed into the lions' den, a stone was rolled in place, and the king's signet ring was placed on top as a seal. After a long sleepless night, the king came out the next morning to find Daniel alive. God closed the lions' mouths and spared Daniel.

Today's verse is the king's response — "he was exceedingly glad for him." I'm sure the king was also happy for himself because one of his best men was still alive. When they removed Daniel from the lions' den, they couldn't find a single scratch on him. That's a miracle! Hungry lions would have devoured Daniel, but God closed their mouths. God delivered Daniel for one reason — "because he believed in his God." God delivers every person that places his/her faith in Him!

## December 2 — Why Hasn't Jesus Come Back?

*"The Lord is not slack concerning His promise, as some count slackness, but is longsuffering toward us, not willing that any should perish but that all should come to repentance." (2 Peter 3:9)*

We live in a very skeptical world. People doubt many things, and sometimes we only have ourselves to blame. Humans are skeptical of politicians, promises, and many other things that never come to fruition. We've had to adopt the phrase, "If it sounds too good to be true, it probably is." Christianity is not immune from the skepticism of our age. One of the main arguments skeptics make against Christianity is that Jesus has not returned like He said He would.

The skeptics are right about one thing — Jesus certainly did promise to return. He told His disciples, "I go to prepare a place for you. And if I go and prepare a place for you, I will come again and receive you to Myself; that where I am, there you may be also" (John 14:2-3). Critics of Christianity like to remind us that Jesus said those words about 2,000 years ago. They say, "If Jesus was going to come back, surely He would have done so by now."

So if Jesus is real (and He is), and if He did rise from the dead (and He did), then why is it taking Him so long to come back? Peter answers that question in today's verse. "The Lord is not slack concerning His promise" — that is, He is not late. Rather, He is "longsuffering toward us." Our Lord is so longsuffering that He is "not willing that any should perish but that all should come to repentance." Our Lord has intentionally delayed His coming so that more and more people can receive Him as Savior and be cleansed of their sins. So then, accept the Lord as your King while there is still time!

## December 3 — How Can I Be Forgiven?

*"If we confess our sins, He is faithful and just to forgive us our sins and to cleanse us from all unrighteousness." (1 John 1:9)*

Today's verse highlights the absolute necessity of confession. We live in a world where some people think they are without sin. In the verse preceding this one, John says, "If we say that we have no sin, we deceive ourselves, and the truth is not in us" (v. 8). We can act like we've never done anything wrong, but deep down we know that's a lie. Each of us was born with a disposition toward sin, and given enough time every human being willfully sins against God. We fall short daily!

The good news is that we don't have to stay in our sins. There is a way that we can be forgiven for every wicked thing we've ever done. "If we confess our sins." What does it mean to confess? The Greek word for "confess" is *homologeo*. Literally, it means to say the same thing as another, or to agree. When we confess our sins to God, we're agreeing with God that our failures fall short of His perfection. We agree that our actions prove His perfection and demonstrate our imperfection.

If we're willing to confess our sins to God by the conviction of the Holy Spirit, the Bible says that "He is faithful and just to forgive us our sins." That means God is faithful to His Word — if He says He will forgive those who repent, that's exactly what He means. God's justice demands that He is compassionate and fair — healing our broken spirits. And not only that, He will even "cleanse us from all unrighteousness" — ridding us of unrighteous desires and molding us into the image of His Son!

## December 4 — Our Advocate with the Father

*"My little children, these things I write to you, so that you may not sin. And if anyone sins, we have an Advocate with the Father, Jesus Christ the righteous. And He Himself is the propitiation for our sins, and not for ours only but also for the whole world." (1 John 2:1-2)*

God's perfect will for us is that we will not sin, but sadly we succumb to temptation every day. We should never use our fallen condition as an excuse for sin — "the devil made me do it." No, the Bible is very clear — "But each one is tempted when he is drawn away by his own desires and enticed" (James 1:14). If we want to know who to blame for our sins, we simply need to look in the mirror. Each day, it is our job to deny ourselves, take up the cross, and follow our Savior Jesus (Luke 9:23).

The good news is that our God has made a provision for our weakness and wickedness. "If anyone sins, we have an Advocate with the Father." What is an advocate? Legally speaking, an advocate pleads the cause of another before a judge — someone who comes to the defense of another. So then, the Bible is very clear that we have Someone who comes to our defense before the Heavenly Father. Praise the Lord!

Who is our Advocate? "Jesus Christ the righteous." Only Jesus can advocate for fallen sinners! Why? Because His very name means salvation (Yeshua). His name also reminds us that He is the anointed Messiah of God (Christ). And this verse calls Him "the righteous" — because He was at all points tempted but never fell into sin (Hebrews 4:15). This Jesus, our Advocate, is the "propitiation for our sins and … also for the whole world." He advocates for all those who trust in Him!

## December 5 — The Antichrist and antichrists

*"Little children, it is the last hour; and as you have heard that the Antichrist is coming, even now many antichrists have come, by which we know that it is the last hour." (1 John 2:18)*

Many false prophets have incorrectly predicted the end of the world, and consequently their "ministries" have been discredited. We need to be clear — only God in heaven knows when the end of time will be. Jesus said, "Of that day and hour no one knows, not even the angels of heaven, but My Father only" (Matthew 24:36). While no one can predict exactly when Jesus will return, we know for certain that He is coming back and that the signs of His coming are already visible (Matthew 24:4-14).

In today's verse, John underscores an important truth — we are living in the last age before the return of Christ. God has given us His Law, He has given us His grace, and now we are simply waiting for the promised return of Jesus. Because we're in earth's "11th hour," we know that "the Antichrist is coming." Who is the Antichrist? The Bible tells us the Antichrist will be something of a messianic figure who will emerge just before the Second Coming of Christ (see Revelation 6 and 13).

The Revelation tells us the Antichrist and the False Prophet will be defeated at the end of time, but prior to their defeat they will mislead many people. But in today's verse, John wants us to understand something — deception will not be contained to the Antichrist. In fact, "even now many antichrists have come." How do we know if someone is a modern-day antichrist? "He is antichrist who denies the Father and the Son." Stand your ground against those who deny our God!

## December 6 — Test the Spirits

*"Beloved, do not believe every spirit, but test the spirits, whether they are of God; because many false prophets have gone out into the world. By this you know the Spirit of God: Every spirit that confesses that Jesus Christ has come in the flesh is of God."* (1 John 4:1-2)

Have you ever noticed how many people in the world are spiritual, but how very few give their lives to Christ? Eastern religions are built around the "spiritual" — self-realization, meditation, auras, etc. Many people take a cafeteria approach to spirituality — take a little from Christianity, take a little from Buddhism, take a little from Hinduism, etc. As a result, they end up with something that is very "spiritual" but not very biblical.

Jesus was clear — "God *is* Spirit, and those who worship Him must worship in spirit and truth" (John 4:24). Our God is Spirit, and it is He who has given life to every other spirit. When we're born again, God blesses us with the abiding presence of the Holy Spirit who confirms that we are God's children (Romans 8:15). That said, not every spirit is heaven-sent. The devil and his demons are also spirit, and by no means do they bring glory to God.

So then, we live in a spiritual world, but not every spirit is a Christ-honoring influence. How can we know the difference between a heavenly spirit and a satanic spirit? "Every spirit that confesses that Jesus Christ has come in the flesh is of God." Any spirit that manifests itself in a way that discredits Jesus or His Word is NOT of God. Know the difference — "the fruit of the Spirit is love, joy, peace, longsuffering, kindness, goodness, faithfulness, gentleness, self-control" (Galatians 5:22-23).

## December 7 — Assurance of Salvation

*"These things I have written to you who believe in the name of the Son of God, that you may know that you have eternal life." (1 John 5:13)*

When I was a young seminary student, I had the privilege of preaching on Sundays, but during the week I had to go to class and earn a living for my family. The Lord opened a door for me to work at a Winn-Dixie grocery store very close to my seminary's campus. Working in the "secular world" was a good thing for me — I got to witness to atheists, cult members, nominal Christians, and many others. We had many long conversations about a wide variety of issues.

I distinctly remember witnessing to one sweet lady who was a lifelong Catholic. I had a great deal of respect for her because she was hard-working, and as a mother she was always concerned about her family. Once I asked her, "Do you know for certain that you'll go to heaven when you die?" She said, "No, and I don't think anyone can know that." As soon as I heard her response, the words of this verse crossed my mind and I got to share with her that she could be sure.

Dear friend, you CAN know for CERTAIN that you are a child of God and that heaven will be your eternal home when you die. That kind of knowledge is called "assurance of salvation." If you have placed your faith in Jesus — if you truly believe that He is the Son of God — then you will absolutely spend your eternity worshiping the Father in heaven. But consider this — the evidence of salvation is surrender. Believing in God means you've surrendered your life to Jesus. Are you surrendered to Him?

## December 8 – Think Before You Speak

*"Do you see a man hasty in his words? There is more hope for a fool than for him." (Proverbs 29:20)*

"Impulsive" is defined as "acting or doing without forethought." Sometimes being impulsive is a good thing. I remember watching a video of a child walking out into rush hour traffic. There was an adult standing close by, and as soon as he saw the boy toddling into oncoming traffic he rushed into action, picked the boy up, and saved his life. At the ocean, I've seen lifeguards do the same thing — acting with no thought to their own safety so that someone else's life could be saved.

Unfortunately, there are many times when acting impulsively can be very bad. That's especially true of the words we say and the manner in which we say them. All of us have been guilty of blurting out the first thing that came to mind. Refusing to think before speaking has cost many people their relationships, their jobs, and their credibility. The old saying "sticks and stones may break my bones, but words will never hurt me" — we all know that's not really accurate.

Today's verse encourages us to think before speaking. And what should run through our minds? Paul left us a verse that can help — "Let no corrupt word proceed out of your mouth, but what is good for necessary edification, that it may impart grace to the hearers" (Ephesians 4:29). We should ask ourselves, "Is what I'm about to say going to build someone up or tear someone down? Is this going to help or hurt the situation?" Let's not be found playing the fool. Think and PRAY before you speak!

## December 9 – No Greater Joy

*"I have no greater joy than to hear that my
children walk in truth." (3 John 4)*

Joy is "a feeling of great pleasure and happiness." There are a countless number of things that bring us joy. How about marrying the man/woman of your dreams? How about the birth of your first child? How about the time your favorite team won the championship? A trip to the mountains, a trip to the beach, a trip to your favorite restaurant — all of these things are sure to put a smile on your face. For many people, life is nothing less than the pursuit of perpetual joy.

In today's verse, the Apostle John tells us what brought the biggest smile to his face. No, it's not a lot of money, worldwide notoriety, or even planting a huge amount of churches. The apostle's greatest joy was "to hear that my children walk in truth." Why is truth so important? Because without truth we can't even worship the Heavenly Father (John 4:23-24). Jesus Himself is the Way, the Truth, and the Life. When we operate outside the bounds of truth, we cease to serve Jesus Christ.

I've got six children. All of them are enrolled in school and have big dreams concerning all that the future holds in store. My dream for each of my kids is not that they would make a lot of money. It's not that they would marry the most beautiful woman or handsome man. It's not that they would drive nice cars and live on the nicest side of town. My dream is that my children walk in God's truth each day of their lives. How about you? Are you walking in truth or are you perpetuating a lie?

## December 10 – Search Me and Lead Me

*"Search me, O God, and know my heart; try me, and know my anxieties; and see if there is any wicked way in me, and lead me in the way everlasting." (Psalm 139:23-24)*

Today's passage takes us to Psalm 139 — a psalm of David praising God for His omniscience and omnipresence. After standing in awe of God throughout the psalm, David asks God to do several things for him at the conclusion. First, he says *search me*. In other words, "God, please analyze my life as only You can!" That sounds like something a little intimidating, doesn't it? When was the last time you asked God to search through the secrets of your life? FYI — He already knows our secrets anyway!

Next, David asks God to *know me* — to "know my heart" and to "know my anxieties." God knows every fiber of your being. David is simply asking God to understand all his frailties. It's good to know we serve a God who knows everything we struggle with, and yet He loves us anyway! David also asks for the Lord to *try me*. In this context, to "try" something is to prove its integrity. David essentially asks God to prove his character — whether or not he is really a man of God.

David then asks the Lord to *see me* — "see if there is any wicked way in me." In other words, he asked God to point out any inclinations toward sin — any areas where a root of wickedness could be rising up. If we ask God to point out our impurities, He certainly will! And finally, David asks the Lord to *lead me* — "lead me in the way everlasting." This is an earnest prayer to be led by God rather than the influence of the world. May we all ask God to search us and lead us as well!

## December 11 — Readers, Hearers, and Doers

> *"Blessed is he who reads and those who hear the words of this prophecy, and keep those things which are written in it; for the time is near." (Revelation 1:3)*

Today's verse takes us to the Revelation — God's prophetic Word to the Apostle John concerning the end of time. Revelation is one of the most widely-read and widely-debated books of the Bible. After reading its words, scholars have come up with terms like premillennial, amillennial, and postmillennial. Some speak of being pretribulation, mid-tribulation, or post-tribulation. Subjects such as the Antichrist, the mark of the beast, and the kingdom of God are hot topics of Revelation conversation.

All those discussions are fine and necessary, but from the outset of the book our Lord wants to make one thing very clear. The only ones who can expect a blessing are those who deal faithfully with what God has revealed. So how do we do that? First, we must be *readers* of the Word — "Blessed is he who reads." You will not get very far in your relationship with God if you are not an avid reader of His Word. We must constantly safeguard our time spent reading the Scriptures.

Further, we must go beyond reading to *hearing* the Word — "those who hear the words of this prophecy." It's one thing to read the Bible, but it's another thing to understand it. So then, we can't just read the Bible — we must study the text for comprehension. And of course, we must be *doers* of the Word — "keep those things which are written in it." Remember, God gave us His word for information AND transformation! The end is near — make certain you read, hear, and apply the Word of God!

## December 12 – Forsaking Your First Love

*"Nevertheless I have this against you, that you have left your first love." (Revelation 2:4)*

There's a good chance you have a significant other, and if not you can probably remember a time when you did. If you have a significant other — a spouse, fiancée, or special friend — I bet you can look back and remember what it was like when the two of you met and began to date. Remember the butterflies in your stomach. Remember the way you were afraid to eat in front of him/her. Remember how you used to hold hands and talk for hours at a time.

Perhaps you've been with that significant other for months or years. Answer this question honestly: What is the current status of your relationship? Do you love that person just as much as you used to? Do you love them more? Have certain barriers hindered your relationship, or have you forsaken your first love through unfaithfulness? I think we'd all have to agree it is entirely possible for someone to forsake his/her first love by substituting other "loves" in their place.

Today's verse is Jesus speaking to the church at Ephesus. They had done many amazing things for the glory of God (Revelation 2:2-3), but just because you're "busy for God" doesn't mean you're really in love with Him. So how is your love for the Lord? Is it as strong as it used to be, or have the distractions of life and sin kept you from loving Him with all your heart, soul, mind, and strength? If so, Jesus has one word for you — "repent." Do whatever it takes to make Him your first and greatest love!

# December 13 — Lukewarm Christians

*"I know your works, that you are neither cold nor hot. I could wish you were cold or hot. So then, because you are lukewarm, and neither cold nor hot, I will vomit you out of My mouth." (Revelation 3:15-16)*

When it's hot outside, there's nothing better than a nice tall glass of water, lemonade, or sweet tea. Likewise, when it's a bitter cold winter day, there's nothing more soothing than a tall mug of hot chocolate or a bowl of piping hot soup. But in both cases — hot or cold — the last thing we want is something lukewarm. Room temperature water really doesn't satisfy our thirst on a hot day, and lukewarm hot chocolate really doesn't warm us up when we're freezing cold.

Today's verse comes directly from Jesus directed to the church at Laodicea. We need to understand something about Laodicca to rightly interpret this verse. Laodicea was known for its hot springs. People came from all around to soak in the hot springs for medicinal purposes. Likewise, the city was also the beneficiary of an aqueduct that carried cold water into the city. So then, hot water had a medicinal purpose and cold water had a physical purpose — both were good!

One thing that served no real purpose for the Laodiceans was lukewarm water — it wasn't warm enough for healing and it wasn't cold enough for refreshment. When Jesus calls the Laodiceans "lukewarm," essentially He's saying that by trusting in their own prosperity they've become useless for the cause of Christ. I wonder, have you allowed circumstances to render you useless for the cause of Christ? If so, here is Christ's command to you today: "Be zealous and repent."

## December 14 — Dealing with Correction

*"Let the righteous strike me; it shall be kindness. And let him rebuke me; it shall be as excellent oil; let my head not refuse it." (Psalm 141:5)*

Did you parents ever tell you, "This is going to hurt me worse than it hurts you"? Did you believe them? Probably not — it was hard to believe that our parents could actually hurt when we were the ones receiving the punishment. When we were kids, correction probably hurt us more physically. Where I came from, it was not uncommon for a disobedient child to get a "whooping," or maybe even some correction involving a belt or switch. Those things usually got my attention quickly.

As we grow older, we don't get too many spankings, but we still need correction. Sometimes correction comes by way of your spouse. Sometimes it could be through a parent. Still other times it could be the warm rebuke of a teacher. No matter who corrects us, sometimes it's hard for us to accept. Why? Because we are prideful people — we don't like to admit we're wrong and someone else is right. For that reason, when we're corrected we often get upset.

Today's verse reminds us that the correction of a righteous person should not be resisted. If a godly man/woman takes the time to correct you, receive it as a blessing, not a burden. Why? Because "it shall be kindness" and "excellent oil." If you listen to the correction of someone who loves the Lord, you'll be more like Christ by heeding their counsel. So then, the next time a godly friend corrects you, put your pride aside and make the necessary adjustments for the glory of God.

## December 15 — Worthy Is the Lamb

*"And they sang a new song, saying: 'You are worthy to take the scroll, and to open its seals; for You were slain, and have redeemed us to God by Your blood out of every tribe and tongue and people and nation, and have made us kings and priests to our God; and we shall reign on the earth.'" (Revelation 5:9-10)*

The Revelation is an amazing book. In Chapter 1, we're introduced to the glorified Jesus Christ. In Chapters 2-3, Jesus instructs and encourages the seven churches of Asia Minor. In Chapter 4, we get a glimpse of the glory of heaven. In Chapter 5, the Apostle John sees a scroll with many seals that need to be broken in order for God's will to be done. The heavens were searched to find someone worthy enough to break the seals and read the scroll, but no one emerged. As a result, John wept bitterly.

But just then, one of the twenty-four elders reassured John that "the Lion of the tribe of Judah ... has prevailed to open the scroll and to loose its seven seals" (Revelation 5:5). Jesus Christ — the Lion of Judah — is worthy to reign over heaven and earth! Through their new song, the elders of heaven explain why Jesus is worthy. "For you were slain" — like a lamb to the slaughter, Jesus died for us! "And have redeemed us to God by Your blood" — through His blood, Jesus paid the price for our sins!

"Out of every tribe and tongue and people and nation" — in other words, the ground is level at the foot of the cross. It's doesn't matter your color, nationality, or economic status — if you've placed your faith in Jesus, you are a child of God! "Have made us kings and priests to our God" — we will reign with Jesus and even now we can offer Him the sacrifice of praise. "Worthy is the Lamb ... to receive power and riches and wisdom, and strength and honor and glory and blessing!" (Revelation 5:12).

## December 16 – Tribulation Terror

*"And the kings of the earth, the great men, the rich men, the commanders, the mighty men, every slave and every free man, hid themselves in the caves and in the rocks of the mountains, and said to the mountains and rocks, 'Fall on us and hide us from the face of Him who sits on the throne and from the wrath of the Lamb!'" (Revelation 6:15-16)*

There are many prophecies found in Scripture. Many have already been fulfilled, but some are yet to come. In Revelation, nearly all the prophecies revolve around the second coming of Christ and His kingdom. While there is some disagreement among Bible scholars about all that Scripture predicts, no true believer doubts that Jesus is coming back. Prior to His second coming, the Antichrist will usher in a seven-year period known as the Tribulation.

Most commentators believe the rider on the white horse at the beginning of Revelation 6 is the Antichrist, identified as "the man of sin" in other portions of Scripture (2 Thessalonians 2:3-4). Paul tells us the Antichrist "opposes and exalts himself above all that is called God or that is worshiped, so that he sits as God in the temple of God, showing himself that he is God." Daniel 9 leads us to believe that he will strike a treaty, gain the trust of many nations, then finally reveal his true character.

Most agree that the coming of the Antichrist will set off a seven-year period of horror and misery on the earth. According to the words of Jesus in Matthew 24, the Tribulation will grow worse and worse as the years march on. Followers of Christ look forward to the second coming of Jesus, but most of the world's inhabitants will not see it that way. They will attempt to flee the "wrath of the Lamb," but there will be nowhere to hide. Only God's children will be spared at the end of time!

## December 17 — No More Suffering

*"They shall neither hunger anymore nor thirst anymore; the sun shall not strike them, nor any heat; for the Lamb who is in the midst of the throne will shepherd them and lead them to living fountains of waters. And God will wipe away every tear from their eyes." (Revelation 7:16-17)*

Suffering is an all-too-real part of the human experience. Just think for a moment about many of the ways we suffer. There is physical suffering — hospitals are typically full as they treat those experiencing bodily suffering. There is emotional suffering — the internal duress that comes from heartbreak, loneliness, etc. There is mental suffering, especially when Satan attacks our thoughts. Other forms of suffering include relational, vocational, spiritual, etc.

People are hurting all over this fallen world, but the good news is that this world won't be fallen forever. Jesus Christ is returning to make all things new. The end of Revelation tells us that Jesus is going to provide a new heaven, a new earth, and a New Jerusalem. In the New Jerusalem, "they shall neither hunger anymore nor thirst." Hunger and a lack of clean drinking water are worldwide problems, but all those problems will be long gone in heaven.

The Bible tells us that "the sun shall not strike them" in heaven. Why? Because "the glory of God illuminated it. The Lamb is its light" (Revelation 21:23). Jesus Christ — the Lamb of God — "will shepherd and lead them to living fountains of waters." In other words, God Himself will provide everything we need in heaven. We will never lack anything! And of course, "God will wipe away every tear from their eyes." Leave the Kleenex on earth because there'll be no more sorrow in heaven.

# December 18 — Running from God

*"Now the word of the LORD came to Jonah the son of Amittai, saying, 'Arise, go to Nineveh, that great city, and cry out against it; for their wickedness has come up before Me.' But Jonah arose to flee to Tarshish from the presence of the LORD."* (Jonah 1:1-3)

I admire runners. I know some people who run in all sorts of weather — hot/cold, dry/rain, calm/windy, etc. Some of my friends run many miles almost every day. Sometimes on TV I catch the coverage of a marathon. It blows my mind that someone could run twenty-six miles without stopping! Running is a wonderful thing because it comes with many great health benefits. Most runners are able to maintain their weight while experiencing a boost of energy and metabolism.

Yet, there are times when running is the worst thing we can do, especially when we're running from God. That's exactly what the prophet Jonah did about 3,000 years ago. I'm sure you remember the story from Sunday School. We tend to emphasize the fact that he was swallowed by a whale, but probably don't take enough time to consider his initial mistake. When God commanded Jonah to go east to Nineveh, Jonah went as far west as he could go — to Joppa (modern-day Spain).

Jonah was a man of God. Why would he run from a preaching assignment in Nineveh? Because his people, the Jews, had been severely harassed by the Ninevites and he wanted them to die. He didn't want the Ninevites to repent because he wanted them to die and go to hell. That's a horrible attitude for a man of God, but even God's men can get in the flesh. Jonah didn't have a good reason to run from God, and neither do you! What has He called you to do? Don't run away — do it today!

## December 19 – Don't Wait Too Late

*"But the rest of mankind, who were not killed by these plagues, did not repent of the works of their hands, that they should not worship demons, and idols of gold, silver, brass, stone, and wood, which can neither see nor hear nor walk. And they did not repent of their murders or their sorceries or their sexual immorality or their thefts."* (Revelation 9:20-21)

In my years of ministry, I've attempted to witness to lots of folks. Most have been receptive, but some have been strong-willed and skeptical. Rarely I've had people say things like, "If what you're saying is true, I'll just wait for Jesus to come back. When Jesus comes back, then I'll place my faith in Him." I encourage them not to wait too late because there will be very little opportunity for repentance after the rapture of the church.

Let me explain. Revelation 7 tells us that a good number of people will be saved during the seven-year period known as the Tribulation — 144,000 Jews and many other Gentiles. But sadly, today's verses tell us it will not be easy to repent during the Tribulation. Why? Because Paul tells us that by this point in human history, "the one who restrains" (2 Thessalonians 2:6) will be removed from the earth. I take that to mean that the Holy Spirit will not be present to convict men of their sins.

If that's the case, then it's easy to see why so many will not repent during the Tribulation, even after they've experienced some of the worst plagues in mankind's history. They won't cease worshiping demons and idols, nor will they repent of their rampant wickedness. So then, if you're one of those people who thinks you'll wait around until Jesus comes back before you get right with God, you need to reconsider immediately. Like Paul said, "now is the day of salvation" (2 Corinthians 6:2).

## December 20 – Talking 'Bout My Generation

*"There is a generation that curses its father, and does not bless its mother. There is a generation that is pure in its own eyes, yet is not washed from its filthiness."* (Proverbs 30:11-12)

In 1965, well-known rock band The Who released a song that set the stage for much of the teenage revolution that permeated the 1960s. The song is called "My Generation," and it says, "People try to put us down just because we get around. Things they do look awful cold, I hope I die before I get old." Basically, the song was an anthem of teenage rebellion. It empowered an entire generation of young people to disregard the counsel of the older generation in pursuit of their own pleasures.

The song sounds much like today's verses. "There is a generation that curses its father and does not bless its mother." In the 21st century, sadly this is a recurring theme. We live in a day where children are raised with many modern conveniences. In some cases, they are awarded with many comforts without having to work for them. And the ones who they should be thanking for all their blessings are often the objects of their unkindness and disdain.

Unfortunately, this same generation "is pure in its own eyes, yet is not washed from its filthiness." We live in a time where most seem to do what is right in their own eyes (Judges 21:25). We've celebrated sin and vilified truth. Please don't hear me saying that only the young are susceptible to this wickedness. The sad truth is that many young people are only repeating what they've learned from their parents. And yet, there is good news — Jesus is STILL the answer for this and every generation!

## December 21 — The Two Witnesses

*"And I will give power to my two witnesses, and they will prophesy one thousand two hundred and sixty days, clothed in sackcloth." (Revelation 11:3)*

The Bible is very clear that Jesus is coming back to rapture His church and take them to heaven (1 Thessalonians 4:13-18). When He does, the Bible tells us that a seven-year period of judgment will be unleashed on the earth. This seven-year period is known as the Tribulation. Daniel 9 and other passages seem to indicate that the first half of the Tribulation will be relatively peaceful, but the last three and a half years — "one thousand two hundred and sixty days" — will be more like hell on earth.

In the midst of rampant wickedness during the last half of the Tribulation, God will raise up two witnesses who will "have power to shut heaven, so that no rain falls in the days of their prophecy; and they have power over waters to turn them to blood, and to strike the earth with all plagues, as often as they desire" (Revelation 11:6). The two witnesses will have one purpose — to share the Gospel one last time so that everyone will have the opportunity to be saved before the Second Coming of Christ.

At the height of their ministry, Scripture tells us that the Antichrist (the Beast) will strike them dead (Revelation 11:7) and that they will remain dead for three-and-a-half days (Revelation 11:9). At the end of that three-and-a-half days, God will raise them back to life and take them to heaven (Revelation 11:11-12). Many speculate about who the witnesses will be. Some say Moses, Elijah, or maybe Enoch. Their identity is not important, but their message is — Jesus is LORD, and we MUST receive Him before it's too late!

## December 22 — The Woman, the Child, and the Dragon

*"Now a great sign appeared in heaven: a woman clothed with the sun, with the moon under her feet, and on her head a garland of twelve stars. Then being with child, she cried out in labor and in pain to give birth. And another sign appeared in heaven: behold, a great, fiery red dragon having seven heads and ten horns, and seven diadems on his heads." (Revelation 12:1-3)*

One of the keys to understanding any passage of Scripture is to identify its genre. In other words, what sort of literature is it? There are many different genres in the Bible — historical narrative, wisdom, didactic, etc. The Revelation belongs to a genre known as apocalyptic — it utilizes a lot of imagery and makes many statements about the future. Yet, apocalyptic texts also take a look back into the past. That's exactly what we have with today's verses.

Revelation 12 introduces the story of a woman, her child, and a menacing dragon. The text tells us she was "clothed with the sun, with the moon under her feet, and on her head a garland of twelve stars." The twelve stars indicate the woman's identity — she is Israel, the nation of twelve tribes. Revelation 12:5 tells us "she bore a male Child who was to rule all nations with a rod of iron." Who could that Ruler be? None other than King Jesus! So then, the Child is Israel's Messiah — Jesus.

But what about this dragon? Revelation 12:4 says that "the dragon stood before the woman who was ready to give birth, to devour her Child as soon as it was born." Clearly, the dragon represents the devil who was banished from hell along with a third of the angels (Revelation 12:4). The devil did everything he could to destroy Jesus and thwart God's plan of salvation. But regardless of all his effort, the devil was unsuccessful in stopping the Lion of Judah. The dragon is great, but our God is greater!

## December 23 — The Number of the Beast

*"Here is wisdom. Let him who has understanding calculate the number of the beast, for it is the number of a man: His number is 666." (Revelation 13:18)*

Revelation 13 introduces us to two beasts — one lesser and one greater. The first of the beasts is also known as "the Antichrist" or "the man of sin" in other portions of the New Testament. Chapter 13 tells us he has "seven heads and ten horns, and on his horns ten crowns." The seven heads are representative of seven great world empires that fell before his time, and the ten horns represent the strength of those empires. The Antichrist will sway the scepter of the world at the end of time.

The Bible is clear that the Antichrist will be empowered by "the dragon" — the devil. The Antichrist will be very winsome, and most speculate that he will even appear to rise from the dead after suffering a mortal wound (Revelation 13:3). Helping the Antichrist in his worldwide conquest will be the other beast of Revelation 13, otherwise called "the false prophet." He, too, will be empowered by the devil and will perform signs and wonders intended to confirm the satanic message of the Antichrist.

But what about the number of the beast? Perhaps you've heard this called the mark of the beast. It is very simple — 666. In the Scripture, "6" is the number of man and consequently a symbol of imperfection since man fell into sin. "Three" is the number of completion and is pictured in the three Persons of the Trinity — Father, Son, and Holy Spirit. So then, the number of the beast represents the complete wickedness of the Antichrist who will force all unbelievers to receive his mark at the end of time.

## December 24 — The Beauty of Praise

*"Praise the Lord! For it is good to sing praises to our God; for it is pleasant, and praise is beautiful." (Psalm 147:1)*

Our God is worthy of praise! Over and over, the Bible commands us to praise the Lord, but really what else could we do? When we think about how holy He is, when we think of how loving He is, when we think of how merciful He is — what else can we do but praise Him? In today's verse, the psalmist uses three words to describe the praise of God's people. First, he tells us that praise is "good." In other words, it is right, appropriate, and totally reasonable (Romans 12:2). Praising God is never wrong!

Notice he says it is good "to sing praises to God." I take that to mean that all able-bodied believers should sing praise to God. I've heard some use the excuse that they can't sing so they just remain silent during worship. It's been well-said that God doesn't require a pleasant noise. Rather, He simply commands that we make a "joyful noise" (Psalm 100:1). Singing praise to God is good because it is simply the choral outpouring of a praise that rises as we serve Him.

The psalmist also tells us praise is pleasant. That means praise is not hateful or contentious — it is like a cool breeze that blows across your face on a hot day. Praise will revive your spirit and refresh your soul. And of course, the writer tells us that praise is beautiful. It's an amazing thing when God's people praise the Lord "in the beauty of holiness" (Psalm 96:9). When the praises go up, the message of Christ's victory reverberates through all of hell.

# December 25 — Make God First

*"This people says, 'The time has not come, the time that the LORD's house should be built.' Then the word of the LORD came by Haggai the prophet, saying, 'Is it time for you yourselves to dwell in your paneled houses, and this temple to lie in ruins?'" (Haggai 1:2-4)*

About 2,600 years ago, Israel (Judah) was besieged by the Babylonians. The Babylonians destroyed nearly everything in Jerusalem, including the temple that Solomon built for the glory of God. Not only that, but practically all of the males, along with some of the women and children, were carried away to Babylon. Just a few decades later, the Persians overcame the Babylonians, and the Persian king allowed the Jews to go back home and repatriate their homeland.

Upon their return, the Jews were shocked and saddened by the devastation they found. So where did the Jews begin their rebuilding efforts? They started with their own homes, and for that reason God cursed their efforts and sent a prophet named Haggai to confront them. Today's verses are the words God spoke through His servant. Essentially, God asked, "Why have you finished your own houses while the house of God lies in ruins?"

That's a problem we still have today — we give ourselves the first and best, while God receives anything that's left. Think about it — one example is the way people give to the Lord's work. Instead of tithing biblically (the first 10 percent to the Lord), some people elect to pitch in a few dollars if there's anything left. We give God the leftovers of our time, our effort, our thoughts, etc. Instead of making God last, let's vow to keep the Lord and His work first in everything that we do!

# December 26 — Armageddon

*"And they gathered them together to the place called in Hebrew, Armageddon." (Revelation 16:16)*

Israel is a breathtaking place. Though it's not the largest country in the world by any means, it features just about anything you want to see — the Mediterranean, the Dead Sea, beautiful cities, harsh desert, etc. One of the ancient cities in Israel is Megiddo, which is located in Galilee. Of particular interest is what the Jews call Har Megiddo — the hill just outside the current city where the ancient town was located. In English, we call that location Armageddon.

Today's verse tells us that at the end of time, the armies of the world will gather at Armageddon for one final battle. Who will be fighting against one another? Keep in mind that this battle will transpire at the end of the Tribulation — the seven-year period initiated by the rapture of the church when the Antichrist will reign. Empowered by the devil and aided by the False Prophet, the Antichrist will convince the world's armies to gather for battle in the valley of Armageddon.

The good news is that the Antichrist and all the world's armies will not be victorious. Why? Because they will go to battle against Jesus and all the armies of heaven. Revelation 19 tells us the outcome — "the beast was captured, and with him the false prophet ... and the rest were killed with the sword which proceeded from the mouth of Him who sat on the horse" (Revelation 19:20-21). That Man is Jesus Christ, and with one word He will strike the nations and prove that He alone is King of kings and Lord of lords!

## December 27 — The Mother of Harlots

*"And on her forehead a name was written:*
MYSTERY, BABYLON THE GREAT,
THE MOTHER OF HARLOTS
AND OF THE ABOMINATIONS
OF THE EARTH." *(Revelation 17:5)*

There were many powerful civilizations in the ancient world, and not many could rival the powerful Babylonian Empire. For about 200 years the Babylonians ruled the world, and even after their demise to the Persians, Babylonian culture and ideas affected each proceeding culture. For instance, it's been well-said that the Romans perfected crucifixion, but it actually originated with the Babylonians. The invention of such a heinous death tells us a little about their wicked culture.

Idolatry began in Babylon (Babel) with a man named Nimrod (Genesis 10:8ff), and later the cult of mother and child — Semiramis and Tammuz — was initiated there as well. This cult was conserved by the Greek and Roman religious systems. So then, when we think about today's verse, we can begin to make sense of "Babylon the Great, the mother of harlots." More than likely, this will be more of a spiritual revival of Babylonian wickedness that will fuel the new world order at the end of time.

Revelation 17 tells us this "harlot" will be responsible for the death of many Christians (Revelation 17:6). But what exactly is this harlot? While the Bible does not answer every aspect of that question, many have speculated that this last great Babylon will be the religion of the new world order. It will be steeped in ecumenism and its only absolute will be this — Jesus Christ is not Lord, and all those who worship Him must die. The good news? Jesus Christ will crush Babylon the harlot once and for all.

# December 28 — The Blood of the Martyrs

*"And in her was found the blood of prophets and saints, and of all who were slain on the earth." (Revelation 18:24)*

At the end of time, Babylon the Great — the ecumenical spirit of a wicked empire — will resurface and many will die. Among them will be many Christians who will choose death rather than receiving the mark of the beast. Christian persecution is nothing new — from Christians being thrown to the lions in the Roman Coliseum to Christians being beheaded in the Middle East in our modern time. Early church father Tertullian once said, "The blood of the martyrs is the seed of the church."

Consider these worldwide numbers. Every year, 245 million Christians experience high levels of persecution for their decision to follow Christ. Over 4,000 Christians are killed in the top fifty persecution countries. Over 2,600 Christians are detained annually in those same countries without a trial or due process. In seven of the Top Ten WWL (World Watch List) countries, the primary cause of persecution is Islamic oppression. One hundred five churches are attacked, burned, or vandalized each month.

Does God really care about those who have died for the cause of Christ? Revelation 6 helps us answer that question. John says, "I saw under the altar the souls of those who had been slain for the word of God and for the testimony which they held ... a white robe was given to each of them" (Revelation 6:9, 11). Not only does God care about the sacrifices of those who are persecuted, but He has prepared a place for them in heaven. Let us continue to "remember the prisoners as if chained with them" (Hebrews 13:3).

## DECEMBER 29 — KING OF KINGS AND LORD OF LORDS

*"And He has on His robe and on His thigh a name written: KING OF KINGS AND LORD OF LORDS." (Revelation 19:16)*

Since the beginning of time, the world has been on a wicked course. Ever since Adam and Eve sinned in the Garden, sin has been reigning over the human race. We see the evidence of our fallen condition all around us. States are creating abortion-on-demand laws, municipalities are forced to recognize marriages that God calls an abomination, etc. Everywhere you turn, the battle is raging and it looks like Satan is winning. The Bible calls Satan "the god of this age" (2 Corinthians 4:4).

Something amazing is going to happen. At the end of time, just when it seems all hope is lost, Jesus is going to come back to earth with the "armies of heaven" (Revelation 19:14). When He does, He is going to strike a devastating blow to the Antichrist, the False Prophet, and every person that takes the mark of the beast. With just a word from the mouth of our Savior Jesus, the enemies of God are going to be overthrown at Armageddon and Jesus is going to establish His kingdom on earth.

At the beginning of the Tribulation, the Bible tells us the Antichrist — the man of sin — will come riding in on a white horse. In doing so, he will attempt to mimic the work of Christ and he will successfully mislead many people. But at the end of the Tribulation, the true Christ will come riding on a white horse. He will have a clear identity — KING OF KINGS AND LORD OF LORDS. Our King Jesus will gain the victory and we will reign with Him forevermore.

## December 30 — One Last Rebellion

*"Now when the thousand years have expired, Satan will be released from his prison and will go out to deceive the nations ... fire came down from God out of heaven and devoured them." (Revelation 20:7-9)*

At the end of the seven-year Tribulation, the Antichrist, the False Prophet, and all those who served them will be defeated and cast into hell. With that, there's only one real enemy left to defeat — Satan himself. Keep in mind that after Christ is victorious at Armageddon, Jesus will reign with His followers on earth during the "Millennial Reign" — 1,000 years of peace on earth. During that millennium, Satan will be locked up in the bottomless pit (Revelation 20:3).

Today's verses take place after the millennium. God will allow Satan to be let loose one more time. Immediately, he will begin to deceive anyone he can into joining one final rebellion. Many have speculated about who the devil will have left to deceive, since it is believers who will reign with Christ during the millennium. While the Bible doesn't provide a clear answer to that question, many believe that it will be the children of those who began the millennium with Christ.

No matter their identity, the Bible says that "Satan will be released from his prison and will go out to deceive the nations." Bringing his rebels to Jerusalem, Satan will try one last time to overcome the Lord Jesus. He will fail miserably, as fire from heaven will devour the rebels, and Satan himself will be cast into the lake of fire where he will be tormented forever. With the final rebellion squashed, our Lord Jesus will usher in a new heaven and a new earth.

## December 31 — No More Night

*"There shall be no night there: They need no lamp nor light of the sun, for the Lord God gives them light. And they shall reign forever and ever." (Revelation 22:5)*

I can't say that I understand very many of the complexities of cosmology or space, but I do know this — the earth rotates on its axis over a period of twenty-four hours. Depending on where you live, that rotation means you get more or less sunlight. Where I live, across the seasons we average about twelve hours of sunlight each day and twelve hours of darkness. Of course, we know the Lord set this course in order at the beginning of time. The light He called day and the darkness He called night (Genesis 1:5).

While night and rest are a necessary part of the human condition, the Bible tells us there will be no more night in heaven. But how can that be? Because "the Lord God gives them light." How does He do that? John also answers that question — "The glory of God illuminated it. The Lamb is its light" (Revelation 21:23). Jesus will reign from His throne in heaven, and His radiant glory will drive away any hint of darkness. In heaven, there will be no literal darkness or spiritual darkness.

Not only that, but the Bible tells us about many other things that won't be in heaven. There will be no sorrow in heaven. There will be no death in heaven. There will be no sickness in heaven. There will be no separation in heaven. There will be no fatigue, no hunger, and no poverty. In that place where the streets are paved with gold and the walls are made of jasper, we will never lack anything as we worship our Risen Savior Jesus. "Even so, come, Lord Jesus!" (Revelation 22:20).

CPSIA information can be obtained
at www.ICGtesting.com
Printed in the USA
JSHW081937091122
32829JS00001B/3